DUBLIN

ALSO AVAILABLE IN THIS SERIES:

Sligo, Michael Farry (2012)
Tyrone, Fergal McCluskey (2014)
Waterford, Pat McCarthy (2015)
Monaghan, Terence Dooley (2017)
Derry, Adrian Grant (2018)
Limerick, John O'Callaghan (2018)
Louth, Donal Hall (2019)
Kildare, Seamus Cullen (2020)
Leitrim, Patrick McGarty (2020)
Antrim, Brian Feeney (2021)
Roscommon, John Burke (2021)
Donegal, Pauric Travers (2022)
Mayo, Joost Augusteijn (2023)
Fermanagh, Daniel Purcell (2023)
Armagh, Donal Hall & Eoin Magennis (2024)

Dublin

The Irish Revolution, 1912–23

Brian Hughes

FOUR COURTS PRESS

Typeset in 10.5 pt on 12.5 pt Ehrhardt by
Carrigboy Typesetting Services for
FOUR COURTS PRESS LTD
7 Malpas Street, Dublin 8, Ireland
www.fourcourtspress.ie
and in North America for
FOUR COURTS PRESS
c/o IPG, 814 N. Franklin St, Chicago, IL 60610.

A catalogue record for this title
is available from the British Library.

ISBN 978-1-80151-119-3

Printed in England
by CPI Antony Rowe, Chippenham, Wilts.

Contents

Illustrations

PLATES

Credits

1, 8: National Portrait Gallery, London; 2, 5, 7, 9, 11, 14, 15, 20, 21, 22, 24: National Library of Ireland; 3: Royal Society of Antiquaries of Ireland; 4, 6, 19, 23: Kilmainham Gaol Museum; 10, 18: Royal Irish Academy Library; 12: Dublin City Library and Archive; 13: Fingal Local Studies and Archives; 16, 17: National Museum of Ireland.

MAPS

Abbreviations

ADRIC	Auxiliary Division, Royal Irish Constabulary
AG	Adjutant General
ASU	Active Service Unit
ATIRA	Anti-Treaty IRA
BMH	Bureau of Military History
CAB	Cabinet Office, TNA
Cd./Cmd.	Command paper
CD	Contemporary document, BMH
CDUA	City of Dublin Unionist Association
CI	County Inspector, Royal Irish Constabulary
CID	Criminal Investigation Department
CSORP	Chief Secretary's Office Registered Papers
DATI	Department of Agriculture & Technical Instruction
DE	*Daily Express* (Dublin)
DÉ	Dáil Éireann
DED	District Electoral Division
DÉLG	Dáil Éireann Local Government department
DI	District Inspector, RIC
DIB	*Dictionary of Irish biography*
DMP	Dublin Metropolitan Police
EH	*Evening Herald*
FCCA	Fingal County Council Archives
FJ	*Freeman's Journal*
GAA	Gaelic Athletic Association
GHQ	General Headquarters, IRA
GOC	General Officer Commanding
GPO	General Post Office
Hansard	House of Commons debates
HO	Home Office, TNA
ICA	Irish Citizen Army
IFS	Irish Free State
IG	Inspector General, RIC
II	*Irish Independent*
IMA	Irish Military Archives
IPP	Irish Parliamentary Party
IRA	Irish Republican Army
IRB	Irish Republican Brotherhood
IT	*Irish Times*

ITGWU	Irish Transport and General Workers' Union
IUA	Irish Unionist Alliance
IWFL	Irish Women's Franchise League
IWSLGA	Irish Women's Suffrage and Local Government Association
LGB	Local Government Board
MP	Member of Parliament
MRA	Municipal Reform Association
MSPC	Military Service Pensions Collection
NAI	National Archives of Ireland
NLI	National Library of Ireland
O/C	Officer Commanding
PR	Proportional Representation
PRONI	Public Record Office of Northern Ireland
RDC	Rural District Council
RDF	Royal Dublin Fusiliers
RIC	Royal Irish Constabulary
SF	Sinn Féin
TCD	Trinity College, Dublin
TD	Teachta Dála
TNA	National Archives, London
UCD	University College Dublin
UCDA	University College Dublin Archives
UDC	Urban District Council
UIL	United Irish League
VAD	Voluntary Aid Detachment
WO	War Office, TNA
WS	Witness statement to Bureau of Military History

SPECIAL ACKNOWLEDGMENT

This book has been published with the support of Dublin City Council under its Commemoration Programme.

Comhairle Cathrach
Bhaile Átha Cliath
Dublin City Council

Acknowledgments

The writing of this book has taken several years and over that time I have accrued many debts. Thanks must first go to the series editors, Dr Daithí Ó Corráin and Professor Mary Ann Lyons, for inviting me to take on the task of writing a book on Dublin during the Irish Revolution and for their continued guidance, support, feedback and patience as the book was delayed by a growing family and a global pandemic. Any temptation to curse taking on the project in the first place (a frequent enough occurrence) was always quickly allayed by their encouragement across many draft chapters and many, many hours of their time.

I was first inspired to study modern Irish history seriously by Professor Vincent Comerford's teaching at the National University of Ireland, Maynooth (now Maynooth University), and later the Irish Revolution as a postgraduate at Trinity College Dublin by Dr Anne Dolan and Professor Eunan O'Halpin. This work is in large part a culmination of much of what I have learned on that journey. It also draws on the scholarship of the many scholars of Dublin and the Irish Revolution cited in what follows, to whom I am indebted for doing so much of the heavy archival and analytical lifting. I hope to have been able to add some fresh snippets of my own.

Several colleagues and friends were generous with their time to read draft chapters, offer feedback and corrections, discuss the project or suggest sources: Dr Seamus Cullen, Dr Anne Dolan, Dr Ian d'Alton, John Dorney, Dr Seán Gannon, Dr Brian Hanley, Lar Joye, Dr Jack Kavanagh, Dr Eve Morrison, Dr Deirdre McMahon, Dr Conor Mulvagh, Aaron Ó Maonaigh, Dr Thomas Tormey and Dr Ciarán Wallace. The book is all the better for their input. Innumerable discussions about the project with colleagues and fellow series authors have also contributed in their own important way to shaping this study. My thanks in particular to Dr Mel Farrell, Dr Darragh Gannon, Dr Pat McCarthy, Dr Patrick McGarty and Dr John O'Callaghan and all who have indulged me over the last number of years. Any errors that remain in these pages are my own.

Mary Immaculate College has been a constant source of support and collegiality since 2017. Particular thanks to colleagues in the Department of History, Dr Liam Chambers, Karen Fisher, Dr Richard McMahon, Dr Úna Ní Bhroiméil, Dr Clodagh Tait and Dr Cathy Swift. The Research and Graduate School at MIC also provided funding to support research undertaken for the book, for which I am grateful.

Thanks to all at Four Courts Press for their expertise and professionalism, in particular Anthony Tierney and Martin Fanning. The maps produced in the book are the expert work of Dr Mike Brennan.

This work would not have been possible without the librarians and archivists who have made the source material for this book accessible to historians, including all those involved in digitizing archival collections that have been essential in my efforts to research Dublin's revolution. Thanks to the archivists, librarians and support staff at Dublin City Library and Archive, the Irish Military Archives, especially Cécil Chemin, the National Archives of Ireland, the National Library of Ireland, The National Archives, Kew, Trinity College, Dublin, UCD Archives, and Fingal Local Studies and Archives. My time working on the Letters of 1916 project, first at Trinity College Dublin and then at Maynooth University, allowed me to engage with material that has been utilized in this book, including several letters in private collections that were generously shared with the project team and digitized. I remain indebted to Professor Susan Schreibman for giving me my first post-PhD employment. Aoife Torpey was particularly helpful in my efforts to source images for the book in the Kilmainham Gaol collections, and additional thanks to images and reproductions staff at the National Library of Ireland, RTÉ Archives, Dublin City Library and Archive, the National Museum of Ireland, Fingal Local Studies and Archives, the Royal Irish Academy Library, the Royal Society of Antiquaries in Ireland and the National Gallery of Ireland.

My parents, Seamus and Jacinta – both adopted Dubliners like so many others – were unfailingly supportive over my years as a history student, and remain so.

Finally, this book is dedicated to Michelle, Cian and Dara for filling a home and always reminding me of the most important things in life.

The Irish Revolution, 1912–23 series

Since the turn of the century, a growing number of scholars have been actively researching this seminal period in modern Irish history. More recently, propelled by the increasing availability of new archival material, this endeavour has intensified. This series brings together for the first time the various strands of this exciting and fresh scholarship within a nuanced interpretative framework, making available concise, accessible, scholarly studies of the Irish Revolution experience at a local level to a wide audience.

The approach adopted is both thematic and chronological, addressing the key developments and major issues that occurred at a county level during the tumultuous 1912–23 period. Beginning with an overview of the social, economic and political milieu in the county in 1912, each volume assesses the strength of the home rule movement and unionism, as well as levels of labour and feminist activism. The genesis and organization of paramilitarism from 1913 are traced; responses to the outbreak of the First World War and its impact on politics at a county level are explored; and the significance of the 1916 Rising is assessed. The varying fortunes of constitutional and separatist nationalism are examined. The local experience of the War of Independence, reaction to the truce and Anglo-Irish Treaty and the course and consequences of the Civil War are subject to detailed examination and analysis. The result is a compelling account of life in Ireland in this formative era.

Mary Ann Lyons
Department of History
Maynooth University

Daithí Ó Corráin
School of History & Geography
Dublin City University

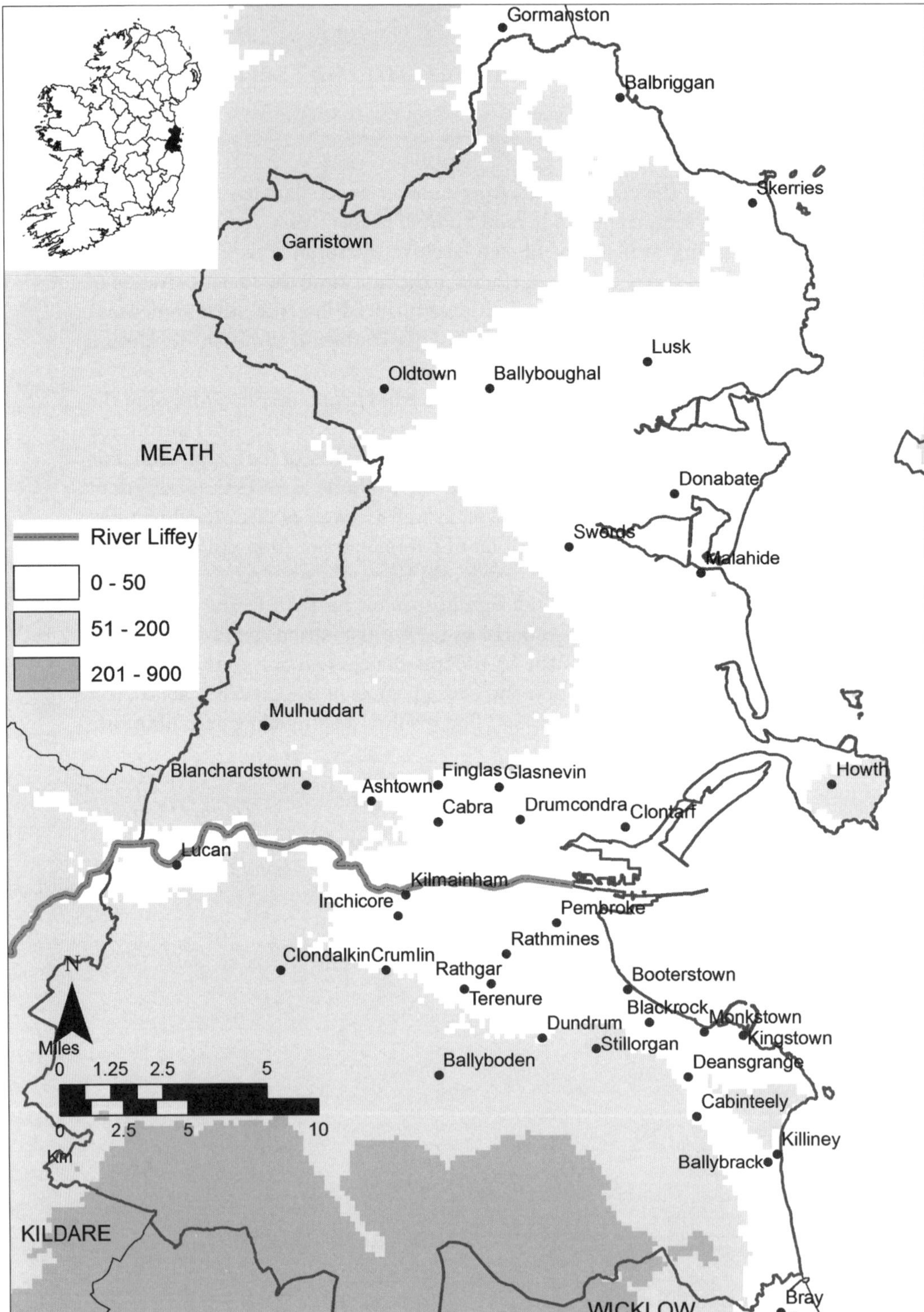

1 Places mentioned in the text

1 Dublin in 1912

'On the whole, given fair weather, no place can look brighter, livelier, or more lovely than the much-maligned City of Dublin, and its ample squares, noble public buildings, not to mention the surpassing loveliness of its environs, fully entitle it to rank as the second city of the Empire.'[1] Thus a guidebook described Ireland's capital in 1908. Three years later, when King George V and Queen Mary paid a visit during the coronation year, the *Irish Times* proclaimed that it had 'vindicated Dublin's ancient claim to be ranked as "second city in the Empire"'.[2] Widely accepted in the eighteenth century, it was a rather more dubious claim by the turn of the twentieth. Dublin was not even the most populous city in Ireland, having been overtaken by Belfast, which also outpaced the capital in commercial and industrial growth.[3] Edinburgh, Glasgow, Birmingham, or Liverpool made their own claims to second city status. Furthermore, some in Dublin rejected the notion outright. These included Arthur Griffith's Sinn Féin, then fronted by a small number of radical separatist city councillors; the nationalist-dominated Dublin Corporation that refused to present an address to the king and queen; the Nationalist Women's Association and the Dublin branch of James Connolly's Socialist Party of Ireland, both of which protested against the royal visit.[4]

But even within nationalism there was no easy consensus and in advance of the monarch's arrival in July 1911, the moderate nationalist *Irish Independent* printed a photograph of Union Jacks adorning Grafton Street and 'hints for spectators'.[5] The *Independent* and *Freeman's Journal* joined the unionist *Irish Times* in devoting considerable space to the decorations and the 'enormous crowds' that greeted the royals.[6] If the crowds – which included an estimated 35,000 visitors and 10,000 extra troops – were not necessarily representative of blind loyalty, they did reflect Dublin's imperial links, the allegiances of at least a portion of society, and a wider (and enduring) curiosity about the trappings and ceremony of royalty.[7] Few in 1911 would have predicted that this would be the last visit by a British monarch for over a century, but over the coming decade the dissidents who opposed the visit came to dominate politically.

Kevin O'Shiel, then a law student at Trinity College and later a barrister and Dáil land commissioner, remembered several 'different Dublins' around this time. There was the 'Castle Dublin' of government, police and law; the professional class of doctors, lawyers and academics; the 'intelligencia' of writers and artists; the world of commerce; the world of local ward politics; and, finally, the 'proletariat of the narrow streets and tenements'.[8] There was more variety again beyond the boundaries of the metropolis. North and south county Dublin, the former including the rural regions to the west of the city, in many ways

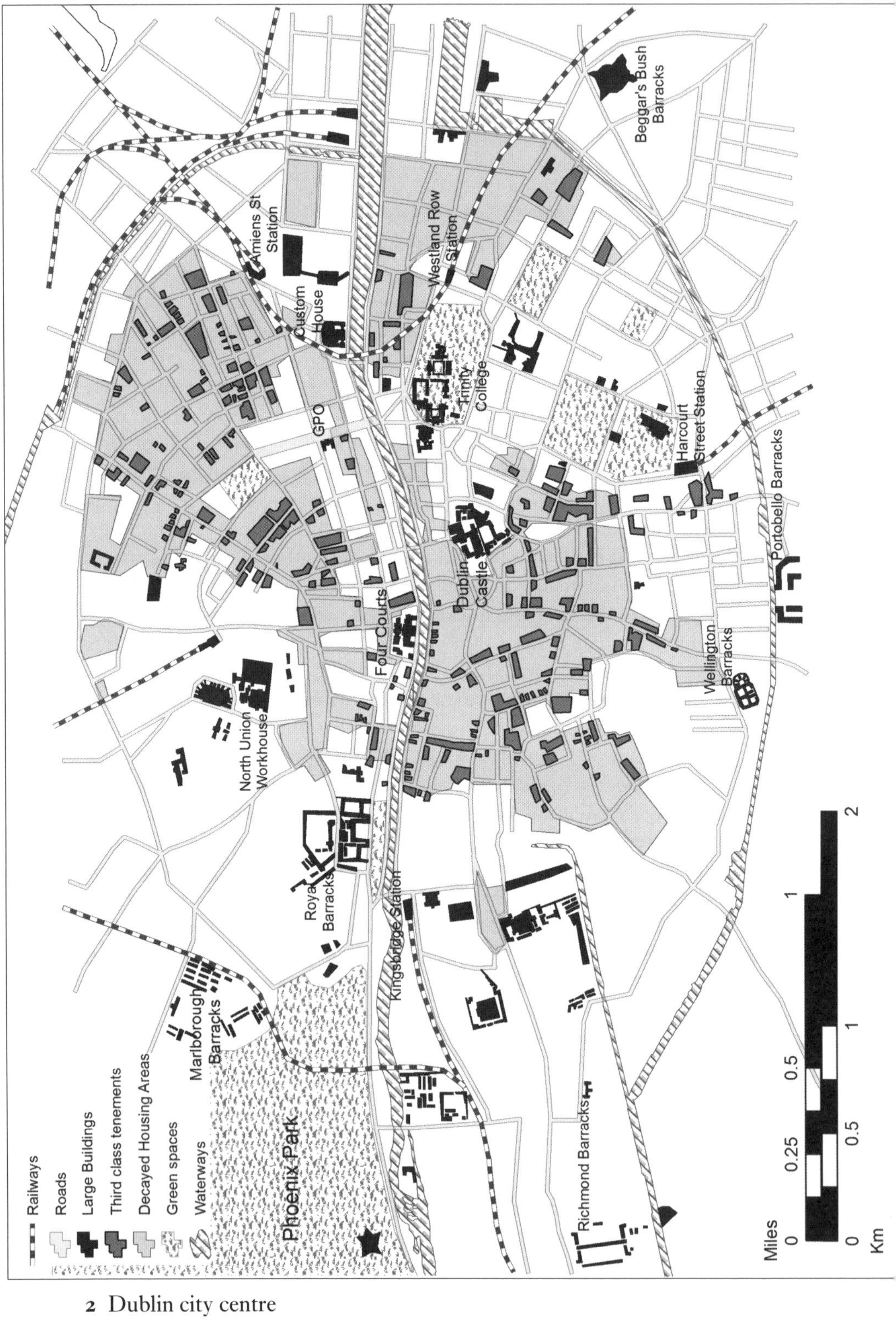

2 Dublin city centre

resembled neighbouring counties more closely than each other. At the same time, rural Dublin was closely linked to, and often economically reliant on, the city; the cattle market on the North Circular Road at Stoneybatter (nicknamed 'Cowtown') being one point at which county and city met.

Like much of Leinster, the land in the county was generally good and most of rural Dublin was under grass or crops. To the south were 'unmatched vistas of natural beauty in the Dublin hills and the Wicklow mountains' and in 'Ireland's "Bay of Naples" – Killiney'.[9] Between the mountains and the city were six suburban townships, designated as independent urban district councils (UDCs): Rathmines and Rathgar, Pembroke, Blackrock, Dalkey, Killiney and Kingstown (Dún Laoghaire from 1920). The Clontarf, Drumcondra and New Kilmainham townships on the northside had been amalgamated into Dublin Corporation in 1900, but their southern counterparts continued to defend their autonomy.[10] These suburbs 'looked and felt quite different to the city, with each township having its own distinctive identity.'[11]

Many defining features of Dublin city's geography were remnants of the eighteenth century. According to one early twentieth-century essayist, 'Dublin, unlike other towns, seems to have settled down in the eighteenth century and to have gone little further in the next hundred years'.[12] The Four Courts and palatial Custom House were city landmarks (see map 2), alongside the early nineteenth-century General Post Office and Clery's department store on Sackville (later O'Connell) Street. None would survive the revolution intact. The Royal Canal on the northside and the Grand Canal on the southside, essentially marking the boundaries of the inner city, were also completed in the early nineteenth century. With its own herd of fallow deer, the 1,700-acre Phoenix Park provided welcome green space, public amenities, sports pitches and a zoological garden. Situated a kilometre north-west of Sackville Street, it was, as Stephen Gwynn put it, 'the chief glory of Dublin' and 'one of the finest parks in Europe'.[13] The Phoenix Park also housed the principal residences of the lord lieutenant (or viceroy), the chief secretary and the under-secretary. The viceroy held a largely ceremonial brief, but the chief secretary – from 1907 to 1916 the increasingly disengaged Augustine Birrell – usually had a seat in the British cabinet. The under-secretary was in command of day-to-day administration. Dublin Castle, a complex of courtyards and buildings behind City Hall, served as the 'hub of an ever-expanding government machine and the ceremonial centre of viceregal entertainment'.[14] A short distance away, the Four Courts was home to the national court of appeal and high court, and the Public Record Office. Multiple small hospitals in the city catered for local and rural patients. Retaining the highest concentration of Irish banks, Dublin continued to serve as the capital of business and commerce. It was also a terminus for all four major Irish railway lines. These railways, and a port directly facing Liverpool, made Dublin an ideal location for both internal and external transport, particularly cross-channel shipping and mail services.[15]

While remaining the administrative centre of British rule in Ireland, the loss of Dublin's short-lived parliament in 1801 under the Act of Union had contributed to a century of decay. There were some international successes – notably Guinness and W. & R. Jacob – but most industry was limited to providing food and related products for internal markets. Brewing (Guinness), biscuit making (Jacob's), distilling (Jameson, Powers, George Roe) and soda water production (Cantrell & Cochrane, Thwaites, O'Brien & Co.) comprised Dublin's main industrial output. Dressmaking and shoemaking had been contracting since the 1860s and 1870s (except in the suburbs where female employment in dressmaking rose). Bakeries and confectioners were common but catered mostly for local needs, and while printing thrived in the city – focused on pamphlets and stationery rather than fine book publishing – the number of paper mills in rural county Dublin had fallen considerably by the late nineteenth century. Several railway companies, concentrated in Inchicore, built locomotives and provided engineering jobs. Growing demand for plumbing, gas-fitting and electricity also helped the engineering industry to survive, but was generally limited to local service and repair. While shipbuilding grew in North Wall between 1902 and 1920, in comparison to Belfast it remained modest.[16] Decline could, in turn, be detected in the city streetscapes, often poorly paved and filled with dust, mud, or manure. Worse was the noise, dirt and the state of the many neglected small lanes, alleyways and courts off the main thoroughfares.[17] Rows of fine Georgian terraces had fallen into decay, subdivided and filled with an expanding working class. While Merrion Square and Fitzwilliam Square remained 'a world of doctors, lawyers, senior civil servants and army officers' in 1912, formerly fashionable terraces on Henrietta Street, Mountjoy Square and Parnell Street had been abandoned by elites lured to London or the expanding Dublin suburbs.[18]

The traditional (nationalist) narrative of inner-city decline fostered under the Union had much truth to it but was an oversimplification. For all its issues, the variety of economic activity in early twentieth-century Dublin was closer to London than any other British or Irish city.[19] Belfast-born, London-based journalist Robert Lynd, who took a keen interest in Irish nationalism and the Irish language, described Dublin as 'a grave and aristocratic witness to what Ireland was beginning to do for herself in the pre-Union days'. However, it was also

> A city of grave dignity. It is a national capital, a place of leisure and statues and wide streets and squares, with brick-faced venerable houses which in the radiance of sunset have a colour at times as beautiful as old wine. As one walks its pavements, one is always, as it were, under the shadow of history as of some high wall.[20]

Ephraim MacDowel Cosgrave and Leonard R. Strangways' 1908 dictionary and guidebook sought to highlight the improved cleanliness of the principal streets, a 'fine water supply', and the absence of 'smoke-laden' skies. They challenged impressions of a 'decayed capital' by emphasizing that the city needed to be viewed on a sunny day to be fully appreciated. The visitor to Dublin might be surprised, they suggested, 'to find a bright cheerful city, with plenty going on, and with streets well filled with well dressed and busy people'.[21] Even if one did not have to look far beyond the thoroughfares to find squalor in the lanes and alleyways, and many of those well dressed and busy people lived outside the city centre, some effort was made to dispel the negative connotations associated with the popular 'dear, dirty Dublin' sobriquet.

Another issue on which there were divergent views was the extent to which Dublin felt 'British' or 'Irish' (a question irrelevant beyond the city and suburbs). C.S. 'Todd' Andrews later claimed that Dublin at the turn of the century was 'a British city and accepted itself as one. Its way of life, its standard of values, its customs were identical with those of, say, Birmingham or Manchester'. The only difference, as Andrews saw it, was religion: 'the [Dublin] population was divided into … the rulers and the ruled. The rulers were mainly Protestants, the Catholics the ruled.'[22] For Lynd, however, 'in one respect it is an English fort and in another a provincial town', though 'no intelligent Englishman can feel that in Dublin he is in a British city.' His prediction that the increasingly common sight of bilingual signage 'foretells of the day when she will be [an Irish-speaking city]' was overly optimistic, but the conflict between two competing visions for Dublin (and Ireland) was played out in the built environment.[23] The shamrock was a common motif on the street furniture in the city, but not in Rathmines. Pembroke's electricity junction boxes displayed a large earl's coronet.[24] Nationalist councillors succeeded in renaming Great Britain Street as Parnell Street and Carlisle Bridge as O'Connell Bridge but failed to do the same with Sackville Street, which was colloquially rather than officially known as O'Connell Street until 1924. By 1912 statues of constitutional nationalists Daniel O'Connell and Charles Stewart Parnell stood at either end of that street, but between them stood Admiral Horatio Nelson on a forty-metre-tall column. There were also the equestrian statues of William of Orange on College Green, George I in the yard of the Mansion House and George II in St Stephen's Green. Queen Victoria sat on the lawn of Leinster House.[25]

There were just over 304,000 individuals counted in Dublin city on census night in 1911, with another 172,000 in the county from a total population of 4.3 million on the island. Although the city had over 80,000 fewer people than Belfast, Dublin was the most densely populated Irish city by some margin.[26] The population of the southside townships and rural north and south county had increased by almost 10 per cent between 1901 and 1911, and half of the Dublin population outside the city lived in Blackrock, Dalkey, Killiney, Ballybrack, Kingstown, Rathmines, Rathgar, or Pembroke (see map 1). The less densely populated north county saw much smaller growth, while the only districts with less than 1,000 houses were all in west Dublin (Castleknock, Finglas, Lucan and Clondalkin).[27] When whole counties are considered, only Dublin and Kildare experienced an increase in population between 1901 and 1911 and Dublin's percentage rise was almost twice that of Kildare.[28] It was expansion in the suburbs rather than the city that made the difference.

Demographic trends often varied considerably between the city, the suburbs and the county. Dublin county, for instance, had the lowest proportion of married women in Ireland in 1911 and the highest proportion of single women aged over twenty. The city's proportion of so-called 'spinsters', on the other hand, was among the lowest in Leinster and its proportion of married women among the highest.[29] Indeed, one commentator in 1914 suggested that the 'girl of the working-class districts is the mother of a household at an age when the girl of the suburbs is engaged in nothing more serious than tennis or term examinations.'[30] Albeit a generalization, this hints at key differences related to class and lifestyle in various parts of Dublin. Religion was inevitably relevant too. Just over 83 per cent of the city's population were Roman Catholics in 1911. The vast majority of the remainder were Protestant Episcopalians (12.9 per cent of the total, primarily Church of Ireland) and there were also much smaller numbers of Presbyterians, Methodists, Jews and others.[31] Minority religions tended to cluster, like the Jewish community around Portobello and the South Circular Road, or Presbyterians and Methodists in Clontarf.[32] In the county, the Catholic population fell to 71 per cent, but Protestants were most prominent in the southside townships where up to 40 per cent were Episcopalian or Presbyterian. In Rathmines, less than half of the population were Catholic. By comparison, Tallaght, further south, and Balrothery, in north Dublin, were over 90 per cent Catholic.[33]

About 60 per cent of the city's population was working class by 1914.[34] One in every five workers between the canals was classified as a general labourer; this figure was far greater than in similar-sized British urban centres. Among unskilled workers there were generally two categories: those in relatively secure employment with steady (though sometimes low) wages, and those in casual work. Native Dubliners were disproportionately represented among the latter because outsiders who were unable to find stable work tended to emigrate. Dublin Corporation, the railway companies, the tramways and the breweries were the main sources of stable, unskilled employment. Relative security and generous conditions made jobs with Guinness particularly desirable, though the dominance of unskilled labourers (over 2,000 out of a total of 2,500) had implications for wider living standards as there was a significant gap between the wages of skilled and unskilled workers.[35] In 1914, D.A. Chart told the Statistical and Social Inquiry Society of Ireland that the average unskilled worker in Dublin earned 18*s*. per week, with some earning as little as 15*s*. or 16*s*. Many of those who earned closer to £1 a week, such as building labourers, were subject to irregular employment and 'broken time' for poor weather or other reasons. After paying rent and providing food, fuel and light for a family, Chart estimated that the average worker had only 3*s.* 1*d.* remaining each week for 'provision or renewal of clothes, furniture, insurance, amusements, etc.',[36] at a time when a full-price weekday trip to the zoo cost 1*s.*[37]

Also 'impoverished and vulnerable to economic and personal crises' were the semi-skilled who, with the exception of engine drivers, were often poorly paid – tram company employees in particular. Next was the largest cohort in Dublin city's social hierarchy: skilled workers, shop assistants, apprentices and clerks. They comprised the upper end of the working class and with their dependants made up a third of the population. The number of artisans had, however, declined by 1912 as semi-skilled and unskilled work had increased. Their wages stagnated between 1905 and 1912 before builders, printers and other tradesmen saw rises in 1913. By 1914, the average wage for a skilled worker was double that of a general labourer. This gap was greater than in London and also exceeded the UK average. But skilled labourers in building trades, in particular, were still vulnerable to disruption, piece work, or changes in working hours. The rise of the professional class in Dublin (about 9 per cent of the workforce), meanwhile, included a doubling of the number of civil servants between 1891 and 1911.[38]

Only a quarter of Dublin women were engaged in an occupation recognized by census enumerators – a proportion almost identical in both city and county. Over 60 per cent of men were engaged in paid work, though in reality the gap was closed somewhat by the range of unpaid, casual, or unrecorded work – such as street selling and prostitution – carried out by women. Of those women who were counted, a large proportion worked in textile or clothing, and there were 7,955 skilled female tailors, drapers, mercers, milliners, dressmakers, staymakers, shirtmakers and seamstresses in Dublin city in 1911, with 2,228 more in the rest of the county.[39] National school teaching was the only profession in which women outnumbered men nationally, and this was also the case in Dublin.[40] Both men and women were likewise engaged in domestic service, but it was an especially important source of paid employment for women who made up the vast majority of servants. In County Dublin there was one female servant for every 12.9 persons (many of these in the suburbs), and in the city there was one for every 24.9 persons. This reflected both a lack of alternative work for unskilled women and a willingness among a significant number of people to enter domestic service. Though it could often be lonely and uncomfortable work, senior domestic servants like cooks, housekeepers and butlers could earn more than national school teachers.[41] Only 8 per cent of female domestic servants were members of the Church of Ireland but this figure rose to 16 per cent among male domestic servants, with Protestants appearing to prefer to hire domestic servants of their own faith.[42]

While there had been some progress towards a 'greening' of the Irish civil service, making it more representative of the Catholic nationalist population, in 1911 senior positions remained largely the preserve of middle-class Protestants with links to the old Ascendancy.[43] The proportion had declined since the 1870s, but the Church of Ireland still accounted for 35 per cent of the professional class and public servants in 1911 with Presbyterians making up another 3 per cent. Dublin Protestants were also overrepresented in white collar clerical and banking jobs, in law, in medicine and in the upper ranks of the army. The number of skilled Protestant workers had also declined, but Protestants were significantly underrepresented among city labourers.[44] Protestants also accounted for two-thirds of the city's justices of the peace in 1911 (an unpaid, honorary title) and in the county it was almost 70 per cent.[45] Many senior civil servants were members of Dublin's overwhelmingly Protestant and unionist gentleman's clubs such as the Kildare Street Club or the Dublin University Club.[46] There was thus often a perception that Protestants were universally well-off, one that ignored the significant Protestant working class in the city. Todd Andrews offered an important distinction: 'there were many poor Protestants in Dublin but never destitute Protestants'.[47]

Unlike Belfast, Dublin did not have recognizable Catholic or Protestant 'areas', and a person's address gave no indication of their religion but could reveal their socio-economic class. Middle-class Protestants and Catholics lived side by side in the suburbs, as working-class Protestants and Catholics did in the inner city.[48] There was also noticeable clustering of workers with the same trades or occupations. Grafton Street's status as the 'great shopping street in Dublin' is reflected in the many milliners, dressmakers, shop assistants, grocer's assistants and clerks returned there on the 1911 census.[49] There were also concentrations of milliners and dressmakers on Henry Street and Mary Street.[50] Employers like Guinness, Watkins & Co. distillers, the Great Southern & Western Railway, the Midlands Railway and the Dublin United Tramways Company built hundreds of houses between them for employees.[51] The Square in Inchicore, for example, built in the 1840s by the Great Southern & Western Railway to house employees at its works in Inchicore, was home to drivers, coach makers, fitters, coppersmiths, boilermakers, firemen, clerks, apprentices and their families.[52] The bulk of the Catholic community in Terenure were employees of the Dublin United Tramways Company or the Blessington Steam Tramway Company, renting houses owned by their employers.[53] Clontarf attracted clerks and salesmen, while Drumcondra was home to a significant number of priests and theology students from the All Hallows and Clonliffe seminaries.[54] While more than 70 per cent of the males over the age of fifteen years living on Church Street in 1911 were unskilled workers, a significant cohort on the South Circular Road worked in banking, in finance, as clerks, or as insurance agents.[55]

In rural Dublin, a large proportion of workers were, unsurprisingly, employed in agriculture, while a smaller but still substantial number worked as coachmen, grooms, or domestic gardeners, on poor wages that could vary from farm to farm. Payment was sometimes in the form of housing, food and clothing.[56] The number of agricultural labourers had been in decline since the 1840s but remained an important part of the workforce of big farms in Leinster and Munster, including Meath, Kildare and Dublin county. Wages for farm labourers were also low (much lower than in England) and living conditions relatively poor, while the economic gap between labourers and the farmers who employed them had widened significantly. Though there had been little agitation prior to 1912, farm labourers would engage in significant strike action in north County Dublin in 1913 and again in 1919.[57] The only industry in north of the county was centered on Balbriggan. There were two large hosiery factories in the town and over one hundred men and a similar number of women were enumerated in the 1911 census as working in 'hosiery manufacture'. Elsewhere there was a significant mixing between classes and occupations, especially in the suburbs. Rathmines and Rathgar, for instance, were home to large numbers of civil servants, soldiers, commercial clerks and shopkeepers and also returned over 600 male general labourers and 2,500 female domestic servants in the 1911 census.[58]

Migration between counties was relatively rare in Ireland and while Dublin attracted people from other Irish counties to many of its urban jobs, it did so less intensely than similar sized cities in Britain. Most migrants came from the surrounding counties or other parts of Leinster.[59] About 70 per cent of those recorded in the city in the 1911 census, and 65 per cent in the county, had been born somewhere in Dublin. This was roughly similar to Belfast and Derry, but a much lower proportion than Cork where 90 per cent of the county's population had been born there. Moreover, though the figures were not divided between city and county, Dublin-born men and women were among the least likely to be living in another county in Ireland after natives of Cork and (perhaps more surprisingly) Mayo.[60] Dublin's port was a regular point of departure for emigrants, though much more often for outsiders passing through than for Dubliners themselves. Between 1901 and 1911, less than 10,000 of the 430,993 emigrants from Ireland were Dublin-born.[61] Dubliners again made up the smallest proportion of natives of Ireland who left to settle abroad permanently in 1912. Dublin thus remained largely a city and county of natives. In keeping with broader national patterns, the majority of Dubliners who did leave Ireland in 1912 emigrated to the United States and Canada, while more went to Australia than to Britain.[62]

As most Irish migrants chose to go abroad rather than settle elsewhere in Ireland, about 25 per cent of all migrants in Dublin had come from outside the island.[63] On census night 1911, Dublin county recorded the second-highest percentage of people born in England and Wales, the second-highest proportion (after Belfast) of people born in Scotland, and the highest proportion of non-natives from elsewhere in the world.[64] Jewish immigrants from Eastern Europe like the Jacobsons, who included a house painter, an engineer and 'mineral water manufacturers', had been well established on Camden Street in the south inner city by 1912.[65] Among the foreigners in Dublin on 2 April 1911 were almost 1,800 non-British Europeans, fourteen Chinese, twelve Egyptians, thirty-six South Americans and a Samoan.[66] In every census between 1841 and 1911 Dublin had a higher proportion of foreign nationals among its general population than any other county. Americans were the largest group of foreigners in Ireland on the eve of the First World War, but as the numbers of Americans in Ireland grew, the proportion of those who settled in Dublin diminished significantly. Importantly, the American-born children of emigrants were apparently more likely to return to the counties that had seen the most emigration in the nineteenth century (probably to the county from which their parents had left).[67]

Another distinct feature of Dublin life was the 'lodger phenomenon'. In both 1901 and 1911, one in twenty individuals in the city on census night was returned as a 'boarder' or 'lodger', the highest proportion in Ireland. Subletting was especially important to the finances of lower middle-class households, providing an often vital boost to the suburban economy and to widows in particular. Women were also dominant among the 'boarding house keepers' and 'lodging house keepers' returned on the 1911 census.[68] Fluctuations in earning meant families often moved frequently from their rented accommodation. Worse still, the quality of housing remained at the core of Dublin's social problems. By 1913, the corporation had provided accommodation for 7,500 people in just over 1,300 houses, as well as a lodging house for one hundred on Benburb Street. Employers, private enterprises and charities had contributed over 5,000 other dwellings between them. The majority were built by the Artisans' Dwelling Company, a profitable business that housed almost 14,000 people in just over 3,000 dwellings.[69] The Iveagh Trust, founded by Edward Cecil Guinness (Lord Iveagh) of the brewing dynasty in 1903, was the other main source of private housing. The Trust's buildings were designed by London architects, built to high specifications, and included bath houses, play centres and shops.[70] Robert Lynd was less impressed with their aesthetic quality and described how Lord Iveagh – 'a patriotic Irishman in all but his politics' – had 'displaced many picturesque hells of poverty and disease in the surrounding parts by huge barracks of inimitably ugly brick – model tenements for the poor – which are no doubt much pleasanter to live in than to look at'.[71]

Tenements remained a defining feature of inner-city housing and an embarrassing stain on the city's reputation. About 30,000 people in total had benefitted from public or private housing schemes by 1912. The Artisans' Dwelling Company, however, had never sought to house the city's poorest and while the Iveagh Trust's rents were kept reasonably low, with an income cap for prospective tenants, they were never intended for the unemployed or destitute.[72] Housing thus served to both create and define the key characteristics that divided the different strata within Dublin society. In November 1913 Chief Secretary Augustine Birrell called for an inquiry into the housing conditions of Dublin's working class, carried out by Local Government Board (LGB) officials. This was prompted by the tragic collapse of 66 and 67 Church Street, causing the deaths of seven residents. The inquiry report, published in early 1914, estimated that about 60 per cent of Dublin's working-class population were living in tenements. Of these, over 20,000 families were living in one room with an average of 6.1 occupants per room. Just shy of 10,000 more were living in what census enumerators defined as 'second and third class small houses', scarcely any better than the tenements.[73] When the corporation's sanitary staff tabulated tenement housing, the categories meant something very different: 'second class' was on the borderline for human habitation, 'third class' was unfit for living purposes and 'incapable of being rendered fit', while being structurally sound was enough for a house to be considered in the 'first class'. There were 6,831 families, or 22,701 individuals, found to be living in 'third class' tenement buildings. Dublin had – by some distance – the highest number of one-room tenements and the highest average number per room of any principal city in Britain or Ireland. Officials found one house occupied by 98 individuals.[74] Two years earlier, on census night 1911, 107 people were recorded in 3 Henrietta Street, 104 in number seven, and 92 at number fourteen.[75]

The dire living conditions and poverty in Dublin slums have been well-documented.[76] Dignity was also present, however. The housing inquiry report provided shocking details of overcrowding, faulty infrastructure and unsafe sanitation arrangements, but also recorded that in a number of places 'an effort is made by the occupants to keep their room tidy', with walls 'often decorated with pictures', and decorations hung for Christmas.[77] Thomas Kelly, a Sinn Féin (SF) councillor, described tenements on Church Street where 'the houses are clean and the rooms look comfortable. The windows are neat, and nice curtains are in evidence'.[78] Even still, the city's poorest were subject to stigma and stereotyping, viewed by some of their supposed social superiors as curiosities to be examined or victims of their own moral degradation and vice.[79] Their diet was meagre and insufficient, especially when compared to rural areas (including rural Dublin) where even the poor had access to safer and more nutritious food.[80] It might have been tempting for middle-class observers to blame intemperance for a family's deprivation, and it certainly could play its part, but poor nutrition, inadequate sanitation and unfit housing all contributed to Dublin's illness and mortality rates. There had been a reduction in the overall death rate in 1911, but it remained higher than any large centre of population in England, Scotland, or Wales.[81] Whereas infant mortality was comparatively low in Ireland, death registers show that in Dublin city infant mortality ranged from 13 to 20 per cent of recorded live births. Disease and poor sanitation explain most of these deaths, but the 'urban penalty' – undernourished mothers and resulting low birth weight – also contributed.[82]

Outside of the inner-city, living conditions were often very different indeed. The average number occupying a house in the county was 5.2 in 1911, only slightly above the national average family of 4.6 persons.[83] The sharing of a single house between multiple families was most obvious in the city, and more common in the suburbs than in rural Dublin. Almost all of the families deemed to be living in fourth-class accommodation in the suburbs were sharing first, second, or third quality houses with one or more others.[84] Less than one in five suburban families, in fact, lived in first-class housing like the desirable Victorian-era properties in Rathmines or Pembroke. But where tenements existed in the suburbs or the county, they were generally less cramped than in the city – if still providing far from ideal living conditions.[85] The vast majority of families in rural Dublin lived in what census enumerators deemed to be second- or third-class accommodation, with only a tiny minority sharing a house with another family.[86]

There were over thirty mansion houses ('Big Houses') in rural Dublin. The most significant included Old Conna House in the south of the county, Howth Castle and Kenure House in the north, and Abbotstown House, seven kilometres north-west of the city. The three-storey, twenty-five room Bracketstown House in Swords was destroyed by an accidental fire in November 1913.[87] Some county estates had been broken up and purchased by their tenants. This created a large cohort of independent small farmers – a major source of employment – but more than eighty separate untenanted demesnes of more than 100 acres remained.[88] Wilson Hutchinson Reynell Heard, a Protestant from County Clare and Royal Irish Constabulary (RIC) county inspector (CI) for Dublin, routinely reported to Dublin Castle that farmers throughout the county were prosperous and well-to-do, with plenty of employment for labourers and artisans, and significant tillage, factories and mills.[89] Living in rural Dublin, therefore, had its advantages. The existence of houses no better than mud cabins in the county, however, suggests that the best place to be amongst the very worst off may have been in the suburbs – and across Dublin wealth and poverty were often in close proximity.

Unusually, Dublin had two different police forces: the RIC and the Dublin Metropolitan Police (DMP) existed side by side but operated separately.[90] The DMP policed the city and a large part of the county, divided into six lettered divisions with an additional detective (G) division based at Dublin Castle. A and B Divisions covered the south inner city, C Division incorporated the north-east of the city, and D the north-west as far as, and including, the Phoenix Park. While the northside suburbs were policed by the RIC, Rathmines and Pembroke fell under E Division, and F Division covered the coastal suburbs and parts of

Ballybrack and Killiney. There was also a consistent army presence with 5,346 British army troops (of a total in Ireland of 25,887) stationed in Dublin's four army barracks in January 1912: Portobello, Beggars Bush, Wellington and the Royal barracks (see map 2).[91] The remainder of the county was policed by the RIC with 167 police of all ranks in thirty stations and a CI based in Howth.[92]

In 1912 the DMP area ranked highest per 100,000 people for criminal offences and charges though it had fewer policemen per head than Belfast city. The county fared somewhat better. It had the tenth-highest rate of offences and charges but was one of the more heavily policed areas per head of population outside of the major urban centres in Ireland.[93] Cases of simple or minor larceny were by some margin the most common form of indictable offence in both city and county but, as might be expected, the number was significantly higher in the city.[94] The city court's first quarter sessions of 1912, for example, recorded twenty-nine cases for consideration by the grand jury and the majority of those were for theft, burglary, or fraud. There were two cases of malicious wounding, one of negligent driving causing injury and one of manslaughter. The county grand jury were only asked to deal with one case for the same period, a burglary, and the recorder emphasized the 'almost total and complete immunity from [serious] crime which the county of Dublin possessed'.[95] Drunkenness was the most common form of non-indictable offence nationally, but was less common in Dublin than elsewhere.[96] Most Dublin drunks were also reasonably placid and only ninety-six offenders were arrested in 1912 for more serious offences, including assault and wilful damage, while under the influence.[97] At a time when violent crime was low nationally, Dublin's average rate was only second to Longford, and only behind Wicklow and Kildare for the even less numerous 'crimes again morals'.[98]

Use of the motor car had grown slowly since its introduction to Ireland in 1894 but by 1915 there were 1,500 cars registered with Dublin Corporation and an additional 140 being added each quarter.[99] Most relied on the impressive transport system, with 330 trams running for sixty miles around the city. The move to an electrified tram system had been led by William Martin Murphy, businessman, former Nationalist MP, and vice-president (1911–12) and president (1912–13) of the predominantly unionist Dublin Chamber of Commerce. His Dublin United Tramways Company absorbed a number of independent companies, investing in relaying tracks and overhead wires, and by 1914 was boasting that it offered one of the finest services in the world, carrying fifty-eight million passengers a year. Trams facilitated quick access to the city from the suburbs (though the routes favoured the wealthier southside townships).[100] Fares ranged from 1*d.* to 5*d.* and, while often controversial, were affordable to at least some of the working class.[101] The railways, meanwhile, opened up travel beyond the county boundaries. The Dublin and Kingstown Railway ran from Westland Row to Dalkey, while a steam tram connected with the railway at Terenure and served Blessington and Poulaphouca in Wicklow. Four other railway lines terminated in Dublin: at Amiens Street in the north-east of the city, Broadstone to the north-west, Kingsbridge (now Heuston Station) at the western end of the city, and at Harcourt Street in the south-east (see map 2). By 1906 a 'loopline' connected all four, at the price of a bridge obscuring downstream views of the Custom House.[102]

Murphy had been involved in the construction of the 'loopline' and combined his ownership of the Dublin United Tramways Company with several other business interests, including control of the *Irish Independent*, which he had relaunched in 1904.[103] The Irish public were well served with affordable Irish and British newspapers offering local, national and world news. As well as Murphy's *Independent* (Ireland's most read newspaper) and his *Evening Herald*, the *Freeman's Journal* and *Evening Telegraph*, which supported the moderate nationalist politics of the Irish Parliamentary Party (IPP), had a combined readership of about 66,000. The unionist *Irish Times* sold around 45,000 issues and the conservative *Daily Express* about 11,000, in addition to the sales of its ally, the *Evening Mail*. Both the *Irish Times* and the *Freeman's* had popular weekly editions and added to these were a series of publications of more robust opinion like Arthur Griffith's *Sinn Féin*, which had reverted from a daily to a weekly by 1912 but remained an important organ for the promotion of Irish-made products and services. The irascible D.P. Moran's popular *The Leader* was responsible for coining or popularizing terms such as 'Sourface', 'Castle Catholic', 'West Briton' and 'Shoneen' to deride unionists, loyalists, or Catholics who did not meet Moran's rigid definition of Irish Irelander. James Larkin's labour newspaper *Irish Worker* was launched in 1911 and soon had 90,000 readers, and the Irish Women's Suffrage Federation's *Irish Citizen*, first issued in May 1912, promoted women's suffrage and feminism, as well the rights of workers and Irish self-determination.[104]

The religious and political make-up of the population had a significant influence on daily life and culture in Dublin. Catholics and Protestants often operated in completely separate spheres. Todd Andrews wrote that during his childhood in Summerhill he 'rarely met and never mingled with Protestants'. Indeed, there was 'only one Protestant couple living in Summerhill'. Nevertheless, he claimed that from 'earliest childhood I seem to have been aware of their presence and influence in the community'.[105] Catholic and Protestant children attended different churches, usually attended different schools, and where Catholics attended Protestant schools or vice versa they were part of a tiny minority.[106] There was, however, more mixing than might initially be imagined. Protestant households, for example, often had both Protestant and Catholic lodgers and Protestants frequently lodged in Catholic houses. Mixed marriages were surprisingly common.[107]

Importantly, Dublin Protestantism was never monolithic and beyond the Church of Ireland there were at least six other independent denominations. Even within Anglicanism, there were tensions between those with High and Low church tendencies. The Plymouth Brethren attracted many Church of Ireland members to its gospel services in Merrion Hall, and this could divide loyalties within families. While Dublin Protestants of all shades were not quite as diligent in attending Sunday services as their Catholic neighbours, their average attendance levels were higher than their equivalents in urban England. The Church of Ireland provided the most visible forms of Protestant associational culture. In addition to schools, churches and hospitals across the greater Dublin area, there were also church-based voluntary organizations like the Boys' Brigade, the Temperance Association, the Mothers' Union and the Church of Ireland Young Men's Christian Association.[108] In 1900 the 1,132 membership of the Boys' Brigade in Dublin was the fourth largest in the United Kingdom; by contrast, membership in Belfast was 740.[109]

The city's reputation for providing venues for entertainment was poor, especially in comparison to London. The relative lack of indoor or outdoor amusement, it was suggested by the city coroner in 1900, contributed to the popularity of the public house, 'the only meeting place for the poor'. Theatre goers had the Gaiety, with a capacity of 1,800, the 2,300-seater Theatre Royal and the smaller Queen's Theatre on Great Brunswick (now Pearse) Street. The Abbey Theatre was opened in 1904. The Antient Concert Rooms provided classical music and opera, as did the Royal Dublin Society's Dublin Music Society and the Dublin Orchestral Society, though less frequently and to apparently declining audiences. Entertainment was inevitably linked to class and income and it was Dublin's two music halls – the Empire Palace and the Tivoli – that provided cheap, popular entertainment for the masses. For the same reasons, the cinema had become a prominent part of urban life and there were twenty-seven cinematographs subject to corporation by-laws in 1910.[110] Other unlicensed or unregistered cinema houses cropped up around the city in the 1910s and were only recorded if and when their owners were prosecuted.[111] The extent to which entertainment was potentially divisive was illustrated in January 1907 when audiences in the Abbey, outraged by the play's depictions of the Irish peasantry, rioted at performances of J.M. Synge's *Playboy of the Western World*. The Abbey sought to promote Irish plays on Irish themes (including those written in English), but whereas an earlier play like W.B. Yeats' and Lady Gregory's nationalist allegory *Cathleen ni Houlihan* had electrified Dublin, by 1912 the Abbey had chosen to avoid political themes. Rejection of the Abbey's approach, and its particular emphasis on 'peasant plays', encouraged the foundation of the Irish Theatre Company in 1914. Literary critic Mary Colum recalled Dublin in this period as 'drama-mad', but a later scholar suggested that while Dublin produced talented painters, musicians, writers and artists, the city 'proved unable to develop the cultural ambience that one should expect from a capital city of ancient lineage'.[112]

Trinity's famous library was closed to the general public and the National Library of Ireland on Kildare Street was more likely to attract University College Dublin (UCD) students than working-class readers. Marsh's Library, adjacent to St Patrick's Cathedral, was also open to the public but a contemporary guide suggested that few Dubliners were aware of its existence 'and fewer still have ever handled its musty tomes'. The Royal Dublin Society had a 'fine and increasing library for the use of its members.' There were also a number of lending libraries and the available volumes in Dublin's free public libraries – which all included reference libraries and newsrooms – increased five-fold. The number of books being borrowed trebled between 1884 and 1912, but this was slow growth in comparison to other urban centres and the service remained chronically underfunded.[113]

Games and play were an integral part of life across all social classes. Rugby, generally the preserve of the middle class, was the longest established organized sport in Dublin. Cricket, meanwhile, had reverted from the most popular game in mid-nineteenth-century Dublin to a minority interest in the wealthier suburbs.[114] Any of the other forms of sport and recreation found in Ireland were available in Dublin but association football was the most widely played contact sport, mainly owing to its growth among the working class – both Catholic and Protestant. Soccer was, for instance, the most popular game among members of the Boys' Brigade in Dublin, all Protestant and drawing more than half of its membership from working-class families.[115] Bohemian Football Club, based at Dalymount Park, was founded in 1891 and Shelbourne in 1895 in Ringsend. Both clubs played in the Irish League alongside teams from Belfast, where the organized game was administered until soccer – like the island – was partitioned. Soon after professionalism was legalized by the Leinster Football Association in 1905, Shelbourne had its first professional players (though Bohemians remained fully amateur). Shelbourne was also the first southern team to win the Irish Senior Cup in 1906 when they defeated Belfast Celtic, followed by Bohemians in 1908 who beat Shelbourne in the final after a replay, before Shelbourne repeated the feat in 1911 in a reversal of the 1908 final. These victories on a national stage were significant in boosting the popularity and profile of the sport in the capital. The 1906 final was played at Dalymount before a crowd of 7,000 people, with 10,000 people attending the 1911 game at the same venue.[116]

By then Dublin had been the GAA's administrative centre (as far as this existed) for a decade. The former racecourse on Jones' Road (which had hosted All-Ireland finals since the 1890s) was purchased for the association in 1908 and renamed Croke Park in 1913. Ultimately, though, the GAA was 'in Dublin but not of it'. Home to about a quarter of clubs nationwide in 1888, by the 1910s the organization was having much less success growing its membership in Dublin city.[117] In 1913 there were 2,272 applications for the use of playing areas for soccer, fifty-eight for Gaelic football and thirty-eight for hurling.[118] Twenty-nine of the Phoenix Park's thirty-one football pitches were used for association football.[119] Golf and tennis were more exclusive, but also visible, sports – particularly in the suburbs and county. The Royal Dublin Golf Society was founded in 1885 and by 1914 there were over 190 golf clubs in Ireland, including several in Dublin. Lawn tennis clubs, including the Fitzwilliam Tennis Club, were popular among Ireland's elites and club culture 'owed much to the culture of the British Empire'.[120]

Many Dublin republicans rejected widely articulated notions about so-called 'foreign games' as inherently British and 'un-Irish'. Soccer players were later prominent members of the Dublin city IRA as the sport was particularly popular among the lower middle-class shop assistants and clerks that fed readily into the movement.[121] Individual sporting pursuits were ultimately personal, linked to class, and to some extent geographical. Todd Andrews described how the limited range of pastimes available to Irish Volunteers in Rathfarnham included 'playing or watching Gaelic or soccer football' and 'hurling was seldom played or watched and rugby was neither played, watched nor read about'.[122] Yet the iconic image of Kevin Barry, executed in 1920, has him wearing the rugby jersey of Belvedere College, and he also played some hurling.[123] Dick McKee, from Finglas, played handball (a GAA game) but was also a keen cyclist.[124] McKee's successor as O/C of the Dublin Brigade, Oscar Traynor, played association football professionally for Belfast Celtic between 1910 and 1912 and later insisted that 'the game a man played did not influence his convictions one iota'.[125]

Dublin was a city and county large enough to contain a variety of social, economic and political groups, views and opinions. As will be seen, the years between 1912 and 1923 served to highlight and reinforce the variety and complexity of Dublin life. Any simple narrative of Dublin's revolution ultimately has to contend with a range of overlapping, competing and sometimes contradictory expressions of preference or identity. This was viscerally evident in the large crowds that for over a decade routinely gathered in the city to march, protest, celebrate, or mourn. In the space of a few weeks, for instance, Dublin could witness both bitter mourning for the victims of shootings by the British army and enthusiastic goodbyes for members of that same army heading off to war. Few other places in Ireland could accommodate this sort of activity on the same scale. Dublin's Mansion House was similarly a space that facilitated meetings of nationalists, unionists, labour activists, suffragists and more over the course of a decade from 1912 – some of which had national significance and many more that were decidedly local. The unique demographics and socio-economic conditions of Dublin – city and county – also ultimately had a significant influence on the nature of revolution in the capital. The capital was often the organizational heart of nationalist, republican, labour and suffrage activism – all at the same time and even when their various demands were in competition. Indeed, one of the defining features of Dublin's revolution might be its range and dynamism. In a southern Irish context, the extent and energy of unionist organization in Dublin was remarkable. It was also unique in many respects, unmatched elsewhere in Leinster, Munster or Connacht, but wholly different from what could be found in the unionist heartlands in Ulster. Just as their lifestyles could vary, and affluence and poverty could be very near neighbours, those who lived in the city and suburbs experienced the revolution very differently to their more rural counterparts. There was also space for those who hoped to ignore it altogether, even if they were not always successful. Neither Dublin's wealthiest nor, especially, its poorest, had the desire or – in the case of the latter – the time and space to fight for Ireland. Most Dubliners were never members of an active political or paramilitary organization, and many of those who did join up remained largely inactive or failed to last the course. One was more likely to join an angry, jubilant, or simply curious crowd in the street than fire, or even hold, a weapon. Nevertheless, as this book demonstrates, political activism and violence affected the lives of many in some way or other in the decade after 1912.

2. Politics and activism in Dublin, 1912–14

On 11 April 1912, Herbert Asquith, the British prime minister, introduced a third home rule bill in the House of Commons. Offering a Dublin parliament and a limited form of independence, the measure was rejected by the House of Lords. The 1911 Parliament Act limited the Lords' powers of veto to two years, which meant that, in theory at least, home rule legislation for Ireland would become law in 1914. Two years of political crisis followed the introduction of the bill, with the threat of civil war between nationalists – intent on forcing through home rule – and unionists – determined to scupper it. The foundation of the Irish Volunteers and Cumann na mBan in Dublin reflected the capital's status as a key administrative centre for activism and mobilization between 1912 and 1914. In some respects, Dublin shaped national events. At the same time, large parts of the city and county mirrored broader national trends, while others were dominated by minority interests. The capital also had a significant and well-organized unionist minority, which played its own part in the home rule crisis. Furthermore, in 1913 Dublin was the site of the largest industrial dispute on the island. Demands for women's suffrage, meanwhile, managed to both coexist and compete with the desire for legislative independence. The political landscape in Dublin was complicated with overlapping, intermingling and sometimes clashing nationalist, unionist, suffragist and labour currents.

The growth of the Irish Volunteers and Cumann na mBan during the third home rule crisis was a challenge to the old order, and the dominance of constitutional nationalism. Like most of Leinster, the city's four parliamentary constituencies elected IPP candidates in the December 1910 general election (the second to take place that year). John Redmond's party was the dominant force in Irish nationalist politics and two of its Dublin city candidates had been unopposed. In addition, John Joseph Clancy was returned unopposed for the IPP in County North, and William Francis Cotton won his contest in County South for the party. Defeat for the Unionist candidates in 1900 in the previously safe Dublin Stephen's Green and County South constituencies – ultimately the result of militant unionist sabotage even though Nationalists won the seats – had been a tipping point. Thereafter, a gradual unionist decline occurred in the south and west of Ireland, and the election 'marked the end of unionism as an effective electoral movement outside of Ulster'.[1] In subsequent elections, Dublin (south of the Liffey at least) remained the sole – albeit severely diminished – challenger to nationalist hegemony in 'southern' Ireland. If its wider impact was increasingly minimal, unionist grassroots activism remained sincere and committed to the end.

Unionists continued to hold the two Dublin University seats and Walter Long had won the County South seat in 1906. It was retained by Captain Bryan Cooper in January 1910, but Cooper's tenure was brief as he was defeated by Cotton by 133 votes in December. The latter election saw a turnout of 93 per cent, suggesting high levels of political engagement in the capital, albeit from a limited franchise that continued to exclude women entirely. Protestant nationalist William Abraham had a comprehensive victory for the IPP over the All-for-Ireland League candidate in the Harbour constituency in that election, while P.J. Brady defeated Unionist Lord Reginald Hubert by just over 800 votes from a poll of 6,359. H.D. Connor, another Unionist candidate, had pushed Brady even closer in the same constituency in January. In College Green, meanwhile, J.P. Nannetti was returned unopposed in December 1910, having faced a stern Unionist challenge in January. He was the only Irish trade unionist in parliament. When he died in 1915, his party successor was faced for the first time with a Labour challenger, Thomas Farren, president of the Irish Transport and General Workers' Union (ITGWU), who was unsuccessful but gained 1,816 votes out of 4,261.[2]

The complexity of the various strands of nationalism and trade unionism can be seen at the inaugural meeting of the Irish Volunteers. Lorcan Sherlock, the lord mayor and a moderate nationalist member of the IPP, had refused the use of the Mansion House for the meeting. As Laurence Kettle read out the Volunteer manifesto at the Rotunda Rink, Parnell Square, he was drowned out by 'perfect pandemonium' caused by trade unionists ('the "Liberty" Hall element'), apparently a protest against Kettle's father – a prominent nationalist and land leaguer in his own right – who had hired non-union labour to harvest his crops.[3] But the Dublin Irish Volunteers also contained prominent trade unionists in its ranks, such as house painter Peadar Macken and bricklayer Richard O'Carroll who had both represented labour on Dublin Corporation. Macken spoke at the Rotunda Rink – declaring to the noisy trade union crowd that 'I am not a blackleg' – and had founded two Gaelic League branches in Dublin. There were also large numbers of skilled workers in both the Gaelic League and the underground separatist Irish Republican Brotherhood (IRB).[4] The Irish Citizen Army (ICA), a Dublin rather than national organization, was formed as a workers' vanguard during the 1913 lockout (discussed below) and drew primarily from the unskilled working class.[5] Sean O'Casey later contended that the lack of support for the ICA among Dublin artisans was 'the old lingering tradition of the social inferiority of what were called the unskilled workers'. The 'socially superior tradesmen' were thus liable to 'shy at an organization which was entirely officered by men whom they thought to be socially inferior than themselves'.[6]

Like most of his flock, William Walsh, the Catholic archbishop of Dublin, was overtly nationalist.[7] His Church of Ireland counterpart, Joseph Ferguson

Peacocke, in turn reflected the politics of the majority of his own congregations in condemning home rule at a special synod in April 1912. A year later, Peacocke told the Dublin Diocesan Synod that home rule was 'a menace to religious and civil liberties', though this was an unusually forthright contribution.[8] When the Presbyterian General Assembly met during summer 1912, it opted against putting the home rule question to a vote, deciding that the views of its membership had been adequately expressed elsewhere and did not require discussion.[9] There was, however, disagreement in Dublin about the extent to which the Presbyterian Church should involve itself in political matters. The senior minister of the church on Donore Avenue suggested that over 100 Presbyterian clergy had declared that they would refuse to join their co-religionists at an anti-home rule protest in Belfast in early February 1912 and were indignant at being politicized in that way. But the letter drew opposition from correspondents to the *Daily Express* and over 200 Dublin Presbyterians were reported to have taken a special train to Belfast for the meeting.[10] An April 1913 motion before the Dublin Presbytery to the effect that 'our people live on friendly terms not only with their Protestant neighbours, but also with their Roman Catholic fellow-countrymen, and that our people are not apprehensive of hostility in the future' was lost by eighteen votes to four. The governing body of the much smaller Methodist Church was similarly divided.[11] At its Representative Session in Stephen's Green in June 1912, the Methodist Conference voted seventeen for and eleven against a resolution declaring that splitting members on a political issue was best avoided and home rule would not be discussed.[12]

Reliant on the promise that successful Ulster resistance would derail home rule for the whole island, Dublin unionists, nevertheless, looked to Britain and the Crown for their allegiance in the first instance and saw themselves as citizens of the empire as well as citizens of the Union. This unionism, and particularly working-class unionism, was also almost always Protestant. The Church of Ireland was the most visible Protestant culture in the capital and Dublin was 'the organizational and cultural centre of the Church of Ireland political community.' Indeed, Dublin boasted some of the largest concentrations of Protestant fraternal associations outside of Ulster. The city was home to a Grand Lodge and about seventeen local lodges of the Orange Order which made their own 'fire and brimstone speeches' on 12 July each year to mark the Williamite victory at the Boyne. Their headquarters was the Fowler Memorial Hall on Rutland (now Parnell) Square which was eventually evacuated and destroyed in 1920. Orange membership tended to be lower-middle or upper-working class rather than suburban, but Freemasonry was overwhelmingly middle class. The Freemasons' Grand Lodge was first opened on Molesworth Street in 1869.[13]

Dublin was one of the few places outside Ulster to hold signings of the Solemn League and Covenant and Women's Declaration on what became known as 'Ulster Day', 28 September 1912. In the north-east this was a carefully managed piece of street theatre, replete with staged ceremony, enthusiastic crowds, flags and symbols.[14] At the request of the Belfast-based organizing committee, the Irish Unionist Alliance (IUA) opened its offices on Grafton Street for signings. Signatories were required to prove a connection to Ulster, and the aim was to facilitate Ulster-born permanent or temporary residents of Dublin as well as Ulster people 'passing through the city'.[15] Scenes in Belfast were displayed on newsreels and reported in great detail in the Dublin press, both nationalist and unionist. But the limitations of what a minority population could achieve were obvious. As the *Daily Express* acknowledged, Ulster Day was 'quite different in Dublin. There was an absence of flags or any outward demonstration of that kind ... quite fit and proper in the circumstances'.[16] Indeed, there was a stark contrast between the photographs of Edward Carson – born on Harcourt Street, a Trinity graduate, and MP for Dublin University – signing the covenant over a large Union Jack in the ornate Belfast City Hall, and of a group of men cramped in a small room on Grafton Street, that were published side by side in the *Independent*.[17] The *Saturday Herald* reported that a call to 'display tokens of their approbation of the Carson movement was not generally followed out by Dublin commercial men, though in a good many instances shopkeepers with Unionist tendencies displayed the Union Jack'.[18]

Special ceremonies were limited to afternoon and evening services in Fowler Hall and another in the Presbyterian Church's Sackville Hall. At St Patrick's Church of Ireland Cathedral, the preachers 'made no reference to the covenant', but the hymns – particularly 'O God, Our Help in Ages Past', which was sung elsewhere that weekend – were 'specially chosen for the occasion'. The afternoon service ended with 'God Save the King'. The Dean of St Patrick's, Charles Ovendon, an Ulsterman, instead took up the subject at the regular Sunday service in Harold's Cross where he offered an optimistic and defiant sermon:

> They were not going to fight with anyone, but they were not going to allow their privileges as British citizens to be taken from them ... 'We have ... our transverse line on the Union Jack, and we are not going to have that flag altered.'[19]

Ovenden was typical in distancing himself from politics and politicians, instead framing the 'crisis' in religious terms, using Biblical analogies. Theirs was a flock that would be saved from injustice and persecution by God and prayer.

Perhaps the most provocative pronouncement, however, was made on the eve of Ulster Day at Kingstown when the rector of the Mariners' Church told a 'devout congregation' – drawn from 'every part of South County Dublin' – that while their Catholic neighbours' natural instincts were towards kindness and generosity, they were obliged to obey an 'intolerant – nay, more a persecuting Church'.[20] Archbishop Peacocke had been reticent about having his church associated with Ulster Day, fearing hostility towards members outside Ulster. He did, though, devise a special form of prayer against home rule – later denounced by Thomas Kettle as blasphemous – that was read at Church of Ireland services in the southern province of the Church of Ireland.[21] The Dublin-based *Church of Ireland Gazette* had described a 'united' front among members on political issues, but the speeches it printed in its issues actually demonstrated more mixed or muted attitudes. During a sermon in Booterstown, for instance, Canon Berry cautioned against interference in political matters and insisted that the power to conquer foes came from the 'uncomplaining sufferance of wrong'.[22]

The signing of the covenant and declaration offered some evidence of considerable enthusiasm, albeit confined to two rooms in the IUA's offices. Ulster men and women 'anxious' for an opportunity to record their feelings gathered outside 109 Grafton Street, where signing began half an hour early to facilitate the crowd. Separate rooms were offered for men and women to sign, assisted by several 'prominent unionists', including Captain Bryan Cooper – 'the Unionist candidate for South County Dublin' or the 'defeated candidate at the last election', depending on who was reporting. The *Saturday Herald* noted that about 2,000 had signed by 4 p.m., while the *Daily Express* claimed there were an estimated 3,000 signatures by 6 p.m.[23] Only the original women's declaration signatures from Dublin survive, and these show that 763 women signed – a figure not explicitly reported in the contemporaneous press. Less than twenty per cent were resident outside of Dublin and most of these, unsurprisingly, gave Ulster addresses. Dublin does not appear to have served as a centre for Leinster signatories and only a small number had travelled from neighbouring counties, alongside a group from Carrigallen in County Leitrim. Three others gave Dublin hotels as addresses. Large numbers of the Dublin-based signatories came from the southside townships where Protestants were most numerous, though there was also a small cluster from Skerries.[24]

The total number of male and female signatories across Ireland and Britain on Ulster Day were broadly similar, so it might be suggested that if the same applied in Dublin the total number of signatories at Grafton Street, male and female, was around 1,500 – or at least closer to 2,000 than 3,000. A request to Belfast for extra covenant forms may have been the result of substantially greater demand from male signatories but was perhaps as likely to reflect initial pessimism on behalf of the organizers. Some Dublin residents had also gone north to sign.[25] Even taking the higher figure and assuming the numbers reported only included male signatories, there was far from universal participation. There were around 15,000 Ulster-born men and women over the age of twenty years in Dublin city and county in 1911. More again may have claimed familial Ulster connections and others aged between sixteen and nineteen years were also eligible to sign.[26] But beyond the 'thousands of Ulster men and women resident in the metropolis' who were eligible to sign the covenant and declaration, there was support from 'southern' unionists in the capital.[27] Bryan Cooper claimed there would have been thousands more signatories in Dublin had southerners been allowed.[28] The separation of Ulster and southern unionists was already becoming increasingly apparent.

Grassroots unionist organizations were dominated by the upper and middle classes. Peers like Lord Longford, Lord Holmpatrick and the earl of Pembroke filled honorary or chairing roles. Officers and other prominent figures were overwhelmingly Protestant professionals – often born outside Dublin – like Bryan Cooper, who was born in India. Two other prominent spokesmen were native Dubliners, Anglicans and king's counsel: Charles Louis Matheson and William Jellett. The latter was a prominent member of the IUA and was elected MP for Dublin University in 1919. The general secretary of the City of Dublin Unionist Association (CDUA), Hugh Robert Topping, was a former solicitor's managing clerk.[29] When Topping was appointed secretary and agent to the South Glamorganshire Conservative Association in November 1912, he was replaced by Arthur Pomeroy, another Dublin-born, Anglican clerk.[30] There were no women on the board in 1913, though they made up five of the fifty members by 1919.[31] Lists of attendees at Dublin unionist meetings were filled with king's counsel, justices of the peace, deputy lieutenants, barristers-at-law, solicitors, or medical graduates from Trinity or the Royal College of Surgeons, while serving or retired British army officers were also well represented.[32] Dublin's business elite – with some exceptions, including William Martin Murphy – remained opposed to home rule. Guinness and Findlater's were owned by unionist families. Andrew Jameson, the distiller, was a prominent member of the IUA. Maurice Dockrell, head of a leading hardware merchants, and Sir John Arnott of Arnott's department store were also members. Furthermore, the chairman and managing director of Jacob's contributed to a 13-point economic argument against home rule in 1913. The Great Southern & Western and Great Northern railways were under Protestant unionist control, while the Catholic families who owned T. & C. Martin timber merchants and Power's whiskey similarly supported the status quo.[33] Catholics or working-class Protestants interested in unionist activism did not occupy leadership positions.

Prominent unionist women were from a similar socio-economic background to their male counterparts. Lady Holmpatrick was from the landowning class, while Marie Clothilde Guinness, Margaret Dockrell, Caroline Arnott and Ethel Craig Davidson were all married to prominent unionist businessmen. Though unable to match the numbers of the Ulster Women's Unionist Council, or the Women's Unionist Clubs in Ulster, Dublin women were increasingly prominent in grassroots unionism during the home rule crisis. Fifty members of the Kingstown and District Women's Unionist Club attended an anti-home rule demonstration on 10 January 1913, organized by the CDUA's Women's Central Committee in the Antient Concert Rooms. The women's committee deemed a demonstration 'foreign to its usual activities', but believed it expedient to allow all Dublin unionist women express their views.[34] The event saw the 'very large hall crowded in every part', as a scroll bearing the inscription: 'We will not have home rule' was displayed on a platform 'draped with Union Jacks.'[35] In May 1913 the CDUA, through its Women's Central Council, formed the first Dublin Women's Unionist Club, 'a new era for the work of the Association'.[36] In March 1914 it hosted a series of lectures on home rule and boasted that it 'now contains 2,000 members'.[37]

An event at Lord Iveagh's residence on St Stephen's Green demonstrated the scale of unionist organization in Dublin. Andrew Bonar Law, leader of the Conservative Party, visited Dublin in November 1913.[38] As part of his visit, Bonar Law was presented with a series of addresses from thirty-nine unionist organizations in southern and western counties. First to present was the Women's Committee of the IUA, followed by the Junior Branch (which had held its first meeting in the Antient Concert Rooms in January 1912),[39] and the City and County of Dublin Branch. Also among the thirty-nine were the CDUA, the South County Dublin Unionist Registration Association, the City of Dublin Grand Orange Lodge, the City and County Conservative Club ('comprised mainly of professional and business men in the city'), the City and County of Dublin Conservative Workingmen's Club,[40] the Primrose League in the City and County of Dublin, and over 400 'Ulster Unionists resident in Dublin'.[41] The Primrose League was 'effectively the "tea and sandwiches" wing of the Conservative Party'. It drew members from across the social spectrum, while the City and County of Dublin Conservative Workingmen's Club attracted the Protestant working and lower middle class and similarly prioritized Protestant ascendancy.[42] There were also two Unionist clubs in Kingstown, though this raised a debate about whether a second club, founded in September 1912, was necessary.[43] Even if this range of support and activism only masked unionism's minority status, and there was significant crossover among membership of related organizations, the breadth of organization is still noteworthy amid a city and county otherwise dominated by support for home rule or some variant of nationalism.

The Orange Order in Dublin has been characterized as 'inert', engaging in only 'fitful and desultory' political activity.[44] The CDUA, though, was more energetic and undertook substantial reorganization during the home rule crisis. As well as forming its Women's Central Committee in 1912, the CDUA was restructured to increase the appeal and impact of the movement in areas with significant numbers of unionists.[45] Its strategy of remaining determined but tactful was reflected in the public speeches that along with voter registration work formed the pillars of unionist activism in Dublin. In some spaces, however, like the Conservative Workingmen's Club on York Street, there was room for more militant rhetoric.[46] More surprisingly, there was even an attempt to arm. On 10 November 1913 the *Irish Times* reported that 'While Ulster is preparing to resist home rule, by force if necessary, and is busy building up a great citizen army, the spirit of militarism that has gripped that province … is also at work in Dublin'. The paper reported that 2,000 men had enrolled in a Dublin Volunteer Corps. Originally intended only for Orangemen, recruitment was expanded to include 'all who might, upon enquiry, be found suitable'. They received military training three nights a week from retired British army NCOs, and 'intended to be ready at a moment's notice to act as they may be ordered in defence of Protestants who may be in danger in any part of the country' or to act as a reserve for the Ulster Volunteer Force.[47] While the discovery of ninety rifles and 2,000 rounds of ammunition in the 1930s in what had once been Fowler Hall suggests there was some intention to use them, it was claimed much later that the rifles 'would not have been any use in battle'.[48]

As with Ulster Day, this mobilization was remarkable in a southern context but only a pale imitation of Belfast. Carson had reassured southern unionist readers of the *Daily Express* on Ulster Day that they were 'fighting the battle for Unionism on the whole of the island' and that they 'may trust in me as an old Dublin man when I tell them that Ulster has made up her mind that she will accept no separate Parliament.'[49] But while it took until 1920 for the Ulster Unionist Council formally to accept the exclusion of the six north-eastern counties from home rule, this had been in the making since at least 1912.[50] In committing to sign the covenant and women's declaration, unionist men and women had themselves essentially 'prepared through that very Covenant to abandon the far more vulnerable loyalist minority in Leinster, Munster and Connaught'.[51] Whether they realized it or not, Ulster-Dublin unionists had done the same thing. Despite the pleading from southern unionists on his visit to Dublin in November 1913, Bonar Law, as well as Carson and other Ulster Unionist leaders, insisted in their speeches to Dublin audiences that Ulster would go it alone. The Ulster leaders were reportedly drenched in spittle by enraged Dublin loyalists, and Carson merely repeated his assurances that Ulster would not sell out southern loyalists.[52] Southern unionist opposition contributed significantly to the delay in granting home rule that ultimately saw it put on hold until after the First World War. Tellingly, as home rule moved closer to the statute books in 1914, and the exclusion of Ulster became a more realistic possibility, some – like Bryan Cooper – had already proposed safeguards for southern unionists in a home rule Ireland.[53]

Not all of Dublin's Protestants opposed home rule, however.[54] Relatively few seem to have been attracted to the 'non-sectarian' Irish Volunteers, but some did take leadership roles in the movement and a significant proportion of Protestant advanced nationalist women were born in Dublin.[55] The most prominent members of the separatist republican organization Inghinidhe na hÉireann, founded in Dublin in 1900, and the regular contributors to its journal *Bean na hÉireann*, were Protestant women, though the personal religious beliefs of its members were usually unorthodox or less than devout. Generally, religion was kept separate from politics as far as possible.[56] The majority of Protestant men and women engaged in some form of revolutionary activity between 1916 and 1923 were operating in Dublin city, reflecting the unique 'geography of radical Dublin' centred around its large, but intimate, selection of newsagents, shops and restaurants.[57]

Three days before Bonar Law's visit, an event much better remembered in Irish history had taken place. The Irish Volunteers was formally launched on 25 November 1913 at a public meeting in the Rotunda Rink on Parnell Square in the city. Its manifesto was somewhat ambiguous in its stated object of securing and maintaining 'the rights and liberties common to all the people of Ireland', but essentially aimed to defend the home rule bill then working its way through parliament and offering Ireland a limited form of self-government. Originating from a series of meetings at Wynn's Hotel, the first committee was selected, as Michael Joseph 'The' O'Rahilly described it, 'not on Party, Political, or Sectarian lines, but solely because they were amongst the sincerest Nationalists of my acquaintance in Dublin'.[58] Eoin MacNeill, chief of staff until 1916, later claimed that there had been 12,000 to 15,000 attendees, including overflow meetings. Between 3,000 and 4,000 men were said to have enrolled. They were told where to present themselves for training, what was required of a Volunteer, and that they were expected to pay 3*d*. a week towards expenses. The first meetings of Dublin city branches took place between 1 and 5 December 1913, divided into the four battalion areas that would endure up to 1922. Branches were not formed in the county until April 1914, at Swords and Clondalkin respectively (though the Clondalkin branch soon folded again when a drill instructor apparently arrived to find only three or four men and 'left in disgust'). Swords was immediately regarded as the headquarters of what ultimately became the Fingal battalion in north County Dublin with 'a young man named Richard Coleman, an insurance agent', identified by police as the key organizer.[59] Branches at Skerries and Lusk were formed in May before the RIC CI for Dublin, Raynell Heard, recorded a rather dramatic surge in organizing activity in his report for June 1914: 'twelve branches with a total membership of 743 men' and the likelihood of several more to come.[60] In May Heard believed that 'No person of any influence has as yet taken part in the organization of the force and I don't think they will', but by the end of June there were 'a good many men of local influence taking an active part in encouraging the movement'. Those considered to be 'of influence' were all men with good middle-class credentials: Professor Tom Kettle of University College Dublin, three merchants, two medical doctors, a veterinary surgeon, a large farmer, a county councillor and the town clerk for Balbriggan. The rank and file, meanwhile, belonged 'chiefly to the labouring class, agricultural labourers, and mill hands etc. An odd small farmer's son here and there'.[61]

The Irish Volunteers' manifesto, meanwhile, noted that there 'will also be work for women to do'.[62] But none were asked to sit on the committee or speak at the meeting, an early sign that women's participation was not entirely disregarded but not always sought out either. Although its formation was far from spontaneous, Cumann na mBan (the Irishwomen's Council) only held its first 'official' meeting several months after the formation of the Irish Volunteers. The gathering at Wynn's Hotel on 2 April 1914 was chaired by Agnes O'Farrelly, who was joined by a small but representative crowd ('about 100 ladies' according to the *Irish Times*). Aside from its less than clear-cut relationship with the Volunteers, one of Cumann na mBan's key challenges was creating an organization that was 'advanced enough for the radicals, moderate enough for the constitutionalists, feminist enough for the suffragists, and broad enough to appeal to the majority of female nationalists'.[63] Indeed, competing – and sometimes contradictory or conflicting – attitudes and priorities were common within nationalism, unionism, feminism and labour in Dublin.

The diverse range of political movements and objectives was particularly obvious in local government, complicated enough in its own right. Individuals could seek election to Dublin Corporation, responsible for the county borough, and to Dublin County Council. In addition, the borough was divided into ten urban districts, with the county divided into another ten urban districts covering the suburbs, and two rural district councils (RDC) each in north and south County Dublin. The workhouses and poor law relief in the North and South Dublin Unions were administered by boards of guardians, half of whose members were elected. Both men and women could be elected to urban and rural districts and to boards of guardians, which shared responsibility with the county and municipal councils. Unionists were at least partly reliant on Catholic support or abstention for electoral success in south Dublin, with victory in general elections in Stephen's Green and County South dependent upon a coalition of militant Protestants and loyalist Catholics.[64] The United Irish League (UIL) effectively served as the IPP's constituency association and remained the most significant grassroots body in the country, putting forward candidates for election to the district authorities. Successive land acts had, however, removed many agrarian grievances. Attendances at UIL meetings improved after 1910, though Dublin county had only eight branches by 1912 – the same number as neighbouring Kildare and with only 344 members compared to Kildare's 411.[65]

Although IPP MP and county councillor J.J. Clancy remained a dominant political figure in north County Dublin, a significant number of voters in Dublin County Council elections did not vote for, or were not represented by, an IPP candidate. Local politicians in Fingal were primarily focused on representing their local community, family, or class or regional interests.[66] Both Nationalists and Unionists in north and south Dublin often went forward as independents or under other non-party labels. The 1914 county council elections offer a revealing example of the complex interplay of local and national political concerns. IPP, UIL and independents of various shades took seventeen of the nineteen available seats (eleven unopposed). Benjamin Newcombe, a Unionist standing on a 'progressive' ticket, won the seat in the Coolock Division from the Nationalist incumbent, while Captain Charles Nicholas Colthurst-Vesey retained his seat in Lucan as a Unionist. In Rathmines, however, Nationalists took the two available seats for the first time in what was regarded as the most significant outcome of the election. There had been some controversy earlier in the year when a council vacancy arose after a Unionist retired and, in defiance of what unionists saw as 'the traditions of the township', the candidate nominated by Rathmines UDC was overlooked for co-option in favour of a Nationalist, who then retained his seat in the election. The *Daily Express* suggested that was 'a sample of what may be expected of Nationalist tactics under Home Rule', but there was also disagreement about the status of the defeated election candidates nominated by the UDC. The Unionist chair of Rathmines UDC claimed it was a non-political selection, based on representing ratepayers' interests, though both candidates were supported by the Unionist Registration Association. Press reports of the results listed J.C. Anderson, defeated in Rathmines East (having been overlooked for the earlier vacancy), as a Unionist. Francis McBride, the incumbent in Rathmines West, was described as an independent.[67]

The corporation had a large IPP/UIL majority, alongside Labour, Unionist and SF members, and others representing specific interests.[68] The 1912 municipal elections saw women candidates go forward for the first time, while labour candidates stood separately from nationalists. In the late nineteenth century women had been given increasing access to voting and participation in local government. Women in the Blackrock and Kingstown urban districts were allowed to vote in municipal elections and stand in poor law elections by 1896. The 1898 Local Government Act allowed women to vote and stand in all local elections except for city and county councils. In 1911 the latter restriction was finally removed.[69] Sarah Cecilia Harrison, a painter, feminist and nationalist, was the first woman elected to Dublin Corporation when she won the South City Ward seat in January 1912 as an independent.[70] For the majority of the Irish population, however, home rule remained the dominant issue. Calls to have women's suffrage included in the home rule bill, for instance, were commonly seen as a potentially fatal distraction.[71]

Molly Adrien was the first woman elected to a local authority in north Dublin when she joined Balrothery Board of Guardians in 1914 (followed by Cumann na mBan in 1915).[72] While a woman did not go forward as a Unionist for a county council or corporation seat until 1920, Margaret Dockrell (Lady Dockrell following her husband's knighthood in 1905) had been a councillor for the Monkstown Ward of Blackrock UDC since 1898 and was elected its first female chair in 1906.[73] Progress was limited enough, however, that it was still deemed necessary in 1913 to ensure that women knew their voting rights and that they used their vote in local elections. The inaugural meeting of the City of Dublin Women's Unionist Club in May 1913 included 'a concise and detailed popular explanation of franchise qualifications' (from a man), and in advance of local elections in 1914 Lady Dockrell emphasized to the Blackrock and Monkstown branch of the Dublin Women's Unionist Association that 'every one of them who had a vote should exercise the franchise'.[74] Ethel Craig Davidson complained of 'the sleep and inertia which had overspread Dublin Unionism' and 'a great deal of apathy amongst women in exercising their vote at the Municipal Elections. In one district, 99 women for whom they had secured votes failed to turn up at the poll.'[75]

Unionist women were less likely to advocate the suffrage cause openly but were placed in a similar position to nationalist women as home rule dominated the agenda. When promoting the women's anti-home rule demonstration in January 1913, Davidson was keen to avoid 'misapprehension', and wrote that 'our Council has no connection with any society having for its object either the promotion of, or opposing of, women's suffrage. We stand altogether clear of that question, and work for the Union only.'[76] Lady Dockrell was unusual in combining her unionism with suffragism through membership of the Irish Women's Suffrage and Local Government Association (IWSLGA), originally founded by Anna and Thomas Haslam in 1876 as the Dublin Women's Suffrage Association.[77] When Dockrell lost out in the election for chair of Blackrock UDC in early 1905, she declared that 'it is not party … it is sex prejudice'.[78]

There were clearly gendered limits on what unionist politicians expected women to contribute to the anti-home rule campaign – exemplified, as in nationalism, by the very existence of separate organizations or branches for women. Nevertheless, the organization and integration of unionist women in Dublin was well ahead of its constitutional nationalist rivals. While some IPP MPs called on women as voters in municipal elections or as unpaid party workers and benefactors when it suited, the IPP discouraged and even set out to alienate women, refusing offers of time and money and largely excluding them from the UIL. Clontarf UIL had passed a resolution on women's suffrage and home rule in 1911, but the main exception was the Young Ireland Branch established in 1905 and mostly made up of UCD students and graduates, which declared (unlike the League's own constitution) that members would not be excluded on the basis of class, creed or sex. Still, when women attempted to enrol, they were first encouraged to form a ladies' branch before eventually being admitted. By 1912, the branch's suffragist members had become exasperated by both their moderate colleagues and the party hierarchy, and Hanna Sheehy-Skeffington, one of the women on the branch committee, resigned in April. Elsewhere, the closest constitutional nationalist women came to 'formal' support for the IPP was through the ladies' committee of the Ancient Order of Hibernians, a Catholic nationalist organization that was informally aligned to the IPP and had grown significantly enough to supplant the UIL in some places, including in Dublin. Turning away women's assistance, however, made little sense and would ultimately harm the party in the longer term. While it contained pro-suffrage MPs – including Dublin city MPs Joseph Nannetti, William Field and P.J. Brady – John Redmond had publicly declared himself against votes for women by 1912.[79]

As suffragists became increasingly embittered by the IPP's stance, they continued to seek support for their own cause, even when it made them unpopular among those whose priority was home rule. This work was centred on Dublin, underlining the 'centrality of the national capital to women's political activism'.[80] The Irish Women's Franchise League (IWFL) was founded in Dublin in 1908 by Francis and Hanna Sheehy-Skeffington and James and Margaret Cousins. In contrast to the devoutly pacifist Haslam and the IWSLGA, the IWFL adopted militant methods. In November 1910 six members were imprisoned in London after they had smashed the windows of Chief Secretary Augustine Birrell's London home with potatoes. On census night 1911, under the slogan 'No Vote, No Census', a small number of Dublin suffragists managed to evade being returned while others registered resistance by including 'voteless' or 'unenfranchised' under the 'Infirmity' heading. Opposition from more moderate suffragists, and fear of prosecution for refusing to cooperate with enumerators, had made a fuller boycott unworkable.[81] The major turning point in the already uneasy relationship between constitutional nationalism and the women's suffrage movement came the following year. A Conciliation bill aimed at giving women with a vote in local elections the same rights in parliamentary elections was defeated at Westminster, in part by IPP opposition. IWLF policy had been for members to challenge any politician who opposed the suffrage campaign, even if they supported his politics, thus forcing loyal nationalist members publicly to rebuke the leaders of a cause to which they were personally committed. Redmond became a *bête noir* of suffrage campaigners, and also put pressure on Nationalist MPs who wished to support women's suffrage. A final breach between the IPP and the IWFL came in April when IWFL representatives, including members of the Young Ireland Branch, were forcibly denied entry to the party's annual convention at the Mansion House.[82]

Labour activists were also forced to compete with home rule. The increasing power and influence of James Larkin's ITGWU and the trade union movement in Dublin was clear by 1913. Growing labour unrest in the city from 1905, often relating to union recognition and working practices rather than wages, usually resulted in victories for the employers.[83] This success was aided by an ability to break strikes by replacing striking workers with 'scabs' from the vast pool of unemployed or casually employed men in the city. By 1913, Larkin's reputation was at its peak and he had succeeded in persuading thousands of skilled workers on the principle that 'an injury to one was an injury to all', thus tipping the balance in favour of employees. Larkin's organization of farm labourers in the county was also central to stirring agitation from a previously weak and disorganized section of workers.[84] The 'sympathetic strike' – strikes by separate industries in support of other striking workers – became particularly effective in securing pay increases and improved working conditions. Between late January and mid-August, there were thirty major industrial disputes between employers and employees in Dublin. Most involved ITGWU members. There were, for instance, major strikes by workers at the City of Dublin Steam Packet Company, at three of Dublin's largest coal merchants, at J. and C. McGloughlin iron foundry, and at Jacob's biscuit factory.[85]

Another set of striking workers in this period came from among the city's silk weavers, who led an ultimately successful strike between March and June 1913. The leader of that strike, union secretary Michael Mallin, also encapsulated some of the ways in which class, politics, labour and activism could overlap in Dublin. Born into a city tenement, Mallin's adult life was in many ways typical of the skilled working class in Dublin. He often struggled to make ends meet and moved frequently around rented accommodation in the Liberties area of the city, with his wife sometimes keeping a small shop to supplement the family income. Like a significant number of working-class Dubliners, Mallin had also spent time in the British army, including a period of service in India. He was later dismissed as secretary of the Silk Weavers' Union. This was possibly after he had fallen out with colleagues, having become increasingly involved with the ICA. By October 1914, Mallin's drift away from more moderate colleagues was further cemented when he was appointed second-in-command of the ICA by James Connolly. He proved a popular and effective drill instructor. The two were executed in May 1916 for their part in the Easter Rising.[86]

Just over two months after the settlement of the silk weavers' strike, the largest and most famous industrial dispute began. On 26 August 1913, the opening day of the Dublin Horse Show, tram drivers and conductors employed by the Dublin United Tramways Company who were members of the ITGWU abandoned their vehicles. So-called 'scab' labour allowed the company to resume services (during daytime hours at least) and Larkin declared that it was a 'lockout' rather than a 'strike'. William Martin Murphy had already sacked hundreds of workers for refusing to give up membership of the union, and violent clashes between strikers and police followed. This culminated in the first of Dublin's two 'Bloody Sundays' in this period. On 29 August 1913 there were disturbances in Ringsend and around Great Brunswick Street as labourers James Nolan and John Byrne died in Jervis Street Hospital following a beating by police. It was a grim example of the heavy-handedness that came to define the

DMP's response to the dispute. On Sunday 31 August James Larkin made a dramatic appearance at a window of Murphy's Imperial Hotel on Sackville Street, where he was arrested. In the police baton charges that followed (by both DMP and RIC), between 400 and 600 people were injured. Trade unionists later attacked the police and shops were looted and trams burned in rioting around the city, but it was a photograph of policemen baring batons on a panicked and scattering crowd on Sackville Street that best captured the public perception of Bloody Sunday, 1913. On 3 September when James Nolan was buried in Glasnevin Cemetery, Martin Murphy convinced over 400 Dublin employers to refuse to employ ITGWU members and while major firms like Guinness and the railway companies remained non-committal, by October some 20,000 men were locked out of work. If dependants are included, the numbers affected are perhaps four times that figure.

The locked-out workers relied on funds provided by the British Trades Union Congress, which donated over £100,000 in cash, food, fuel and clothing, a much smaller fund raised at home by Lorcan Sherlock, Dublin lord mayor, and charities like the Society of St Vincent de Paul. The underwhelming reaction to Sherlock's appeal revealed the limits of middle-class support for the workers in Dublin. While Labour candidates polled strongly in the local elections in January 1914, this was not reflected in seats on the UDCs or corporation. Efforts to assist workers were also impacted by the Catholic Church's fears of proselytism, as seen in clashes with Protestant food kitchens over the souls of hungry families. A scheme to send children temporarily to foster homes in Britain, devised by Dora Montefiore, an Australian-born suffragist and socialist then living in England, and supported by Larkin, was condemned by Archbishop William Walsh and saw huge efforts to prevent Catholic children leaving Dublin (either by vigilance committee or by public shaming in Martin Murphy's newspapers). Montefiore was arrested and charged with kidnapping but the charges were later dropped. She was also subjected to anti-Semitic attacks in the press. The controversy surrounding the 'Kiddies' Scheme', opposition from within the IPP, and a harsh winter all undermined the workers' cause. Larkin blamed the British Trades Union Congress for refusing to engage in a sympathetic strike, but his attacks on British labour and support for the Montefiore scheme only served to isolate him from wider society. With British financial support contracting, and faced with impending starvation, thousands of employees had little choice but to return to work in early 1914 and sign anti-union pledges.[87]

Living and working conditions in Dublin city were significant factors in understanding the lockout, which coincided with the collapse of tenements on Church Street and a subsequent housing enquiry. But the lockout was not, initially at least, motivated by the slums. It aimed to destroy the sympathetic strike and this framed Larkin's response. William Martin Murphy (a Catholic nationalist among an overwhelmingly Protestant unionist group of employers), meanwhile, did not object to 'respectable' craft unions, rather to the organization of the unskilled worker – indeed, he had raised wages and shortened hours after a strike in 1911.[88] Nor were the reverberations of the lockout restricted to the working class of the city. On the first day of the ITGWU strike, William Shackleton of the Anna Liffey mills in Lucan locked out his employees when they refused to resign their union membership.[89] In mid-October 1913, police baton-charged demonstrators crossing the Liffey Bridge in Lucan and by the end of the month the majority of the strikers had returned to work on the employer's terms. Some of the Anna Liffey workers were from nearby Leixlip and north-east Kildare. There was a strike in a mill there in September, and economic reverberations from the lockout were also felt as far away as Naas.[90]

A strike by almost 600 farm labourers in Fingal, where the ITGWU had actively recruited, had begun before the tram workers' action and came to a negotiated settlement in August with the looming prospect for farmers of losing the harvest. But the agreement between the County Dublin Farmers' Association and the ITGWU also quickly unravelled.[91] The 'farming elite', nationalist and unionist, came together to 'protect the prosperity they had gained on the back of political struggle and land purchase', and to tackle the ITGWU.[92] For most of this period the RIC CI maintained that the farmers 'throughout the county are prosperous and well to do and not given to politics', but by October 1914 'nearly all' had joined the Farmers' Association.[93] In August the police reported that almost 1,000 unionized labourers walked off farms in Balbriggan, Howth and Lucan, and on 12 September the Farmers' Association joined the Employers' Federation in pledging to dismiss continuing ITGWU members or workers wearing the union badge. Police protection was drafted in for farmers and working employees. The police reported 'numerous cases of petty intimidation' in Swords, and a 'serious riot' in Finglas, where the windows of a public house were smashed and a teenager was shot in the back when police fired over the heads of a crowd.[94] By mid-September there may have been as many as 1,600 farm workers on strike in north County Dublin and some 400 in south Dublin.[95] Towards the end of the year, CI Heard believed intimidation and disorderly conduct had been 'more or less abandoned by the strikers' and replaced with incendiarism. Even cases of malicious burning that could not be blamed on striking workers were linked to the strike via a 'spirit of wrecklessness [*sic*]'.[96]

Agitation peaked with nights of rioting in Swords and Lucan in mid-October.[97] It also contributed to growing food prices in the city, as the county's market gardens were its primary source of produce.[98] By the turn of the year, however, the workers were effectively defeated and began drifting back to work over the following months. Around 120 men remained out of work in May, but in his report for June, CI Heard noted tersely that 'unrest caused by the labour strike has ceased' (adding, for good measure, that ITGWU candidates had all been defeated in the local elections).[99] Larkin's moment during the lockout came and went without bringing about any significant changes to working life in Dublin. But while trade unionism in the city was undoubtedly set back by the length and severity of the strike as well as by its crushing defeat, some legacies were visible.[100] The dispute permanently damaged the reputation of the DMP, a force drawn largely from 'labouring stock' but unprepared for the disturbances and unable to maintain discipline as it escalated.[101] A growth in interest in working-class housing among employers and by the corporation may have been prompted by 'the threat of socialism and the aftermath of the 1913 lock-out'.[102] As will be seen later, memories of 1913 remained fresh in middle-class minds during the next major eruption of violence in Dublin at Easter 1916. Larkin was gone from Dublin, having left for the United States, but 'Larkinism' came easily to mind. It may not have been a coincidence that two of the first fatalities on Easter Monday 1916 were DMP men shot at ICA outposts.[103]

Among the farms impacted by the farm labourers' strikes in 1913 was Lord Holmpatrick's Abbotstown estate near Blanchardstown.[104] But by July 1914 Holmpatrick's attention had returned firmly to the issue of home rule and the prospect of civil war on the island. Writing from London in July, he asked his land agent, George Fowler, 'What is going to happen now with Home Rule, will they come out from Dublin and burn the place down. Gilbert tells me there are about 200 nationalist volunteers in Blanchardstown, who drill every Friday night. Things look in a bad way.'[105] Two days earlier he had asked Fowler to 'insure, for a year, against riot & insurrection' as 'being so near Dublin might draw people out there'.[106] Such concern was somewhat understandable. By June 1914, the police considered that the Volunteer movement had the support of 'all sections of the Nationalists' and the Roman Catholic clergy. CI Heard noted that there were by then up to ten 'ex-military' with a 'good knowledge of drill' acting as instructors, with 'considerable activity' taking place in some areas. They were at this point unarmed, though some members were seen to 'wear bandoliers and haversacks and carry sticks'.[107] A rapid growth in the Volunteers within the county was also reported in July and August 1914, with the number of branches growing from 12 to 22 with a membership of 2,130 by the end of July and 32 branches and 4,225 members by the end of August.[108] Volunteers in Dublin finally saw rifles with the landing of 900 (by then obsolete) German Mausers at Howth on 26 July, and 600 more at Kilcoole in Wicklow on 1 August; a much more modest return than their unionist counterparts who brought 25,000 guns into Larne in April 1914. The CI reported that 54 Mausers were distributed to Volunteers in the county, 50 to Skerries, 2 to Howth and 2 to Lusk.[109]

The Howth gun-running had been masterminded by a committee led by former British civil servant, artillery driver and spy novelist Erskine Childers. It was followed by the shooting dead of three Dubliners and the wounding of over thirty more when members of the King's Own Scottish Borderers, a British army regiment then stationed in the city, opened fire on a hostile crowd; one of the wounded succumbed to his injuries in September. Perhaps less well remembered than it might be, especially in comparison to the gun-running affair, the 'massacre' on Bachelors Walk had its own powerful effect on the movement and on attitudes towards British soldiers in Dublin city.[110] The funerals of the first three victims two days later brought the city to a standstill, as the bodies were brought by procession from the Pro Cathedral to Glasnevin Cemetery. The *Irish Independent* described 'scenes of the most impressive character. Seldom in the recent history of Ireland has a more poignant and dramatic scene been witnessed'.[111] On 31 July Dublin County Council unanimously passed a resolution to 'emphatically condemn the action of those responsible for the brutal outrages' and urged the IPP to press the government into taking 'prompt and effectual steps to bring the perpetrators of this gross crime against the Irish Nation, to justice'. This was followed by a vote of condolence to the relatives of those who had lost their lives 'as a result of the cowardly attack made by the Scottish Borderers on an unarmed body of our people'.[112] One of the victims was Mary Duffy, a 56-year-old widow whose son was serving in the British army and wore his uniform to the funeral. The witness account of a former British soldier was also widely reported in the press. The killings generated significant hostility to the army. Soldiers were confined to barracks and when one soldier with a Scottish accent did venture out in civvies he was thrown in the River Liffey. Lord Aberdeen, the lord lieutenant, was advised against visiting the wounded in hospital.[113]

In the end, the feared march on Abbotstown never materialized as the home rule crisis in Ireland was ultimately superseded by developments beyond the island. For two years, Dublin had been at the heart of a major political crisis and the site of mobilization and activism for a number of national causes. Large numbers of Dublin men and women played their part in national and local politics, paramilitarism, suffrage activism and industrial and agricultural disputes. Workers' agitation was not just a city phenomenon and the strike of farm labourers in north and south County Dublin was more significant than an addendum to the lockout. Indeed, agricultural disputes in the county began before the strike of city tram workers.[114] While Dublin was the site of the foundation of the Irish Volunteers in 1913 and the base for its key organizers, it was also the home of one of the triumvirate of leaders of the IPP, John Dillon, who lived on North Great George's Street, and birthplace of another, John Redmond, who was a Trinity graduate and also lived in the city for a period (though neither was an MP for Dublin). In addition, Dublin hosted its own (limited) version of 'Ulster Day' in 1912, large anti-home rule demonstrations in 1913, and witnessed energetic local unionist organization throughout 1912 to 1914. It is also worth considering that Dublin was the designated location of the proposed home rule parliament and so the capital had spent two years awaiting

– or dreading – the return of a constituent assembly and the status that it might bring. All of this, however, came to a rather abrupt halt. Eight days after the shootings at Bachelors Walk, Britain went to war with Germany and its allies. The consequences of 26 July tempered the initial reaction to the outbreak of war in Europe for many Dubliners, but the war itself had its own profound impact on the city and county.

3. Dublin's response to war, 1914–16

On 5 August 1914, Dublin asylum clerk Thomas King Moylan began to keep a diary. Compelled to record the experiences of an 'ordinary man-in-the-street', he wrote of

> an earnestness and impressiveness and a thoroughness about the preparations on foot that can remind one of what the Napoleonic wars must have been like. Of these wars I have never seen the records of the impressions of the ordinary peaceful citizen, the even tenor of whose ways must have been roughly disturbed by the havoc of war … We are just getting a glimmering of what war means. What experience we shall have got by the time peace is again declared I am unable to say. No one at present dares to prophesy what way the map of Europe will be coloured at the end. The great war may 'fizzle' out – it may be Armageddon. No one knows.[1]

The previous day Britain had sent an ultimatum to Berlin, ordering Germany to end its military campaign against Belgium and France – the culmination of a 'July crisis' among the major European powers. When the ultimatum expired at 11 p.m. Britain was officially at war with Germany and Austria-Hungary. The opening entry in Moylan's diary, which he kept intermittently until April 1918, captures the surprise and uncertainty that followed the outbreak of the war. Events in Europe only really drew significant Irish attention away from domestic affairs during the August 1914 bank holiday weekend at the turn of the month, and prior to Britain's official declaration of war most people had hoped it would be avoided.[2] By the time Moylan sat down to write, it was clear that something momentous had happened. In the first instance, war in Europe immediately dissipated the potential for civil war between nationalists and unionists in Ireland. If it – ironically – brought 'peace', it also had a profound impact on the city and county of Dublin. The Easter Rising was the defining event of the war years in Dublin, and fundamentally changed the course of the Irish Revolution. The Rising should not, however, be separated from the wider context of the war, and Dubliners had already experienced that conflict in a variety of ways for almost two years before April 1916. Dublin was a city of mixed loyalties and this was vividly demonstrated by responses to the outbreak of war in Europe. At the outset, open hostility to the war was only obvious among a minority but fears of, and resistance to, conscription grew as the war progressed. Many people were, however, willing to make a distinction between volunteering and conscription. Between 1914 and 1918, tens of thousands of Dublin residents served in the

British armed forces – all volunteers – and a large proportion of Dublin households were touched directly by the First World War. Significant contributions in time and money were also made on the home front. Many more felt the war indirectly, through the impact it had on prices, wages and opportunities for work.

By the first week of August 1914, the Dublin press was full of news about developments in Europe and security preparations at home. Stop press editions of the evening papers 'sold like wild-fire' in the city, as Thomas Moylan put it, with 'as many as five and six separate editions being printed'.[3] In its first editorial after Britain's declaration of war, the unionist *Daily Express* reflected on the inevitability of the declaration of war as a necessary response by 'our Government' to the German invasion of Belgium: 'the last straw in a series of outrages'. 'Party spirit is for the moment suspended', the editorial continued, having noted the departure of troops from Ireland 'with every expression and appearance of good will on the part of Irishmen of all classes and political distinctions.' On 3 August, the day before the official declaration, IPP leader John Redmond had pledged the services of the Irish Volunteers to defend the Irish coast from invasion. This encouraged the erstwhile Unionist MP for South Dublin Bryan Cooper to appeal to fellow unionists to join the Volunteers. But the *Express* was more cautious, and instead hoped that 'Southern loyalists will consider earnestly with one another in what way they may best contribute to insuring the safety of the Empire without foregoing a particle of their intention to make the best stand they can hereafter for the maintenance of the Union'.[4] The nationalist *Irish Independent* similarly blamed German aggression, an early sign of anti-German sentiment (which appeared alongside, but also potentially separately from, pro-British sentiment), and hoped that 'England' would be quickly able to mobilize an expeditionary force for Belgium. The paper also called for 'coolness and calmness' from the people.[5] The *Irish Times* sounded a cheery note, suggesting that a period of suspense and uncertainty in Ireland had ended and, even in the face of 'terrible and urgent danger', had been replaced with a national feeling of courage and confidence. Nationalists and unionists had come together against the 'invader of their common liberties' with two armed camps now one – 'and its menace directed against a foreign foe'.[6]

The immediate response to 4 August 1914 was, however, overshadowed by local events. On 5 August, Dublin Corporation was summoned by five SF and Labour councillors for a special meeting, not about the war in Europe, but to express 'horror' at the killings at Bachelors Walk on 26 July 1914 – a 'savage crime' – and urge the recall of the lord lieutenant and chief secretary. As only sixteen members presented themselves, the meeting fell through, but the lord mayor of Dublin, Lorcan Sherlock, took the opportunity to call for calm and reassure Dubliners that there was no need to panic buy or rush to withdraw money from banks.[7] That day, alongside their reactions to the outbreak of war, the nationalist *Irish Independent* and unionist *Daily Express* had simultaneously editorialized on the inquests into the deaths at Bachelors Walk. The inquest verdicts concluded that the victims were killed by members of the Scottish Borderers and that there was insufficient evidence to implicate individuals. Furthermore, the military action of firing on unarmed civilians was also criticized. The *Independent* considered the verdicts 'fair and reasonable'.[8] Writing on the inquiry into the death of Mary Duffy, the *Daily Express* considered it unsurprising and 'comparatively fair' (given the biases and vindictiveness it saw in the operation of the inquiry) but was less convinced by the 'rider' that criticized the action of the authorities in bringing the military on to the streets. While acknowledging that public opinion was 'inflamed' over a 'deplorable business', it could not resist suggesting that some of the moral responsibility lay with a 'National Press' that had then taken glee in 'hounding down British soldiers'.[9] Such pronouncements were, however, unlikely to have found much sympathy beyond a minority.

While Bachelors Walk firmly overshadowed the initial response to war in Dublin, revulsion at the massacre coexisted with excitement, enthusiasm and support for mobilizing soldiers and sailors. Soon after the declaration of war, Thomas Moylan shared a tram with some soldiers who were 'greeted with boohs and groans', which he suggested was an 'after effect' of Bachelors Walk.[10] But Dublin had long been a site for recruitment to the British armed forces and this military tradition also shaped the capital's interactions with the First World War. There were already thousands of Dublin men serving in the army, particularly in the 1st and 2nd Royal Dublin Fusiliers (RDF). Others were members of the Army Reserve or Special Reserve and joined their battalions immediately after 4 August – often to a rapturous reception.[11] On 5 August, as Royal Dublin Fusiliers reservists gathered at Beggars Bush Barracks, friends and relatives rushed the gates and had to be restrained by police and military. The 1st Battalion of the City of Dublin Cadets, a cadet corps established in 1911, was called to parade at Wellington Barracks, and along with members of the Dublin University Officers' Training Corps and St John Ambulance Brigade were said to have responded enthusiastically to a call to enlist. The *Irish Times* reported that railway stations all along the Dublin coast saw evidence of the general mobilization order as reservists were transported to their regiments, with 'aged mothers and fathers, or young wives, with babes in their arms, parted from the men going to the front'. These 'painful' scenes were witnessed alongside efforts at 'reckless merry-making, singing, and dancing'.[12] Moylan estimated that a crowd of some 50,000 people accompanied a cohort of reservists to North Wall and described how men travelling to mobilization centres were accompanied by large crowds, 'most enthusiastic for England, singing "God Save the King", an unheard of thing hitherto among our nationalists'.[13] One body of reservists from Blackrock was even accompanied to North Wall by the local Irish Volunteers and the township band.[14] A departing British soldier described leaving amid cheers, songs and gift bags containing the words: 'From Irish friends who are proud of you' and 'This inspired us, as a week or so before they would have hung us if possible, as there was some trouble there between the military and the volunteers over the illegal landing of arms.' For much of the first half of August the signs of mass mobilization were unmistakable in the city, with wireless cables dismantled, ship owners warned their vessels could be commandeered, streets crowded with regulars and reservists, and loud sounds of departing ships.[15] 'Soldiers', Thomas Moylan reported, was the 'one and only game of all the youth in the City'.[16]

On 10 August the corporation finally met and passed its resolution condemning the military action at Bachelors Walk. There were no declarations of support for the war effort, but a committee was formed to examine food prices for the duration of the war.[17] To the RIC, at least, the reaction to war in the county was more unanimous and the CI reported in August 1914 that 'all general opinion is on the side of the Government in the present Great War struggle'.[18] In the southside townships, where there was a strong Protestant and unionist population, the UDCs generally supported the war effort, making facilities available for the military and for recruitment efforts. This was the case both in unionist-dominated Rathmines and Rathgar and in nationalist-dominated councils, such as Pembroke, which supported the policy of John Redmond.[19] Dublin County Council passed no votes or resolutions on the war, but responded to a request from the LGB by setting up a large committee 'for the Prevention and Relief of Distress consequent on the war'.[20] On 18 September 1914 the Government of Ireland (or Home Rule) bill was placed on the statute book. Though a Suspensory Act passed on the same day suspended its implementation for the duration of the war, Dublin County Council passed a resolution at its next meeting to record appreciation for the 'noble and indefatigable exertions of the Irish Parliamentary Party' and offered 'heartiest thanks and warmest congratulations to Mr John E. Redmond and his faithful colleagues on their magnificent victory', pledging continued support.[21]

The executive committee of the IUA, based on Grafton Street, immediately passed a resolution declaring it 'the duty of Irishmen to undertake their full share of Imperial responsibility in the present national emergency' and urged members in the 'three Southern provinces' to continue efforts to encourage recruitment.[22] Political activity virtually ceased for the IUA, and no resistance was offered when the home rule legislation became law. The focus instead remained firmly on the war effort and this ultimately weakened local unionist organization.[23] But, as the *Irish Times* suggested, the outbreak of war offered the Protestant and unionist minority in Dublin a renewed purpose and sense of identity; the potential for a sort of unification with the majority through a higher, shared cause.[24] For many, the call to enlist or support the war effort was also a call to duty. There were political motivations, such as the hope that the Irish contribution to the war might encourage Britain to maintain the Union, but for many it was also perfectly natural to come to the defence of the empire in a time of peril.[25]

The experiences of the Holmpatricks of Abbotstown House in Blanchardstown, to the west of the city, are broadly representative of the contributions of Protestant landed elites to the British war effort. Within weeks of the British declaration of war, it was reported in the *Irish Independent* that Lady Victoria Holmpatrick was contemplating 'fitting up a small field hospital to send to the front', with the training of nurses and ambulance drivers already commenced under a 'distinguished instructress'.[26] Irish women like Holmpatrick were central to home front efforts and they raised funds, distributed aid and sent care packages to soldiers. Hans Wellesley Hamilton, the only son who had succeeded his father as Lord Holmpatrick while still a minor, was among the Irishmen to serve abroad as a commissioned officer. In May 1914 Holmpatrick was gazetted out of the 16th Lancers, intending to 'become a civilian & make my headquarters at Abbotstown'.[27] But his retirement was short-lived, and immediately on the declaration of war Holmpatrick re-joined his unit at the Curragh as a lieutenant. Within days, he wrote to inform the manager of the Abbotstown estate, George Fowler, that he would 'start for France any day now' as part of the British Expeditionary Force.[28] Even then, Holmpatrick seemed to fear he might not come home, writing that 'I want my will carried out, although it may be rather a shock to the family.'[29] In March 1916 it was reported that the 16th Lancers had 'suffered severely' at the front in France. Under a photograph of the regiment's twenty-two officers, taken before they had left the Curragh in 1914, the *Irish Times* named four who had been killed and two others who had been wounded.[30] Two months later, Lord Holmpatrick's name was added to the regular, and growing, list of casualties – he was badly wounded in the arm and shoulder and sent to London to convalesce.[31] This time away from the front was ultimately spent between London and Dublin – an experience that perhaps separated Holmpatrick and his class from other Dubliners recovering from injuries sustained in the war. Holmpatrick also continued to do his bit for the war effort while recuperating and, in July 1915, agreed to preside over an open-air recruiting meeting in Tallaght organized by the City and County of Dublin Recruiting Committee, aimed at encouraging Dublin workers to enlist in the army.[32]

Holmpatrick's sister, Lady Clare Hamilton, was 26 years old in 1914. At some stage after the outbreak of war, she enlisted as a Voluntary Aid Detachment (VAD) nurse and was posted to Egypt. VADs were organized by the British Red Cross and the St John Ambulance Brigade, which agreed in September 1914 to cooperate for the duration of the war and formed a joint headquarters in Dublin. Lady Hamilton was one of over 13,000 Irish women who served with the Red

Cross during the war – a proportion of the eligible population (women had to be between 21 and 48 years old to serve as a VAD nurse) comparable to Britain. Nor was this service restricted to privileged women like Lady Hamilton, as volunteers came from a wide social base. While VAD nurses were paid a 'paltry and tokenistic' £20 per year (rising to £30) and required some independent means to fund training and uniforms, women in the Dublin city branch took on a wide range of roles in the Red Cross beyond nursing. These included knitting clothes, providing hospital supplies, fundraising and preparing comfort packages for soldiers.[33] At least twenty-two hospitals were opened in Dublin to treat wounded soldiers returning from the front, increasingly visible in the city as the war progressed, with the most famous set up at Dublin Castle through the efforts of Lady Aberdeen, wife of the lord lieutenant.[34] Aberdeen, who was president of the Red Cross in Dublin city (her counterpart for County Dublin was the countess of Meath), later reflected proudly on the work of her branch, which included over 14,000 garments made and sent to headquarters, over 3,000 students taking first aid and home nursing courses, Christmas gifts, newspapers and magazines supplied to 'every soldier and sailor in the hospitals of the City and County of Dublin', and social clubs for 'the wives, mothers and other relatives of soldiers and sailors in Dublin, of whom were a great number, Dublin having always been largely represented in the British Army'.[35]

A broad coalition of Dublin men and women engaged in other work beyond the Red Cross. Monica Roberts, daughter of a fellow of Trinity College living in Stillorgan, set up a 'Band of Helpers to the Soldiers' with some friends to provide gifts and comforts to soldiers. Over the course of the war, she kept up correspondence with many of the men who received her packages.[36] While the patrons and founders of a range of charitable associations were often upper-class Protestants with the time and resources to engage in such activity, both the Catholic and Protestant middle classes were also extensively involved in fundraising and other forms of war-relief.[37] The German destruction of the Belgian city of Louvain in late August 1914 provoked significant anti-German sentiment and support for 'little Catholic Belgium', and Belgians fleeing the war soon began to arrive in Dublin – including between 50 and 100 in October. Relief committees were set up across the city and county, and women from a variety of backgrounds opened their homes, knitted, provided clothes, or cooked for incoming refugees. There were, however, ultimately limits to the support offered and, over time, some frustration. The Killiney and Ballybrack refugee committees made clear they would 'not take Jews or agricultural labourers', while complaints were made about 'inappropriate behaviour' by refugees in Balrothery in November; by January 1915, rumours were circulating that some were German spies in disguise.[38] Anti-German sentiment was evident in the obsession in some quarters for rooting out 'enemy' aliens, some eight of whom were imprisoned. On 15 August several German pork butchers in the city were looted and around the same time Dublin Corporation voted to withdraw the honorary freedom of the city from German-born Celtic scholar Dr Kuno Meyer.[39]

War work appears to have been uncontroversial in Dublin and was supported by a large cross section of society. Support for Irish enlistment in the British armed forces was more divisive. Joseph Lawless remembered that some political supporters of the IPP had joined 'the Unionist element' in promoting the war effort in return for the promise of home rule, with some young men enticed to join the British armed forces while a 'stauncher national element' had seen through a British 'trick'. Though perhaps benefitting from hindsight, as well as his own convictions, Lawless later claimed that the outbreak of war had caused a 'flutter of excitement' and was immediately recognized as an opportunity to 'strike for freedom': 'In Fingal such talk was on every lip.'[40] The extent to which this conviction was actually shared across the Dublin Irish Volunteers is, however, difficult to ascertain. There is also an important distinction to be made between voluntary support for the war and the wider fear that Irishmen would be conscripted, with nationalists remaining committed to resisting any efforts to apply conscription to Ireland. On 7 August 1914 three of the five Dublin battalions unanimously adopted a resolution, declaring they would cooperate with Ulster to defend Ireland but would refuse to support the British government in a war they believed was not Ireland's. After home rule was placed on the statute book in September, Redmond moved to support voluntary enlistment in the British forces; first, and most famously, at a speech in Woodenbridge in Wicklow in September 1914 when he encouraged the Irish Volunteers to go 'wherever the firing line extends'. Redmond was, however, firmly opposed to conscription and announced that – without proof that it was necessary from a military point of view – he remained 'anchored in my hostility to a system of compulsion'. Nevertheless, the issue of support for recruitment efforts (and by extension for Britain and the empire) continued to provoke tension within the Irish Volunteers. Redmond's Woodenbridge speech ultimately split the Volunteers, with Dublin a pivotal battleground. In June 1914 the provisional committee of the Irish Volunteers had reluctantly bowed to pressure from Redmond and admitted twenty-five Redmondite nominees but twenty of the original members issued a statement after the speech at Woodenbridge. It declared that Redmond had betrayed the aims of the Volunteers and pledged to carry on without the Redmondites. They retained the name Irish Volunteers, while a large majority who supported Redmond and the IPP formed the rival Irish National Volunteers.[41]

Figures compiled by Maurice Moore, inspector general of the Irish and then National Volunteers, on votes for or against Redmond in Dublin city units suggest a wide variation from unit to unit. According to Moore's notes, the 2nd battalion voted for Redmond by 530 to 165, the 4th by 490 to 264, and the 5th overwhelmingly by 321 to 47. The suspiciously round figures for the 6th

Battalion noted that the 50 members of each of the four companies voted for Redmond. But the 1st and 3rd Battalions – based in the north-east of the city and the south inner city respectively – had majorities against (430 to 301 in the 1st and 190 to 125 in the 3rd). Though unlikely to be entirely accurate, Moore's figures suggest over 2,300 votes for Redmond and 1,103 against across six battalions and the (almost entirely Redmondite) Army Service, Ambulance and Banba Hall corps.[42] In the county, Moore recorded near universal support for Redmond: 1,713 to 127 in north County Dublin and 1,796 to 83 in south County Dublin. Only in Skerries, Swords and Rathfarnham were substantial anti-Redmond minorities recorded, and only in Rathfarnham was it more than 50 per cent of the Redmondite total.[43] Moore's county figures, at least, appear reliable enough and align closely with those of CI Heard who recorded a total National Volunteer membership of 3,547 with 247 'Sinn Féiners and others opposed to Mr J. Redmond's policy'.[44]

Far from demoralizing the minority, the split left the remaining Irish Volunteers a smaller but more cohesive and committed movement. Patrick Pearse, a schoolmaster in Rathfarnham and director of organization in the Volunteers, believed that secession had 'pulled the Volunteers straight'.[45] Even before the formal split in September, the police had noted conflicts in branches in Swords, where 'a large number of the members are Sinn Féiners', in St Margaret's and in Lusk.[46] While the split played out differently in different units and in different parts of Dublin, those who remained in the minority widely remembered it afterwards with a sense that the victory was theirs. Joseph Lawless claimed that the split depleted the Irish Volunteers in Fingal, but the National Volunteers 'became a dead letter in the district within a few weeks'.[47] In Lusk, it solved an issue where two companies had been founded amid rivalry between nationalist families in the area. Both had apparently participated in the Howth gun-running but were denied any arms until they could settle their differences and unite (in fact, few companies in the county appear to have had access to arms anyway). After the split, one company joined the Redmondite National Volunteers and the other, led by the Rooney family and drawn from the hurling and football club in Lusk, remained with the Irish Volunteer executive. Thomas Peppard, who joined the Rooney company in 1914, claimed the National Volunteers soon ceased to exist, meaning 'our differences were solved for us by the march of time'.[48] Joseph O'Connor was an officer in A Company, 3rd Battalion – where Moore recorded an even split of fifty men for and fifty against – and remembered finding himself left with nine men out of about 100, but 'we were fortunate in the fact that our officers remained firm and we had sufficient enthusiasm to restart. I was very glad that when the split occurred there was so little bickering.'[49] Gerald Byrne claimed that in the 4th Battalion only six men and one officer 'went to the Redmond side' (a very different picture to that suggested by Moore's figures).[50]

The decline of the National Volunteers in Dublin was not as quick or straightforward as some remembered it, and efforts were made to keep the force going in 1914 and 1915. After a jump in August 1914, the CI noted a decrease in Volunteer membership in the county in September and a 'great falling off in enthusiasm'.[51] Training days and field exercises were held in places like the Phoenix Park and Lusk, and Moore continued to receive requests for rifles and equipment from local companies.[52] There was also enough enthusiasm in early 1915 for a disagreement to emerge between the City of Dublin Committee and the South Dublin Committee over unit boundaries.[53] In August 1915 the 1st Battalion of the National Volunteers organized an excursion to Cashel, County Tipperary, to 'keep the battalion together as well as possible'.[54] But in December 1915 Frank O'Curran, a member of 'F' Company, 2nd Battalion of the Dublin National Volunteers, wrote to Maurice Moore to appeal to him 'to make one more effort' to bring the numbers of the 'Dublin Regiment' up to a 'fair strength'. O'Curran noted a 'considerable decrease' in the ranks as well as a growing lack of interest in training and field exercises.[55] And by early 1916 there were very obvious signs of ill-discipline and apathy from Dublin city officers and men. In February 1916 one officer, who had received a letter demanding an explanation for his absence from a meeting, wrote to Moore and complained that over the previous eighteen months he had 'sent so many letters, postcards, and circulars to members of my Company of which absolutely no notice was taken that I thought I might, without further prejudice to the fortunes (or misfortunes) of the Company, indulge in the luxury of ignoring such communications myself.' Resenting a reference to 'lack of enthusiasm and attention to duty', the officer continued by declaring that 'as long as the half-dozen men who now form the Company attend I shall continue to do so. But a constitutional distaste for futile discussion and sad experience of previous meetings of officers have compelled me to a resolution against attending any more such meetings.'[56] The chief inspecting officer for the city and county of Dublin was sent to interview the officer in question. Moore took from a report of their meeting that the officer 'regrets the statement that he will not attend meetings whether ordered or not and that he will comply in future with any orders received'. But the chief inspecting officer had said nothing of the sort. In any case, the damage was likely already done.[57] In the county there appears to have been a gradual and steady decline in membership and activity, with a drop from 4,226 at the outbreak of war to 2,554 as reported in December 1915 – though most pre-war branches remained nominally in existence.[58]

Redmond's call to arms had a profound impact on the Irish Volunteers in the capital, but the extent to which it encouraged Dubliners to serve is less obvious. By mid-January 1918 police figures recorded that just over 3,000 of the city recruits to the army had come from the National Volunteers, while over 20,000 had no known volunteer background. About a quarter of all Dublin recruits served in the 16th (Irish) Division, one of a number of 'Irish' New Army divisions created after the outbreak of war and seen as most clearly representative of the Redmondite 'project'. Another 15 per cent served in the other unit closely associated with Irish nationalism, the 10th (Irish) Division. But the War Office was unwilling to allow Irish Volunteer units to be converted directly into British army units, therefore the allegiances of all recruits is not clear.[59] And as Dublin city and suburbs had a strong, organized unionist minority it was not only nationalists who were politically motivated to join up. Some 200 members of the Loyal Dublin Volunteers joined the 9th Royal Inniskilling Fusiliers, which formed part of the 36th (Ulster) Division, as a 'Dublin' company.[60] In the county, the transfer from the National Volunteers to the army was poor, with only 103 joining up by the end of November 1914 and a 'few' more in December. The CI believed this was not principally due to the efforts of SF, which had a small following in the county, and was instead inclined to believe that National Volunteers were simply 'shirking their duty through funk'.[61]

Wider recruitment efforts provoked a range of responses in Dublin. Recruiting offices were set up at Great Brunswick Street and, in late September 1914, following a recruiting meeting at the Mansion House attended by Redmond and Asquith, on Grafton Street. Enlistments at Grafton Street were initially slow, and the first man to enroll was said to have been jeered by a large crowd, but the office soon became busier.[62] The city was also awash with both pro- and anti-recruitment literature.[63] In October 1914 the *Irish Times* claimed that setbacks for the Allies usually saw surges in recruitment in the country but that this was not the case in Dublin where anti-recruitment handbills were common and 'peaceful persuasion' was applied to potential recruits.[64] A minor controversy about a fortnight earlier, however, highlighted both the visibility of recruitment talk in the city and the ways that it could engage an audience. On 24 September the *Irish Times* published a letter to the editor complaining about a man standing on Grafton Street with a sandwich board that read 'Irishmen. Don't enlist'. The correspondent was sure that this did not represent the views of the ordinary Irishman and insisted that the sooner the 'authorities in Ireland's capital put a stop to so scandalous an advertisement, the better for Dublin and for Ireland'.[65] The following day, two more letters were published from observers who pointed out that the back of the sandwich board read, 'Until you have been photographed at Messrs. So and So's studio'. One writer considered it an 'objectionable trick', but another – whose initial 'righteous indignation' soon gave way to amusement and relief – suggested that, while in bad taste, the advertisement went to show that 'there are two sides to most questions'.[66]

Archbishop William Walsh had long lost faith in the IPP by 1914 and opposed Redmond's offer of voluntary support for the war effort.[67] The archbishop had much earlier been critical of the army's presence on Dublin streets as potentially promoting 'depravity' among his flock, but was considered an important ally by recruiters and was approached repeatedly in the early months of the war to put his name to appeals. Walsh, though, imposed a rigid policy of refusing any request for help. His private secretary, Monsignor Michael Curran, for instance, claimed that the archbishop refused a military request for permission to place recruiting posters on the railings of Catholic churches in his archdiocese and openly disapproved of the practice. After the liner *Lusitania* was sunk off the Cork coast by a German submarine in May 1915, costing some 1,200 lives, Walsh publicly described it as a 'horrid massacre' and a 'frightful premeditated crime', but was annoyed when the Organization of Recruiting in Ireland used his words on a poster and sent it to him for approval: 'In reply, I have only to say that, in my opinion, your Council, in producing the poster … has taken a very great liberty indeed.' Curran considered that the 'recruiting geniuses' in Dublin had 'got a bad slap in the face from His Grace'.[68] Curran also stated that Walsh had considered war hospital and Red Cross collections as a 'ruse for recruitment', but the archbishop did contribute £10 10*s*. to a relief fund for the *Lusitania* and was a member of various war-relief committees – further evidence of wider nuances in attitudes towards the war and distinctions that could be made between humanitarian assistance and more direct aid to the military campaign.[69]

Notwithstanding some disappointment about overall recruitment figures, Dubliners continued to enlist in the British armed forces for a variety of reasons that went beyond politics or ideology – demonstrating, perhaps, some limits to the Catholic archbishop's influence. Indeed, the poor health of Dublin citizens on its own denied the army a significant number of additional recruits who were rejected on medical grounds. Police figures calculated that between the outbreak of the war and its end in 1918, over 26,000 men from the city volunteered for the British army. This was in addition to between 6,500 and 7,000 reservists and it is estimated that between 35,000 and 40,000 residents of Dublin city ultimately served in the war. The most popular unit for Dubliners was, unsurprisingly, the RDF. Over half of those whose service can be traced to a specific infantry regiment joined it. Over 1,000 served in the 2nd RDF and over 800 more in the 1st. But Dublin recruits were spread widely and can be found in ninety-four separate battalions. About a third served in non-infantry units, including the Artillery, the Army Service Corps (primarily tasked with transport and logistics), the Royal Engineers, and the Royal Army Medical Corps.[70] The range of service and its impacts are evident in the experiences of the family of Edward Lee, a large draper merchant originally from Westmeath, and Annie Lee, of the well-known Shackleton family, who lived in Stillorgan. Two of the four Lee sons received commissions in the Royal Munster Fusiliers and another was commissioned in the Royal Army Medical Corps.[71] Edward and Annie Lee also contributed on the home front, opening premises for use by the Dublin city branch of the Red Cross, and Edward Lee was the only non-council member of Rathmines UDC's recruitment committee.[72]

Of some 23,400 Dublin volunteers recorded by mid-January 1918, 13,254 were known to be Catholic and 3,432 Protestant (with the denomination of the remainder unknown).[73] When compared to their proportion of the city's population, Protestants thus appear to have been disproportionately represented among Dublin recruits. But these figures can be misleading as large numbers of men were not living in Dublin but had travelled into the city to enlist.[74] Figures for the county area – outside the DMP's jurisdiction – are even more difficult to quantify. Recent research has suggested that about 70 per cent of Dublin's volunteers came from the city area, slightly more than its 63 per cent share of the combined city and county population in 1911. Another 20 per cent came from Pembroke or Kingstown, meaning just 10 per cent enlisted elsewhere in the county; over 2 per cent came from Skerries or Swords but the remainder were well spread over the west and south of the county.[75] This seems to be confirmed by monthly reports from the CI, where detailed figures were not regularly recorded but frequent remarks made on the absence of recruits across large parts of the county.[76]

In total, at least 6,568 Dubliners (and possibly over 600 more) were killed or died in service between August 1914 and August 1921, when the Commonwealth Graves Commission stopped classifying deaths as 'war deaths'. Over 4,500 were killed on the Western Front, in France or Flanders, with another 500 at Gallipoli in Turkey and almost 400 at sea. The remainder died on 'home' service, somewhere in Britain or Ireland, including some who died of wounds in hospital.[77] In line with enlistment patterns, the majority of the Dubliners killed in the war were from the city. Though not exhaustive, a list of war dead from Fingal only gives 292 names.[78] Records list 4,858 RDF killed up to 11 November 1918. Over 1,700 were men born in Dublin city and county and the proportion of Dubliners killed while serving in the RDF ranges from 78 per cent in the 9th Battalion to only 35 per cent in the 10th. As the 10th was a 'commercial' battalion, some of its members may have originally come to Dublin for work. The impact of poverty was, though, again evident in the recruits to the RDF who ultimately died and the highest proportion of Dublin-born RDF fatalities were from the north and south inner city. These included eleven men from Francis Street and seven from Gloucester Street. Another cohort of fatalities, however, came from the more salubrious Blackrock, Dalkey, Kingstown and Monkstown where there were large numbers of Protestants.[79]

The British military unit most closely associated with Dublin's experience of the war was the 7th RDF, one of the new battalions raised in August 1914 and part of the 10th (Irish) Division. Though 'Pals Battalions', designed to encourage recruitment through groups drawn from towns, streets, clubs, or organizations, were common in Britain, 'D' Company of the 7th RDF was one of very few 'Pals' units established in Ireland. Organized by the Irish Rugby Football Union, its members were not necessarily all rugby players but were generally young, middle-class Protestants.[80] One of the 'Pals' was Henry Kavanagh, a solicitor's clerk from Merrion Road. He joined in 1914 and was promoted to lance corporal in August 1915.[81] The battalion trained at the Curragh for almost eight months and attracted the attention of the Dublin press until it left Ireland for more training in Basingstoke. In July 1915 it left for the Gallipoli peninsula.[82] RDF and Royal Munster Fusiliers had already fought at Gallipoli as part of the first attack there in April 1915, suffering sufficiently heavy losses that the two battalions were merged and became known as the 'Dubsters'. The 'Pals' in the 7th RDF were part of a second attack on Gallipoli in August 1915, landing at Suvla Bay on 6 August and again suffering heavy losses in difficult conditions. Within a week, 131 of the 200 members of 'D' Company – quickly nicknamed 'the Toffs in the Toughs' – were killed or wounded.[83] Among the Dubliners serving in other units killed at Gallipoli was Joe Lee of the Royal Munster Fusiliers, son of Edward and Annie Lee. His brother, Tennyson, was badly wounded in the arm and witnessed Joe's body being brought back from the front. It was almost three weeks before the scale of Dublin's loss at Suvla was reported at home. Growing lists of casualties were published in late August and early September – including group photographs featuring many by then deceased officers. One photograph published in the *Irish Independent* included twenty-eight officers from the 'Pals' battalion, nine of whom had been killed and another six wounded. Significantly, Gallipoli helped to discredit the war effort in some quarters in Dublin. The loss of young Dublin men was compounded by criticism from the commander of the Mediterranean Expeditionary Force, Sir Ian Hamilton – in stark contrast to praise for troops from Australia and New Zealand – and reports of poor logistical and operational planning. This both gave succour to militant nationalists who opposed the war effort and shook the faith of supporters, while there was also a belief that the sacrifices of Dublin soldiers were insufficiently recognized or that some units were receiving undue attention. Writer Katherine Tynan, whose two sons enlisted during the war, wrote of a sense of bitterness that 'lives had been thrown away and their heroism unrecognized … Dublin was full of mourning'.[84]

The Dubliners who supported the British war effort from 1914 ultimately did so for a wide variety of reasons, once again reflecting the diversity of feeling, allegiances and circumstances in the city and county. Among those who supported the war effort at home, loyalty could lie with Britain, with John Redmond, with the Allies, or just with a husband, brother, or son serving in the colours. There had long been a strong economic rationale behind service in the British armed forces from Dublin city and separation allowances paid to the wives of soldiers were a significant attraction for working-class recruits, whose families would be noticeably better off while they were in service abroad. Dublin's largest employers, such as Guinness, the railways and the corporation, also offered financial incentives to potential recruits (though the latter did so less enthusiastically than unionist-owned businesses).[85] Financial incentives alone were not enough to sustain recruitment, particularly given growing casualty lists. There were also group loyalties and collective pressures that went beyond politics. One common factor that united the 'Pals' was a love of games, and the sporting rhetoric that often accompanied participation in the war had its own influence in encouraging a powerful 'logic of collective sacrifice'.[86] Henry Kavanagh survived Gallipoli, but his war was not over and he was killed at Salonika in Greece in September 1916.[87] Notwisthstanding the fame of August 1915 in the memory of Dublin's war, the worst single day for fatalities was 1 July 1916, the opening day of the Battle of the Somme, when 111 Dubliners were killed (with another five dying elsewhere on the same day).[88] In Dublin, however, the Somme was eclipsed by what had preceded it. The events of Easter 1916 ruptured the experience of the First World War, though the Rising took place very firmly in the wider context of that conflict. The Rising also fatally scuppered John Redmond's home rule project. But that was all to come, and should not detract from the extent to which the declaration of a republic from the front of the General Post Office (GPO) in Dublin city centre on Easter Monday 1916 came as a profound and disorienting shock to the majority of Dubliners, irrespective of their political views or allegiances.

4. Dublin city's 1916 Rising

'Such excitement! Dublin is in the hands of the Sinn Feiners'.[1] The lively opening to Lilian Stokes' diary entry for 24 April 1916 conveys something of the sudden and dramatic way in which the Easter Rising – conceived and executed by 'a minority of a minority of the minority' – was thrust upon the city of Dublin.[2] Planning was led by a (retrospectively titled) 'military council', comprised of members of the oath-bound, revolutionary IRB hand-picked by veteran Fenian Thomas Clarke and his protégée Seán Mac Diarmada; James Connolly, the socialist and leader of the much smaller ICA, was added to the conspiracy in January 1916. Probable opponents within the movement were kept in the dark, including, most significantly, chief of staff of the Irish Volunteers, Eoin MacNeill (not himself a member of the IRB). The original plans, whatever they may have been, were sundered by the failure to land arms in Kerry and the arrest of Sir Roger Casement, by the confusion and disorganization caused by MacNeill's infamous 'countermanding order', and by the decision to delay until Easter Monday. What ultimately transpired in Dublin is well known. Around midday on Monday 24 April 1916, Patrick Pearse read a proclamation on behalf of the 'Provisional Government of the Irish Republic' at the front of the GPO on Sackville Street, marking the symbolic opening of the rebellion. The Irish Volunteers, ICA, Hibernian Rifles and Cumann na mBan occupied a series of potentially strategic but largely unsymbolic buildings around the city, with the GPO as headquarters.[3] An abortive attempt was made to take Dublin Castle, the seat of British government in Ireland.

Five of the signatories of the proclamation were among the occupants of the GPO: Pearse, Clarke, Connolly, Mac Diarmada and Joseph Plunkett. The only other garrison on the north side of the river occupied the Four Courts and was under the command of Edward Daly. Signatories Thomas MacDonagh and Éamonn Ceannt commanded rebels at Jacob's biscuit factory and the South Dublin Union respectively. Seán Heuston marched a group of fourteen from Mountjoy Square to the Mendicity Institution, a charitable home, and Con Colbert occupied Watkins' Brewery and later the Jameson Distillery on Marrowbone Lane. Michael Mallin, meanwhile, led a contingent of ICA men and women, bolstered by some late arrivals from the Irish Volunteers, to St Stephen's Green (later abandoned for the Royal College of Surgeons). Éamon de Valera, ultimately the most senior Volunteer to survive the Rising, commanded a garrison in Boland's bakery and flour mills. In each of these locations and in a number of smaller outposts dotted nearby, rebels waited to repel assault from British forces. After some early skirmishes on Easter Monday and Tuesday, including the shooting of a DMP constable at Dublin Castle who became one of the first Dublin fatalities of the Rising, violence increased as additional units of British troops – who had been training for the Western Front – landed at Kingstown and marched to the city. The most significant concentration of casualties, and the only really significant rebel military victory, was at Northumberland Road and Mount Street Bridge where just over a dozen Volunteers killed twenty-six members of the Sherwood Foresters and wounded some 130 more. Four Volunteers were killed.[4] But within a week the British army had surrounded the rebels and suppressed the Rising as a military event. A more important symbolic victory followed for the defeated rebels, but this was also a week of unprecedented danger, uncertainty and disruption for Dubliners.

Thirty-eight-year-old Lil Stokes was from a prominent Dublin Protestant family. She had been making her own contribution to the war effort ('VAD housemaiding') when she found, to her dismay, that no trams were running: 'No thrams miss, the Volunteers has the city'. Dodging bullets along the way, Stokes eventually returned to her home in Ballsbridge to find that her parents 'had not heard a word of what was going on and had not noticed the firing'.[5] If many prospective rebels had some inkling – however vague – of an upcoming 'scrap', the outbreak of insurrection caught the citizens of Dublin completely by surprise.[6] Many were out on the bank holiday Monday in the county, at the Zoo, or at the races in Fairyhouse. It was only on their way home that day-trippers became aware of the occupation of the city. Other visitors to Dublin found they could not leave.[7] A newly wed serviceman and Trinity graduate, one of many British soldiers on furlough that weekend, was taken with his wife into his alma mater when fighting broke out.[8] This soldier had come to Dublin to escape the First World War. For surgical supply salesman Alf Fannin and others like him, the war – or, at least, a war – had come to them: 'We used to think we were clear enough of the war here in Ireland but we certainly have got it close enough now'.[9]

For those present in Dublin on Easter Monday 1916, the sudden eruption of violence was dramatic and exhilarating. As Fannin put it, there had 'been nothing like this in Dublin in our generation'.[10] Pearse may have been met with indifference at the front of the GPO, but as the day wore on, 'knots of watchful strangers' gathered in Sackville Street and around the city to take in the spectacle.[11] For the remainder of the week, curiosity, an insatiable desire for information, and the necessity of sourcing food continued to bring people outdoors in spite of the risks. Lil Stokes found her way on Easter Monday to the provost's house in Trinity where Elsie Mahaffy, the provost's daughter, later remembered her as a 'foolhardy lady': 'saying to herself "I shall never see another Revolution" she walked all over Dublin'.[12] Another 'civilian witness', whose Westland Row-bound train was suddenly stopped at Lansdowne Road, 'mediated' on whether to return home or push on into the city. 'Personal safety prompted me to return home, but a thrill of adventure rushed through my veins, and, regardless of risk, I decided to proceed at once to Dublin.'[13] Cartoonist and journalist Joseph Robert Clegg was one of many roving reporters who spent the week travelling between rebel garrisons before returning home each evening.[14]

John Dillon MP, the deputy leader of the IPP, was the only senior member of the party in Dublin. He commented on throngs of people walking past his home on North Great George's Street 'without slightest appearance of fear or panic'.[15] The *Irish Times* similarly noted the 'quietness and courage with which the people of Dublin accepted the sudden and widespread danger. In the very neighbourhood of the fiercest fighting the streets were full of cheerful and indifferent spectators.' 'Such courage', it was suggested, 'is excellent, but it may degenerate into recklessness.'[16] On Thursday, the paper commented again on the 'cool and almost indifferent behaviour of the well-disposed crowds in our streets during the last few days', but warned people drawn to areas of fighting 'by mere curiosity and love of excitement' to obey martial law restrictions and stay away.[17] To the *Irish Times*, at least, this seemed a distinctly Dublin response to a sudden and traumatic event.[18]

This must have played its own part in many of the fatalities of Easter week in Dublin; over half of almost 500 dead were non-combatants. At least forty were aged sixteen or under, 2-year-old Christina Caffrey the youngest, shot in the spine in her mother's arms in the family home in Corporation Buildings.[19] Urban war was a new experience for rebels and British soldiers alike, and posed its own problems. As one loyalist commentator put it, 'With Sinn Feiners parading the roofs & loyalists in the houses, there were many mistakes made'.[20] Nervy rebels shot civilians who had (sometimes inadvertently) obstructed them, while British soldiers fired on others for failing to stop at checkpoints.[21] As meagre rations in working-class homes ran low and forced people outdoors in search of food, civilian deaths rose steadily each day from fifteen on Easter Monday to forty-five on Saturday.[22] One tragic case was Margaret Naylor, who was possibly the woman spotted carrying bread near the Barrow Street railway bridge in Ringsend on 29 April when she was shot dead by a soldier. Her husband John, a private in the RDF, was killed in France on the same day, leaving their three children orphaned.[23] The Dublin Fire Brigade responded to ninety-three calls during Easter week as fires were started by looters and worsened by British shelling.[24] Dublin hospitals were overwhelmed with dead and injured rebels, soldiers and civilians. At the end of May it was reported that the busiest hospitals, Jervis Street, the Mater and the Richmond, had treated 600, 300 and 200 individuals respectively.[25] Robert Scott, who offered his services to the St John Ambulance and Red Cross on Easter Monday, finished an account of his experiences by noting 'I was very thankful indeed that I had not a single child to deal with'.[26]

Witnesses were drawn into the events of Easter Monday 1916 by chance. To those living in the south city or its suburbs it was (often second-hand) news of the occupation of St Stephen's Green or Westland Row Station, and not the GPO, that first alerted them to the Rising.[27] Surviving contemporary accounts do not record Pearse's oration from the front of the GPO and Joseph Holloway – a devotee of the Abbey Theatre and not unsympathetic to the rebels – was unusual in seeing a copy of the proclamation ('a long and floridly worded document full of high hopes').[28] Residents of the townships had to travel into the city to witness the fighting, but others were caught up more directly. As Trinity College was defended from rebel attack, the provost's house was transformed from a domestic site to a military one.[29] British soldiers stopped outside Monica Roberts' house in Stillorgan for tea and refreshments, while polite rebels took over Denis Johnson's house in nearby Lansdowne Road.[30] Isabelle Fleming brought wounded soldiers into her home on Northumberland Road, where there was intense fighting on Wednesday, providing tea, water, food, towels and cushions; a wounded adjutant died there.[31] Those closer to the fighting were also more likely to be confined to their homes for prolonged periods. In Sackville Street, the isolation could be acute: 'It is horribly lonely not being able to communicate with any person outside this house.'[32] Notwithstanding the distance that many witnesses lived from the worst of the fighting, the absence of bereavement in surviving contemporary accounts suggests that the more prosperous citizens of Dublin were better insulated from its impact. But death was not the preserve of the poor, and casualties included the president of the Irish Rugby Football Union, Francis Browning, and corps superintendent of the St John Ambulance Brigade for County Dublin, Holden Stodart.[33] Both were shot on affluent Northumberland Road.[34] In the intimate confines of Dublin society, however, acquaintances were not restricted by religion or politics and other middle-class loyalists had similarly known, and even admired, rebel leaders.[35]

Suppression of the rebellion began in earnest with the arrival of infantry battalions from Britain in the early hours of Wednesday morning. Monica Roberts recorded their arrival in her diary and remarked that it was 'grand to see our Tommies & they gave one a great feeling of security' but also feared the fighting that might soon take place and the 'useless waste of our soldiers' lives'.[36] That day the British army began shelling the empty Liberty Hall and by Thursday incendiary shells were being fired at the GPO and its vicinity.[37] James Stephens watched first hand as 'the shells of a heavy gun lobbed' through the windows of buildings on Sackville Street.[38] One resident described Wednesday as 'a nightmare day of nerve-racking sound' with the 'sickening dull boom' of cannon, 'infernal rattle of machine-guns', and the 'incessant vicious snapping of the rifle firing'.[39] Over the course of Wednesday and Thursday, flames engulfed Sackville Street, Abbey Street, Henry Street and Eden Quay, and were widely visible across the city. Meanwhile, British troops began strategically cordoning off the city, using the river as a natural divide. Civilian movement was also increasingly, if not entirely, restricted and as the British response intensified, so too did some of the practical issues facing residents of the city and suburbs. If a business or workplace was lucky enough to avoid the worst of the conflict, getting staff and supplies to premises remained unduly risky or even impossible. Alf Fannin's medical supply shops on Grafton Street and North Frederick Street were able to carry on some limited business on Tuesday. He later reported that he had lost a fortnight's business but, nevertheless, paid his staff in full.[40]

In a letter written over the course of 10 and 11 May, Marion Kelleher recorded the prices of a range of ordinary goods sold during Easter week, including butter at 7*s.* 6*d.* per pound on Baggot Street, loaves of bread for 1*s.* in Monkstown, and the 'coarser parts' of 'meat killed the night before' for 1*s.* 6*d.* per pound. On Tuesday, she had been lucky enough to buy a loaf of bread, some flour, butter, ham, potatoes and biscuits.[41] But by Wednesday (26 April), even those fortunate enough to have well-stocked larders began to grow concerned about potential food shortages.[42] Kelleher had a different lifestyle to many working-class Dubliners (whose experiences were generally not recorded), but her letter demonstrates the supply dilemmas created by the Rising as the city struggled to avert a food crisis. By Friday, Frances Taylor was not alone in fearing that the limited supply of food might soon run out.[43] On Saturday, John Dillon heard that the residents of Barry's Hotel in the city were 'in a terrible position', with one loaf between thirty.[44] Fortunately, the worst of these fears were not realized. Under-secretary Sir Matthew Nathan formed a committee that was tasked with securing and safeguarding food supplies in the city on 26 April, the British army distributed supplies around the city, and the LGB eventually set up thirty-one depots to dispense free food.[45]

Access to necessities varied around the city. On Tuesday Dillon was 'amazed' to see bread and milk carts doing their rounds on North Great George's Street.[46] Margaret Mitchell received a visit from the baker and milkman across the river, at Herbert Park, while Elsie Henry believed the baker on the other side of town was unable to make it to her home in Ranelagh.[47] Near St Stephen's Green, nationalist, Gaelic Leaguer and future president of Ireland Douglas Hyde 'found it quite impossible to get any provisions' on Saturday and sent out two servants in search of 'either bread flour or oatmeal or Indian meal' with no success.[48] One letter writer travelled from Lucan to Howth, some 20 kilometres north of the city centre, and found that food was also getting very scarce there, with Howth completely cut off from supplies.[49] A letter to the editor of the *Daily Express* later described how starvation was narrowly avoided there by the action of the village's 'gentlemen'.[50] Those further away from the worst fighting, and with access to motorcars, could source supplies more easily.[51]

The reflections of Dubliners from more comfortable backgrounds offer a reminder that the Rising did not always act as a great leveller. In spite of their worst fears, none of the writers of surviving letters and diaries went without food for any prolonged period. It was, instead, the limited range of food that drew most complaint. Eileen Chance complained about the absence of fresh milk: 'We hate the condensed … it is horrid muck'.[52] The lack of meat – hardly a staple of the diet of the average working-class Dubliner – caused further grumbling: 'No fresh meat to be had at any price'; 'Butchers meat is unobtainable for several days but we have some hope of a joint today or tomorrow'.[53] A neighbour had given Sarah Harden 'a thick slice of hot ham for dinner' and she informed her nephew that 'the ham was a great treat as we have had nothing but eggs since Tuesday. I don't think we will be anxious for soda bread again in a hurry'.[54] Nellie May Preston joked that she was 'nearly sick of the sight of Rhubarb'.[55]

As rich and poor were forced to jostle for access to limited supplies of bread, resources mattered when it came to paying inflated prices. Eileen Chance approached a baker's cart near Kildare Street and found it 'surrounded by poor women' and, as she pointedly described, 'people like ourselves from Fitzwilliam and Merrion Squares'. She was 'lucky in getting a fair supply of fancy bread' as the poorer women would 'only take plain loaves'.[56] In the under-secretary's lodge in the Phoenix Park, Dorothy Stopford knew that 'we shall be alright' but, she wrote, 'I can't imagine what they are doing in Dublin'. People within the 'cordon' around the city, she was told, would be close to starving in two days and a chef had 'refused to cook while his wife and children are starving in Dublin', throwing a saucepan at an aide-de-camp in protest.[57] Labour leader Thomas Johnson found it 'strange' to see 'well-dressed, middle-class citizens lugging home bags of flour, bundles of vegetables, rhubarb, cabbage etc.' in Drumcondra but recognized that the poor could not afford to benefit from the plentiful supply of four stone bags of flour.[58] Any temptation to take advantage of the disturbances to avoid shortages and high prices remained beyond those who would have considered themselves among the 'well disposed'.

Some writers scarcely hid their fears about what the lower classes were doing or might do. John Dillon was kept awake by a fear that 'the slum people would break into the public houses and that the city at night would be in the hands of a howling drunken mob'.[59] Public houses were restricted to opening between 2 p.m. and 5 p.m., a decision Louisa Hamilton Norway, wife of the head of the Irish postal service, believed was 'just to inflame the mob'. She was 'furious' when her husband was refused whiskey and soda at 8 p.m. or cider with his dinner.[60] Fred Kidd wrote despairingly of 'starvation riots' and wondered, 'When poor people begin to feel the pangs of starvation what frame of mind will they get into?'[61] In doing so, these commentators were repeating – perhaps subconsciously – the derogatory discourses aimed at working-class strikers during the lockout. This captured the chasm that existed between those who deemed themselves the 'respectable' classes and the urban working poor who were routinely treated with contempt based on perceptions about their moral and spiritual inadequacies.[62] This was also visible when middle- and upper-class witnesses described the looting that soon accompanied the outbreak of the Rising.

Waiting in Holyhead to make his way back to Dublin from a trade union conference in Cardiff, Thomas Johnson heard some 'Incredible stories' about what was happening in Dublin, 'most comical if not so tragic':

> Boys with 21/- (£1.05) silk hats mimicking Charlie Chaplin. Old women in rags sitting on the kerb putting on fancy boots and shoes. One man tells of a boy selling an Irish Times in the street with a gold wristlet watch on his wrist. Women taking out suites of furniture from the furnishing shops and finding that they would not fit their rooms – breaking them up or using them to form a barricade. Boys in the midst of real firing playing soldiers, sham fighting with toy guns and wearing uniforms taken from the fancy goods stores.[63]

Witnesses were widely drawn to comment on this looting, and particularly the actions of those they described as the 'rowdy element', the 'mob', the 'riff raff', or the 'inhabitants of the Slums'.[64]

Looting was generally depicted with a mixture of amusement, disgust and condescension and provides revealing insights into class divisions in Dublin that transcended feelings about the rebellion. Indeed, to Presbyterian clergyman Revd Robert Clements, no supporter of the rebels, the behaviour of the lower classes was as galling as the rebellion itself.[65] Louisa Norway described 'ragged women and children' stealing boots and shoes, one particular looter who complained to the police after her own haul was taken, and another who lamented, 'Isn't Clery's broke yet? Isn't it a great shame that Clery's is not broke?'[66] Others witnessed the theft of straw hats alongside gold watches and rings, grand pianos and even a safe.[67] Raids on Lawrence's toy shop and Noblett's sweet shop on Sackville Street drew attention, and James Stephens wrote that the poor children of the city were experiencing 'sweetstuffs they had never toothed before, and will never again taste in this life, and until they die the insurrection of 1916 will have a sweet savour for them'.[68] Looting, and the behaviour of the working class, was thus mediated through the eyes – and prejudices – of those who saw themselves as their social superiors, reflecting wider attitudes towards those who lived in Dublin's tenements. Rebels, their supporters and civilian commentators – regardless of religion or politics – were more inclined to condemn the looting than reflect on the dire poverty of many of its practitioners.[69] It appears that looting was not confined to the 'submerged slum population' as the conservative *Irish Life* magazine put it. It was noted that many looters were 'well dressed and belonged to the wage-earning working class', and even some were deemed more respectable still; the eminent Trinity College physicist and geologist John Joly was later willing to 'vouch for the deeply enjoyable nature of looting operations'.[70] This was deemed in some quarters to be its most worrying feature.[71] Most of those later convicted of looting offered rather innocent excuses for their behaviour. One defendant claimed she had 'found' two boys' suits, an overcoat, trousers, a jacket, a piece of tweed, a large enamel kettle and two enamel jugs on the corner of Henry Street and 'knowing the police were making a search she retained them with the intention of handing them over'. Others claimed to have been given items or purchased them from strangers.[72] When asked by a policeman to explain how they came into possession of shoes, clothes, sweets, lemonade and a bottle of rum, two 'respectably dressed women' simply told him that 'We were looting like the rest. We had a bit out of it too'.[73] Over 400 persons were ultimately charged and either fined or imprisoned. Many more were presumably able to retain their loot.[74]

Aside from their thoughts on the looting, residents of the suburbs were frustrated by the impact of the Rising on everyday amenities. As Blair Carphin exclaimed to his sister in Scotland, 'No post in or out, no telegrams, no telephones, no newspapers, no gas & not much to eat all through the Sinn Fein (pronounced Shin Fane) Rising.'[75] Monica Roberts, who spent the war sending care packages to soldiers at the front, complained that they could not get any news of what was 'going on in France'.[76] When it was all over, Joseph Clegg elaborated on that sense of disruption and disjuncture:

> The severance for such a length of time of all communication with places outside the city; the complete collapse of communications inside; the absence of daily papers; the disappearance of the police; the cessation of tramcar and other wheeled traffic; the problem of getting house supplies; the total stoppage of business; the vague and often alarming reports of casualties; the paucity of authentic information; the unfamiliar and menacing detonations, night and day, of rifles, Maxims, and heavy guns – these and other associated features of the time gave an unprecedentedly strange colour to the daily life of Dublin.[77]

The sensory experience of the Rising, the smells and sounds, can be easily overlooked but were central to those who lived through it.[78] Elsie Mahaffy struggled with the noise of gunfire and shelling and found it impossible to sleep in her room in Trinity.[79] Others eventually became strangely accustomed to the noise and amateur ballistics experts began to pride themselves on naming the weapons they could hear in the distance.[80] Witnesses in Dublin also understood and experienced the Rising in the context of the First World War. Gladys Johnson was a trainee nurse in the Adelaide Hospital, close to the rebel garrison in Jacob's biscuit factory. She later went to France as a VAD nurse, but felt she had already had a taste of war in Dublin.[81] For Nellie May Preston, roles had been temporarily reversed with her fiancé, then on active service abroad, as she chided him in a letter: 'you boys won't be the only ones that can tell tales about the war … when you come home we'll have so much to tell you about our war that we won't have time to listen to your Trench a/c'.[82]

In keeping with Dublin's experience as a 'home front', attempts were made to continue with ordinary tasks, if not always entirely successfully, and this was another significant feature of Dublin's Rising. Sir John Ross, a high court judge, later recalled sitting in his south Dublin garden reading Plutarch in the warm weather over the sound of machine-gun fire and cannon.[83] Such nonchalance was perhaps a little easier to portray in hindsight (Ross' memoir was published in 1924), but the Dublin Spring Show – impacted by the lockout, the war and outbreaks of foot and mouth disease in earlier years – was opened at the Royal Dublin Society grounds in Ballsbridge on Easter Tuesday 25 April. Attendees were deprived of the popular horse-jumping competitions, some exhibitors from Britain were affected, and the military occupied part of the grounds, but the quality of the entries was considered above average.[84] On Tuesday a small group of junior sophister students turned up at the dining hall in Trinity to sit scheduled exams. Many of their peers were understandably unable to attend, but Eileen Corrigan – who had travelled from Belfast on Easter Monday – recalled completing (and passing) her three-hour written exam to the sound of gunfire. The provost, John Pentland Mahaffy, had acted as returning officer for the Dublin University constituency that morning and personally carried out *viva voce* examinations the following day. Once the Leinster Regiment arrived in the college on Wednesday, however, Trinity cast aside its normal functions and focused instead on military objectives.[85] At the same time, while Mary Martin recorded the deaths of Francis Sheehy-Skeffington, James Connolly and Constance Markievicz (the latter two of whom were still alive) on Thursday 27 April, she immediately noted afterwards: 'The boys marked out the Tennis Court so I presume play will now begin for the season.'[86]

Accurate information about what was going on in Dublin was denied even to those close to the city centre. Fighting quickly put the press out of action and the *Irish Times* was the only Dublin-based newspaper issued on 26 and 27 April before it too halted production. While the *Irish Times* was able to reappear on 1 May, it was 3 May before the next *Daily Express* and *Evening Mail* were produced and 5 May for the *Irish Independent* and *Freeman's Journal*.[87] Foreign newspapers became almost impossible to come by. Sir Horace Plunkett caught a glimpse of the *Daily Mail* for 28 April ('Nortcliffe meets you everywhere!') but found that it 'greatly under-stated the gravity of the situation'.[88] Copies were apparently on sale for 1*s.* or available to read in a shop for 1*d.*[89] The scarcity of news caused frustration and contributed to the feeling of living in a 'besieged city'.[90] The *Irish Times* issued on Tuesday 25 April was a source of disappointment for those who could get their hands on it. Described by Douglas

Hyde as 'a miserable edition', it contained a government proclamation of martial law and a miserly 'three line notice about the Rebellion'.[91] Still, news vendors were refusing to sell issues for less than 2*d.*, double its retail price, and some went for as much as a shilling (12*d.*).[92] A longer proclamation was produced in an afternoon edition, but a full page of excited and remarkably detailed reportage had been cut by the censor at 8 a.m. that morning and never made it on to the streets.[93] Surviving accounts suggest that issues produced under trying circumstances on Wednesday and Thursday were not widely read.[94] Rumour filled the gaps left by trusted reporting and a wide array of stories were in circulation over the course of Easter week. The most common related to military successes and failures, casualties and the numbers of troops (either British, German, or 'Sinn Feiners') believed to be converging on the city. Many of the same, usually inaccurate, tales revolved around figures well known in the Dublin public sphere. Witnesses were remarkably well informed about the killing of journalist, suffragist and pacifist Francis Sheehy-Skeffington in Portobello Barracks, but even accurate reports could quickly become embellished.[95] Douglas Hyde was informed that Sheehy-Skeffington had exposed a tattoo of the words 'Votes for Women' on his chest and had requested to be shot there.[96]

If military control was well established within a few days, a speedy end to the Rising did not necessarily appear inevitable to onlookers. As late as Friday, Sir Horace Plunkett noted in his diary: 'There will be very hard work before these desperate men (those who will be shot or imprisoned for life) surrender – unconditionally as they must.'[97] Shocked by the scale of civilian casualties, Pearse in fact agreed to an unconditional surrender the following day to 'prevent the slaughter of unarmed people and in the hope of saving the lives of our followers'. The garrisons on the north side of the river surrendered first on Saturday (excluding Seán Heuston's garrison at the Mendicity Institution, which had surrendered on Wednesday). The leaders on the south side followed on Sunday, 30 April.[98] Sniping, though, continued into the following week, signalling to those on the ground that the conflict was not over.

Instead, it was the return of everyday services that marked the end of the Rising for the citizens of Dublin. Elsie Henry described excitement at the first sight of a running tram, while Dorothy Stopford also noted the first baker's cart and delivery of post.[99] By 4 May, many civil servants had returned to work. The GPO staff began operating from the Rotunda while city post offices dealt with applications for separation allowances and pensions.[100] Telephone lines began to operate again on 6 May and further appearances of normality came when gas supplies were finally resumed on 10 May. Theatres opened on 14 May with newsreels showing images of the ruined city. The Theatre Royal showed a film featuring the Irish regiments abroad ('With the Irish at the Front').[101] Some viewed the destruction of the area around Sackville Street in the context of the on-going war, comparing it to images of Ypres or Louvain.[102] Streetscapes had been drastically altered: the GPO was a hollowed shell and fires and artillery had either partially or completely destroyed a number of Dublin landmarks, including Clery's, the Dublin Bread Company on Sackville Street, and the Metropole Hotel. Arnotts' fate was considered 'almost miraculous'; a mere 'couple of thousand pounds would cover the damage to their property'. The company secretary described how the premises was almost alone in remaining standing, though with all of its front windows smashed and some fire damage.[103] While Leverett & Frye on Grafton Street ('entirely looted and wrecked') was unable to resume business at the site for a short period, McBirney's on Aston Quay was keen to reassure customers that its 'premises practically escaped injury, and all their stocks are in perfect order'; Hickey & Co. on North Earl Street offered damaged goods at 'tempting prices'.[104] Areas removed from British shelling fared reasonably well, even where rebel garrisons had been established. Jacob's biscuit factory was practically uninjured after it was occupied by rebels and reopened by 6 May.[105] The registrar of the Royal College of Surgeons reported that 'comparatively little malicious damage has been done' and lectures were scheduled to resume on 10 May.[106]

During less than a week of sustained fighting, hundreds of Dublin homes were left bereaved or denied a breadwinner through injury or incarceration. Dublin Corporation held an emergency meeting on 10 May to allow the North and South Dublin Unions, the latter of which had been taken by rebels, to secure bank overdrafts to deal with destitution caused by the rebellion.[107] Around £2,500,000 worth of damage was done to 200 buildings, mostly in the block around Sackville Street, with businesses and livelihoods temporarily or permanently destroyed. The sums of compensation provided by the Treasury-funded Property Losses (Ireland) Committee, established in June 1916, ranged from the £1 7*s.* 5*d.* awarded to Margaret Kiernan for a destroyed apron and shoes to £77,292 for the destruction of Clery's department store opposite the GPO.[108] Some of the dead had been hastily buried in shallow graves and there were fears about the spread of disease.[109] Elsie Mahaffy recalled how a rebel shot from the roof of Trinity was brought into the college and eventually buried, before being disinterred and sent to the morgue: 'though well dressed and from a respectable street, no one ever came to ask for his body', his friends 'too cowardly or callous to secure him a decent burial'.[110] More than sixty civilians were supposed to have been buried in pits at the rear of Dublin Castle.[111] Soon after the Rising was over, Marion Kelleher told her family that 'No mourners were allowed to go to the cemeteries – only the driver of the hearse'. One man who had died of natural causes was brought 'in an ass & cart as they could not get a hearse'.[112]

In this context, the immediate response to the Rising was understandably mixed. Thomas Johnson made a point of surveying attitudes among both workers and the middle classes and found it was practically unanimously against the rebels, though many were compelled to admire their courage in defending their positions.[113] Loyalists decried the folly of the Rising but were willing to direct the blame towards the leaders rather than the rank and file.[114] There was also respect for the youth, courage and even the politeness of the rebels – and a willingness to separate the rebellion from the rebels.[115] Blame was much more forcefully directed towards the mismanagement and complacency of the Irish administration, especially Augustine Birrell as chief secretary.[116] Catholic asylum clerk Thomas Moylan even went as far as to place responsibility for the Rising on Edward Carson: 'But for him there would be no Sinn Fein Volunteers at all. On him rests the curse of this rising and indeed the whole war'.[117] With 1913 remaining fresh in their minds, however, many middle-class Dubliners were less forgiving of the 'Larkinite' contingent among the rebels, principally the ICA. From an ascendancy background but armed and in uniform in St Stephen's Green, Constance Markievicz drew particularly unflattering attention.[118] To another writer in Lucan, James Connolly was 'one for whom I feel no pity'.[119]

There was seemingly little contemporary criticism of the use of artillery or the infliction of civilian casualties by the British military, though this occasionally followed in later memoirs.[120] Revd Clements wrote about how the 'destruction of our beautiful city' had been 'unhappily compelled to be done by the hands of our own soldiers', and only briefly alluded to the shooting of civilians by British troops.[121] Wesley Hanna similarly noted that it seemed a 'very haphazard thing to do, this shelling more or less indiscriminately, but they know best I suppose ... They have a dangerous and difficult job – One that I am sure is repugnant to them – to do'.[122] If they became aware of events like the summary killing of fifteen civilians on North King Street, these early commentators chose not to say so. Marion Kelleher, whose husband was a moderate nationalist, was unusual in explicitly condemning the shooting of civilians by the Irish Rifles.[123]

Official responses to the Rising were largely hostile, not least because of its economic impact. The 120 members who had defended Trinity College were awarded silver cups and 15*s*. each by the ostensibly 'grateful citizens and traders of Dublin city'.[124] On 5 May the Dublin Chamber of Commerce unanimously passed resolutions assuring 'His Gracious Majesty of the loyalty of the commercial community to his person and his throne' and recording 'abhorrence at the dreadful scenes of carnage, murder, and destruction resulting from the action of a section of the community in the City.' The meeting also agreed that blame should fall on the 'gross and unpardonable laxity, long continued, of the administration of the Irish Government' and called on the Treasury to provide the necessary funds to restore destroyed buildings and property.[125] Indeed, commercial interests, the press and public representatives were united in their conviction that it was the Treasury's responsibility to make good the damage done to the city.[126] The Dublin press denounced the Rising, though the *Freeman's Journal* soon turned on the *Irish Times* and *Irish Independent* for its infamous editorials calling for stern measures against the rebels.[127] On 9 May the postponed meeting of the Dublin Methodist synod expressed its 'grief and shame' at the 'wicked and foolish insurrection'. It had lost two children connected to its Dolphin's Barn church.[128] A few days later, the Presbytery of Dublin put on record its own opposition to the rebellion and the loss of its Lower Abbey Street church and adjoining property.[129] But while John Heney Bernard, Church of Ireland archbishop of Dublin, wrote to the *Times* in London calling for 'swift and stern' punishment for the rebels, his Catholic counterpart, the ailing William Walsh, refused to criticize their actions publicly.[130] By the time it resumed official business on 5 June, Dublin Corporation restricted itself to a series of votes of sympathy acknowledging recent deaths.[131] It was acknowledged that the disruption of the Rising had brought hardship across the city and county. The boards of guardians of the North and South Dublin Unions applied to the corporation and council for permission to obtain overdrafts to distribute relief in exceptional cases 'in view of the destitution caused by the Sinn Fein rebellion'. At a special meeting, Dublin County Council unanimously approved the application to the LGB, 'satisfied that exceptional distress exists in all the District Electoral Divisions situated in the County of Dublin.'[132] Dublin Corporation also approved the overdraft facility, but with objections from two councillors who denied the extent of the distress and sought to protect ratepayers' interests.[133]

Even if there was not necessarily consensus on the Rising's morality or its consequences, there was a wider recognition that this was a historic moment. Demand for both information and souvenirs was evident in the 'colossal circulation' of the special composite issue of the *Weekly Irish Times* published on 13 May.[134] An array of ephemera based on images of the Rising's leaders – including posters, memoriam cards, homemade scapulars and cigarette cases – emerged almost immediately.[135] Valentine & Sons offered a series of 'souvenir postcards of Dublin ruins' and was unable to keep up with initial orders.[136] Charlie Dalton, later a member of the famous Squad, immediately began collecting souvenirs and treasured a photograph of a 'dead leader' with 'a kind of sacred interest'.[137] Elsie Mahaffy, a determined critic of the rebellion, compiled a diary cum scrapbook pasted throughout with images and ephemera enthusiastically gathered in the months after Easter week.[138] Demand was not confined to natives of the city. Tom Dolan, serving with the British army in Dublin, sent a postcard of the destroyed Liberty Hall to his sister in England and was disappointed not to get his hands on a copy of the Sackville Street card.[139] The leaders of the Rising were soon venerated in much the same way as traditional Catholic martyrs, and the Catholic Church was one of the first channels through which sympathy for the rebels was publicly demonstrated.[140] Crowds turned out for requiem Masses in large numbers, particularly month's minds and anniversary Masses. These services were an important public demonstration of support and their popularity provided spiritual comfort for relatives.[141]

The Irish National Aid Association was founded in May 1916, made up of well-known associates of the IPP alongside advanced nationalists, for the dependants of those executed, killed, or sentenced to penal servitude or deported. Around the same time, Kathleen Clarke and other women – primarily women widowed by the Rising – founded the Volunteer Dependents' Fund with money donated from the US. In August 1916 the two associations merged to form the Irish National Aid Association and Volunteer Dependents' Fund. A new executive was roughly balanced between moderate nationalists and republicans, though the balance of power ultimately shifted towards the separatists. After the merger, the association was able to bring in large sums of money, particularly from early 1917, from the US. As well as providing significant aid to those affected by participation in the rebellion, the new Irish National Aid Association and Volunteer Dependents' Fund generated sympathy for the rebels and contributed to the shift in hearts and minds that soon followed the Rising, and facilitated the construction of important revolutionary networks – including those around Michael Collins, who made his name as secretary of the association from early 1917 and was the face of the association in Dublin.[142] At the same time, the conversion of the Dublin public had its limits. Around June 1917 Elsie Mahaffy described how those who were 'sensitive to such things, walking around the streets of Dublin, began to feel a change among the people'. She remained certain that the leaders of the Rising had 'brought the contempt of honourable people'.[143] The family of executed leader Michael Mallin remembered that when his widow, Agnes, was in hospital giving birth to their daughter in August 1916, there were protests outside the Coombe Hospital.[144] After Andy McDonnell was released from Richmond Barracks in May 1916, his neighbours in Rathmines were initially 'inclined to keep clear of our family, cold and distant, while some did not try to hide their hostility'. They were, however, ultimately 'sound nationally and proved it when they got over the shock of the executions'.[145]

There had been some localized activity in the north of the county during Easter week and this also elicited varying responses. The Fingal Battalion had killed the RIC CI for Meath, a district inspector and six other policemen at Ashbourne. Prior to this, after the outbreak of the Rising, Volunteers had taken the RIC barracks and post offices at Swords and Donabate and dismantled telegraph equipment (the police offered some resistance at Donabate but had surrendered without a fight at Swords). On Easter Wednesday men from the battalion had also rushed the RIC barracks in Garristown; it was empty, bar a lone unarmed constable left behind as a caretaker while his colleagues were ordered to decamp to Balbriggan. The post office there was also raided and telegraph equipment again dismantled. Charlie Weston recalled that money was taken and a receipt given to the postmaster by Richard Mulcahy who remarked that 'This money is no longer of any value'.[146] A large number of troops were drafted into Skerries in advance of a feared attack on the wireless station there that never materialized.[147] Just after the final executions in Dublin, the *Drogheda Independent* published a piece in which it happily contradicted a report that there had been a 'branch of Sinn Fein volunteers in Garristown': 'no such branch ever existed, and … not even one person from Garristown was in the ranks of the insurgents'. It also carried a statement from the chairman of Balrothery Board of Guardians contradicting press reports that there had been 'trouble in Rush during the rebellion'. 'The residents of Rush naturally resent the statement, which is calculated to throw discredit on the locality.'[148]

But the RIC also began to note a change in atmosphere almost immediately after the Rising. CI for Dublin, R.G.C. Flower, who had replaced Reynell Heard in February 1916 on the latter's departure for Roscommon, noted for several months after April 1916 that loyalists were 'apprehensive', with a sullen and troubled feeling in the air that was difficult to describe adequately. It was similarly difficult to ascertain the feelings of those Flower described as the 'lower order of Nationalists' – presumably those from less respectable backgrounds than the typical IPP supporter. The CI also believed that there were large numbers willing to 'give trouble' if the opportunity or necessity arose. Sympathy for the rebels was increasing – 'a dangerous condition of things' – but it was initially expressed privately rather than publicly. The Irish Volunteers in the county were considered to be 'practically wiped out' and no efforts to reorganize were noted before the end of 1916.[149] In February 1917, by which time Flower had been promoted to assistant inspector general and replaced by A.A. Roberts, 'Sinn Fein colours' were displayed in Dundrum to mark the return of released 1916 prisoners. But Roberts suggested that this might have been 'temporary brazenness'. In the north of the county – 'where the disloyal element is strongest and where there are many released Sinn Feiners' – the extremists remained 'quiet, but the spirit of disaffection is still there and must always be reckoned with'.[150]

Like so much else in this period, there were many Dublin experiences of the Easter Rising. The events of Easter 1916 upended ordinary life in the city and its suburbs, bringing with it significant destruction of property and loss of life. The Rising also vividly brought to the surface issues of class and class prejudice, highlighting once more the chasm that often existed between the poor of the tenements and the Dublin middle and upper classes. The Rising also encouraged a range of human responses that transcended politics: fear, excitement, curiosity, anger, amusement and bemusement. Nor did immediate reactions to the Rising occur in a vacuum. They were influenced both by still fresh memories of the 1913 lockout and the ongoing war in Europe. There were smaller outbreaks elsewhere but the capital city was the symbolic centre of the Easter Rising, as well as the site of its most sustained and significant fighting. On 8 May 1916, Thomas William Lyster, librarian at the National Library on Kildare Street, was prescient enough to request copies of the proclamation and 'the one issue of the rebel newspaper' (*Irish War News*, published on 25 April), believing they would 'be important for historical purposes in years to come'.[151] Lyster was not alone in quickly recognizing the significance of what had happened around him. If the ultimate trajectory and outcome was less inevitable than it might now seem, it was clear that something significant had changed. Over the two years that followed, the constitutional nationalist project of the IPP was cast aside in favour of the republic declared on Easter Monday 1916. Developments were set in motion that saw SF – previously the party of a small cohort of Dublin councillors – comprehensively defeat the IPP at the first general election to follow the end of the war.

5. Sinn Féin and its enemies: from the GPO to the Dáil, 1916–18

The Easter Rising prompted a profound shift in Irish politics, culminating in the establishment of a separatist counter-state and, beginning in 1919, a military insurgency against British rule. The allegiances of Dubliners were also challenged and, for many, they changed. Dublin was central to wider political developments in Ireland, while at the same time its residents plotted a range of different courses. The rise of SF was not a universally successful process. Following the sudden shock of the 1916 Rising, much of what followed over the next two-and-a-half years was slow and incremental. This included the reorganization and arming of the Irish Volunteers and Cumann na mBan; replacing lost or imprisoned leaders in some places and starting from scratch in others. Other Dubliners engaged with the aftermath of the Rising by protesting on behalf of internees and prisoners, and in marking anniversaries related to the Rising and its leaders. Meanwhile, the First World War continued to have its own tragic impact on Dublin homes. Nevertheless, support for the war effort – rather than the Westminster government, its Irish policy, or, more importantly, conscription – survived among large sections of the Dublin population right up to the end of the conflict in November 1918. SF won a convincing victory in the general election that followed the armistice, the first since 1910, but that victory was also challenged by some sections of the Dublin electorate.

Publicly, the IUA forcibly resisted efforts to bring about a home rule settlement in the aftermath of the Rising, though some sections of southern unionism had already become willing to consider it as the most palatable option available. Immediately after the Rising, Liberal politician Cecil Harmsworth gathered the private views of 'mild' Dublin unionists. The 'broad-minded' G.F. Stewart, vice-chairman of the IUA, believed that Ireland had travelled beyond the point where the Union could be seen as a viable permanent solution for Irish government and favoured a federation. Sir Alfred Callaghan, proprietor of the *Church of Ireland Gazette*, thought that while the Dublin Castle regime would have worked well enough if in strong hands, southern unionists had reconciled themselves to home rule and would 'feel tolerably safe and happy' under John Redmond.[1] But opposition in Dublin to IPP policy – not necessarily tantamount to support for SF – was visible reasonably quickly after Easter week 1916. Shortly after the executions in Kilmainham Gaol, David Lloyd George, then minister for munitions, was tasked with resolving the home rule issue in negotiations with Nationalists and Unionists. He offered the immediate establishment of a Dublin parliament, but with the exclusion of the north-eastern counties of Ulster. The IPP's position was weaker than it had been in

1914, with Unionists holding several prominent positions in the coalition war cabinet established in 1915. In need of an immediate solution, Redmond was willing to acquiesce to the exclusion of Fermanagh and Tyrone – counties he had earlier insisted should be included in the home rule settlement – but the question of temporary or permanent exclusion remained. Edward Carson compromised on the partition of Ulster and the immediate implementation of home rule in the rest of the country, but was satisfied with a promise that there would be no automatic inclusion of the six excluded Ulster counties at the end of the war when an imperial conference would resume the negotiations. The plan was approved by the IPP at the Mansion House in late June, aided by the work of Joseph Devlin in convincing a conference of Ulster nationalists, but by the end of July the talks had collapsed. On 19 July 1916 amendments were tabled that would mean the excluded counties could not be put under a Dublin government against their will and that Irish representation at Westminster would be reduced. Redmond, forced into a corner by the demands of British Unionists and southern Irish Unionist opposition to partition, was left with no choice but to reject the settlement.[2]

The *Irish Independent* proclaimed: 'Every honest Irish Nationalist will rejoice at the disappearance of the nefarious and shameful scheme of Mr Lloyd George and the Government to divide and dismember Ireland', but dismissed any notion that it could be framed as a 'masterly retreat or a stroke of bold and splendid statesmanship' by Redmond. In trying to extricate itself from a 'miserable mess', the paper claimed, the IPP had only emphasized its 'ineptitude, weakness, and inefficiency'.[3] Persistent criticism from the long antagonistic *Independent*, which ran a fierce series of anti-partition editorials in June and July, undoubtedly had some influence on Dublin attitudes towards the IPP over the following two years.[4] The other significant daily published in Dublin, the Redmondite *Freeman's Journal*, had already been struggling financially and was hampered further by the destruction of its premises during the Rising.[5] William Walsh, the Catholic archbishop of Dublin, had also long lost faith in Redmond and the IPP programme.[6] The unionist *Irish Times*, which had a much smaller circulation in the capital, was kinder, and believed that the British cabinet's belated recognition that it would have to reduce Irish representation at Westminster to confirm the scheme had – 'to a slight extent' – allowed Redmond to save face. The paper did not 'grudge him this small measure of good luck', but believed the IPP leader was unlikely to convince anyone that he was an 'injured and betrayed man'.[7]

On 24 January 1917 the maverick nationalist councillor Laurence O'Neill was elected lord mayor of Dublin – the first formal sign of the demise of the UIL's traditional dominance in Dublin civic politics.[8] But there were no contested Westminster by-elections between 1916 and 1918 for Dubliners to express new political preferences. When the South County Dublin seat became vacant in July 1917 on the death of W.F. Cotton, it was held for the IPP without a contest by

Michael Hearne, a barrister. The Unionist Registration Association did not nominate a candidate in line with the 'party truce' it had agreed at the outbreak of the war.[9] But the victories in 1917 of Dubliners Count George Noble Plunkett, father of Joseph executed in 1916, and Rising veteran W.T. Cosgrave in by-elections in Roscommon and Kilkenny respectively were indicative of wider trends. Plunkett went forward as an independent but later aligned with SF, for whom Cosgrave also captured a seat from the IPP. When Plunkett's train arrived at Broadstone Station in Dublin city he was met by large crowds and carried shoulder-high to his residence in Fitzwilliam Square, accompanied by renditions of 'The West's Awake', 'God Save Ireland' and 'The Soldier's Song'.[10] This was, however, as much a demonstration of a growing popular sentiment for the Rising as any clear show of support for SF in the city.

After the first leaders were executed in early May 1916, John Dillon, who was able to gauge opinion on the ground, informed John Redmond that the Dublin working class – many of whom had been initially hostile – were becoming increasingly bitter, even those with no sympathy for the rebels or the Rising. Within six weeks of the executions, Sir John Maxwell complained to Archbishop Walsh about a large demonstration along the quays that followed requiem Masses for the leaders. The arrests of some 3,300 suspected separatists, including many unconnected to the rebellion, caused additional resentment. Though about 1,800 were released almost immediately, the scale of arrests and detention in Britain was probably as important in shifting the public mood, and certainly fed into perceptions about the draconian British response.[11] Alfie Byrne, MP for Dublin Harbour since 1915, was notably vocal in the House of Commons on the post-Rising detentions. On 23 May he asked the under-secretary of state for war, Jack Tennant, if he was 'aware of the dissatisfaction that is being caused in all parts of Ireland, owing to the whole-sale arrests of those of the labour and Gaelic movement; and what steps, if any, are being taken to limit the arrests of innocent persons?'[12] Later in the session, and in the following days, Byrne followed up with more questions about the arrests of apparently innocent men, including members of the Dublin Trades Council (asking if there was 'any charge against them besides being advocates of the working classes'), and conditions in prisons and detention centres.[13] William Field, MP for Dublin St Patrick's, contributed to debates on conditions in Frongoch detention camp in north Wales, and on 12 July 1916 called on the home secretary to release all innocent men who were detained on suspicion.[14] The remaining Dublin MPs were notably quiet on the Rising, but P.J. Brady, MP for St Stephen's Green, did press a question on compensation for Dublin property destroyed in the Rising with reference to a resolution passed by the Dublin Chamber of Commerce.[15]

After Lloyd George ousted Herbert Asquith as prime minister in December 1916, Chief Secretary Henry Duke announced in the House of Commons that all remaining internees would be released. Prisoners released from the north camp at Frongoch just before Christmas included '29 Dublin men in charge of Mr William Tannam', captain of E company, 3rd Battalion, Dublin Brigade. Dubliner Helena Malony and Winifred Kearney, both veterans of the GPO, were released from Aylesbury Prison around the same time. Released internees arriving in Dublin were invited to call into the Irish National Aid Association and Volunteer Dependents' Fund offices on Exchequer Street.[16] But those who had been tried and sentenced, including three members of Dublin Corporation, Seán T. O'Kelly (or Ó Ceallaigh), W.T. Cosgrave of SF and Labour's William Partridge, remained in prison. All three were unanimously co-opted by the corporation after the municipal elections in January 1917, filling the vacancies created by their absence.[17]

In March 1917, Redmond led his party out of Westminster in an effort to force the government to move on home rule. An unimpressed *Independent* declared that the IPP was now 'paying the price for fawning "like nerveless creatures" on successive English governments', and failing to secure home rule. The *Irish Times* unconvincingly suggested that Redmond had succumbed to pressure from John Dillon.[18] An Irish Convention, Lloyd George's next attempt to find a solution to the Irish question, was announced in May. Held in Trinity College between July 1917 and April 1918 and tasked with drafting a new Irish constitution, the Convention has been described as a 'brilliant failure' and, less kindly, as 'utterly futile'. Ultimately, it demonstrated the loss of influence among constitutional movements in Ireland alongside British failures to recognize the shifts occurring in Irish politics. From the beginning, it was restricted by SF's refusal to participate, though this appeared less of an issue early in the negotiations.[19] A delegation of Ulster Unionists largely confined themselves to a 'watching brief', but several shades of Dublin opinion were represented.[20] Among the government nominees was Trinity's fiercely unionist provost John Pentland Mahaffy, alongside William Martin Murphy, Sir Horace Plunkett and George Russell. Church of Ireland archbishop of Dublin John Bernard was among the episcopal delegates; representatives of southern unionism included Andrew Jameson of the distilling dynasty and king's counsel J.B. Powell; while the longstanding MP for Dublin North, J.J. Clancy, was among the IPP representatives. P.J. O'Neill was the appointed delegate for Dublin County Council.[21]

The press reported a good deal of public interest in the first day of the Convention as a crowd gathered at Trinity to watch the arrival of the delegates – many were 'strangers to the ordinary Dublin man' but 'several familiar figures were recognized, and their attitude, bearing, and possibilities in debate discussed in the off-hand manner of the man in the street'. The decline in the IPP's popularity among sections of the Dublin population was, though, already evident. The *Evening Herald* reported that after the Convention adjourned at the end of its first session, John Redmond passed the chair and vice-chair of Blackrock UDC as he left Trinity. When they called for 'Cheers for our Irish leader', there was 'no response from the crowd'. As Redmond walked alone towards Sackville Street, he was reportedly overtaken by '200 youths' who 'groaned and booed' before cheering 'Sinn Féin', 'East Clare' and 'Up, de Valera!' as they passed SF election offices (de Valera had won a by-election in East Clare earlier in the month). This was repeated outside the offices of the *Freeman's Journal*, and again as Redmond left in a hackney car with the lord mayor of Dublin.[22] Inside Trinity, the Convention was a happier experience for Redmond and he was eloquent, judicious and magnanimous, but perhaps only because he was comfortably surrounded by representatives of moderate nationalism and unionism.[23] This was also southern unionism's last big stand. As early optimism faded and the Convention dragged on without securing a settlement, there occurred a demoralizing split between moderate and diehard unionists.[24] The crowds that gathered in Dublin over the course of 1917 were thus more representative of the direction of things than anything that took place inside the walls of Trinity.

On Easter Monday 1917 the *Irish Times* described the presence of SF bunting in Dublin city, along with 'other signs that the lower element was seeking to let itself loose in honour of "Easter Week".'[25] Easter Sunday had been quieter than normal and no attempts were made to defy a proclamation on public gatherings.[26] But on Easter Monday crowds gathered on Sackville Street and a SF flag was 'hoisted surreptitiously' at half-mast at the GPO. By noon, the flag had fluttered down the flagpole but was raised once more and prompted cheering and 'other demonstrations of approval on a wide scale'. Flags also appeared at the Nelson Pillar, Liberty Hall and other sites associated with the Rising. Some of those present wore black armbands surmounted with SF colours. Youths were accused of causing disturbances and damage at Middle Abbey Street, and of throwing stones at DMP and a military guard (in spite of appeals to desist from young men wearing 'Republican badges').[27] Another hint at the changing order was a separate report in the same April 1917 edition of the *Irish Times* on the selection of the SF candidate for a forthcoming by-election in South Longford: 'Mr Joseph McGuinness, a draper in Dublin, who is now undergoing three years' imprisonment in connection with the rebellion in Dublin'.[28] As McGuinness defeated the IPP candidate from prison, Archbishop Walsh played an important part in the SF victory. On the day before the election, 8 May 1917, he was among three Catholic archbishops and fifteen bishops, three Protestant bishops and several chairmen of county councils who signed a manifesto opposing partition. That evening, Walsh wrote a letter that was published in the press reaffirming his view on the necessity of the manifesto. McGuinness' election agent was quick to capitalize on Walsh's intervention, and a handbill declared to South Longford voters that it was 'a clear call from the Great and

Venerated Archbishop of Dublin to vote against the Irish Party Traitors, and Vote for Joe McGuinness.' McGuinness won by 37 votes.[29]

In the county, the anniversaries of the Rising and the executions were marked with scattered displays of flag-waving, requiem Masses for executed leaders and some of the men killed at Ashbourne, and a theatrical performance in Balbriggan with songs and recitations that were 'almost on the borderline of disloyalty'.[30] Flag-waving gradually became more common, and the RIC believed the death in September 1917 of Thomas Ashe – a Kerry native who was principal of a school near Lusk and commandant of the Fingal Battalion of the Irish Volunteers – gave 'fresh impetus' to SF and the Volunteers in the county.[31] In the city, the funeral was an impressively organized and emotive display of 'separatist' spirit with Volunteers taking temporary control of the streets as the cortége made its way to Glasnevin Cemetery.[32] While drilling remained rare across Dublin, there was a new tension in the city that could spill over into physical violence. On 10 June 1917 protests in Beresford Place and Aungier Street about the treatment of prisoners in Lewes Prison culminated in the death of DMP Inspector John Mills. Following the arrest of Cathal Brugha, Mills was struck on the head with a hurl and died from a fractured skull.[33] The following day, Alfie Byrne again raised the treatment of prisoners at Lewes in the House of Commons, pointing to 'the breaking-up of a protest meeting in Dublin yesterday', and asked the home secretary to order the immediate release of prisoners to 'avert further trouble in Ireland'.[34]

Byrne received no immediate commitment in the Commons, but four days later Andrew Bonar Law told the House that all remaining Irish prisoners would be released.[35] The IPP claimed credit, but the lack of enthusiasm that accompanied the opening sessions of the Irish Convention, which had begun around the same time, suggests that the Dublin public were unconvinced. Some 3,000 people, meanwhile, gathered at North Wall to greet returning prisoners on 18 June (less than three years after cheering crowds waved off British soldiers going to war). The released men had, in fact, arrived at Kingstown and then took the train to Westland Row as the crowd rushed across the city to meet them.[36] Photographs captured the extent of the gathering, with the entrance to the station, the platform, Westland Row, and Great Brunswick Street packed with onlookers, and an overwhelmed DMP guard.[37] Having eventually overcome the crowds, the returning prisoners were brought by wagonette to the GPO and then to Fleming's Hotel on Gardiner Street for a celebratory luncheon. To Frank Robbins, a veteran of the St Stephen's Green garrison in Easter week, the welcome had 'well repaid us for our day of surrender and the subsequent insults'.[38] The *Evening Herald* described a 'city aglow with enthusiasm', and declared that the 'scene when the train eventually pulled into the station' would 'never be forgotten'.[39] For some, the enthusiasm extended further and two women and five boys were charged in the southern police court with 'riotous behaviour' and 'malicious damage' after windows were smashed and a Union Jack burned in Boyne Street.[40] A similarly large and excited crowd gathered again at Westland Row to greet Constance Markievicz's return to Dublin on the morning of 22 June. Markievicz was received at Liberty Hall, welcomed by Agnes Mallin, widow of Michael Mallin under whom Markievicz had served during the Rising, and a gathering of wives and relatives of other executed leaders and recently released prisoners.[41]

Meanwhile, the war remained a constant presence. The start of the Somme offensive on 1 July 1916 had received relatively little attention in Dublin, and the city would not again suffer the communal shock of the news of casualties suffered at the Dardanelles a year earlier. Recruitment from Dublin city to the British army virtually dried up and while it recovered in the summer it never again matched pre-Rising levels.[42] In the county, it did not rebound at all. CI Roberts routinely observed that enlistment was 'at a low ebb', 'nominal', or 'practically nil'.[43] But this should not necessarily be interpreted solely as a response to the Rising. CIs around the country had been reporting slack and unsatisfactory recruitment almost universally since early 1916. Nor was this an obvious reflection of a decline in support for the Allied war effort, but rather a drying up of the existing – much smaller – pool of potential, voluntary recruits outside the metropolis.[44] In his July 1918 report Roberts wrote: 'Most of the loyalist young men who can be spared have gone to the Front but the other side still hold sulkily back.'[45] By contrast, he saw support for SF as a convenient 'excuse to avoid joining the Army' among young men, while young women were getting 'carried away by emotional sympathy' for SF.[46]

This pronounced difficulty in finding willing recruits for the armed forces in Dublin county from 1916 seems to have owed relatively little to anti-recruitment activity by republicans. The RIC reported no 'open efforts' to promote 'sedition' or 'injure recruitment for the army' in the months after April 1916.[47] The first – and indeed only – 'clear case' contained in monthly reports was the rather tame prosecution of a Miss Griffin, a school attendance inspector. On visiting a home in Ballybrack, she was alleged to have seen a mother making a parcel for a son at the front and asked: 'Why did they go to fight for England?'[48] In many of the working-class households where men had already joined up, benefits and allowances had appreciably improved living standards. For many others, a growth in wages and opportunities for work meant there was little incentive to enlist during the final two years of the war. In spring and summer 1918, Roberts concluded that the high wages available in the county contributed to poor recruitment.[49]

There was also some resentment, usually directed at the British authorities or at the army, at the impact of the war on the cost and availability of necessities. As priority was given to war industries and the armed forces, coal supplies were limited and prices increased. This was also the case with fodder. Rumours early in the war that fodder would be commandeered for the British armed forces, affecting Dublin's 500 dairies and thus the city's milk supply, were not fully borne out, but in 1915 and 1916 the authorities requisitioned all hay crops within ten miles of Dublin for cavalry regiments and transport corps. In July 1916 Dublin Corporation complained of shortages. The dairies had access to increased supplies of feed from waste produced by Guinness, whose overseas markets were impacted by the war, and this helped keep the price of milk down. But enforced cuts to the output of Dublin's breweries contributed to a decline in feed for the dairies and an inevitable decline in the supply and quality of milk. In October 1916, a quart of milk rose from 3*d.* to 4*d.*; a year later the price was 6*d.* a quart.[50] The issue was regularly raised in the Commons by Dublin MPs. On 7 June 1917 J.J. Clancy, IPP MP for Dublin North, submitted a question to Chief Secretary Henry Duke about a statement made a week earlier by the vice-president of the Department of Agriculture and Technical Instruction (DATI) in Ireland that claimed a serious shortage of milk would occur in a few months' time and that the North Dublin Board of Guardians had proposed the food controller take control of creameries to ensure sufficient milk supply for the poor. Clancy asked what steps the government would take 'before a milk famine actually occurs', but Duke denied that there were any serious shortages or any risk of such a famine.[51] A few days later, Alfie Byrne again referred to the vice-president's statement and asked what was being done to safeguard supplies. The chief secretary claimed not to have read it, but again denied any knowledge from the DATI of issues with supply or recent price increases.[52]

These interventions in parliament had a rather minimal impact, and it appears that IPP MPs received little credit on the ground. In early November 1917 the Dublin dairy trade raised prices again to 7*s.* per quart of milk.[53] On 21 November, Field once again raised the issue of milk supplies in the city and suburbs. Duke promised that regulations on the supply, distribution and price of milk would 'be issued forthwith', and related problems with access to brewers' and distillers' grains to feed dairy cows would be considered.[54] A week later, Field enquired about the delay in issuing the promised food order and was informed that it was due to come into force on 10 December.[55] The order limited the price of milk to 5*s.* per quart if sold at the counter and 6*s.* per quart if delivered, but on 1 December the Dublin City and County Dairy Trade announced that prices would immediately rise again to 8*s.* a quart, ten days before the food order came into effect.[56] This was denounced in the *Irish Independent* as price gouging by an 'ultra-profiteering association which has already exploited the public beyond endurance' and 'brazenly and without any kind of warning' increased the price of 'the prime necessity of the poor'.[57] The *Irish Times* called it an attempt to 'bully the public and to defy the Government' by a 'public menace', a 'monopoly which would rather see the children of Dublin dying by the thousands than abate a farthing of its extortionate profits'. Perhaps significantly for the IPP, the *Evening Herald* accused the Redmondite *Freeman's Journal* of remaining silent while consumers were exploited by the 'Milk Huns', a pointed slur in December 1917.[58] Indeed, the *Herald* compared the prospects of the 'slum children of Dublin' who were 'fed on unadulterated milk' unfavourably with those of 'soldiers fighting in France and Flanders'.[59]

The impact of the war was felt elsewhere, too. Male employment in brewing and distilling was reduced by wartime production controls, while the building industry receded and lesser public servants and members of the DMP saw their wages eroded by inflation. But wages for skilled labourers stayed close to or ahead of inflation, while high prices for farm produce in turn led to increased demand for city trades and services. Record sales of cattle and sheep to the English market similarly benefitted Dublin farmers and those who oversaw their transport out of Dublin ports. Munition factories employed significant numbers of women from 1916, bringing them into the work force for the first time.[60] The impact of increased prices fell most heavily on the poorest Dublin families, especially those reliant on milk as a cheap source of nourishment or with children, fuelling resentment towards the army. The sale of cows to the English market only exacerbated milk shortages, while contaminated milk supplies contributed to the city's shocking infant mortality rates (though one positive development was a sharp decrease in cases of ill-treatment, neglect and abuse of children, which the National Society for the Prevention of Cruelty to Children considered a result of increased employment and wages). Moreover, the price of staples like sugar, meat, eggs and potatoes rose even faster than the price of milk over the course of the war. A pound of tea cost double its 1914 price by 1916 and rose further in 1917 as submarine attacks on shipping lines reduced imports.[61]

Growing lists of war dead may have played their own part in suppressing enlistment as the war continued to visit Dublin homes. In February 1917 the *Constabulary Gazette* announced the death of Corporal Willie Phillips of the Black Watch regiment, son of the RIC head constable in Lucan and brother of another former civil servant serving with the 10th RDF.[62] A year earlier, Mary Martin, from a prominent middle-class Catholic family in Monkstown, began keeping a diary. Her son Charlie, who was a member of the 6th Battalion, RDF, was reported missing in Solonika in December 1915 and she hoped that he would be able to read it on his return. The final entry is dated 25 May 1916. On 1 June she was informed that Charlie Martin had, in fact, died of his wounds after being captured.[63] The Cruess-Callaghan family in nearby Blackrock lost three sons, all members of the Royal Flying Corps (the Royal Air Force from April 1918), between 1916 and 1918. Almost 150 men were killed fighting with the RDF at Langemarck during the first three weeks of August 1917 of whom 39 were Dubliners. Between March and April 1918, at least 136 Dubliners were killed during a major German offensive on the Western Front. Almost half had been fighting with the 'Dublins'.[64] By then, the *Irish Times* caustically suggested that 'Ireland has deserted her regiments at the front. She still praises them in her newspapers and talks about "Irish valour" and the "Irish tradition", but it is mere talk'.[65] The editorial hinted at something important in Dublin's relationship with the war. Opinion against the war or those who chose to fight never fully took hold before 1918, even as numbers willing to volunteer declined, but enthusiasm for active service continued to wane and some, at least, resented an unwillingness to acknowledge fully Irish sacrifice.

The rise of SF was not immediate, even in the context of declining support for the IPP and voluntary enlistment. Only in October 1917 did CI A.A. Roberts consider SF to be the primary political movement in the county; a new branch with sixty-seven members had been founded at Finglas and a meeting in Howth had attracted some 300 attendees.[66] The following month he noted that there were ten branches, but was surprised there were not more – especially after the 'great fillip' provided by Thomas Ashe's funeral.[67] The first SF ard fheis, held in the Mansion House on 26 October, demonstrated the national growth of the organization and a shift towards radicalism. Éamon de Valera replaced the more moderate Arthur Griffith as president, merging the political and the military wings of separatism.[68]

The following day, the Irish Volunteers held a convention in the city and, as SF became the dominant political party, there was a significant increase in Volunteer membership noted by the RIC. The National Volunteers had, it was believed, being trying to reorganize in late 1918 but found that a large number of its members had gone over to the Irish Volunteers.[69] There was also the beginning of a generational shift in active militants in the aftermath of the Rising. Frank Henderson later recalled how the 'majority of the men who had fought in the Rising returned to their Companies, the general feeling among them being that the Volunteers would set about preparing for a second phase of the struggle against England'.[70] About 60 per cent of 1916 rebels in Dublin took some part in the War of Independence. These men were often found in leadership positions and were also among the most active participants in the War of Independence.[71] But while Rising service therefore carried significant weight, veterans did not all transition easily to guerrilla warfare. Todd Andrews joined the Volunteers in 1917 and was initially self-conscious as one of a minority in his company who had not been 'with Pearse in the GPO', but quickly noticed that these older men began to fall away and 1916 veterans 'attended fewer and fewer meetings'.[72] The drop-outs tended to be older, were more likely to work as professionals, merchants, or in a skilled trade, and had no rank in the Volunteers in 1916.[73] A small number of older men, including W.T. Cosgrave and Seán T. O'Kelly, moved to the political wing of the movement, but there was a marked departure in favour of younger volunteers with greater personal freedom.[74] Some others who may have been willing to remain active were prevented from doing so by work or personal circumstances. Henderson acknowledged that the 'lack of employment forced a number to leave Dublin' and 'some who had been born in the country returned to their native counties where their prestige and experience were of great value to local units'.[75] Frank Shouldice, for instance, was dismissed from the civil service and became a full-time organizer in east Mayo; Peadar Dunne was first a battalion and then a brigade O/C in Limerick after losing his job with Guinness and taking a new one with the republican Daly family's bakery in Limerick city.[76]

The ICA lost its most important and charismatic leaders in 1916 – James Connolly, Michael Mallin, Seán Connolly, Peadar Macken and Richard O'Carroll – along with William Partridge, who died from illness a year later, and it declined significantly after 1917. Distrusted by a section of the trade union movement and hampered by internal divisions and apathy, the ICA ultimately lacked decisive leadership and a clear political strategy. Some ICA 1916 veterans joined the Volunteers, with a number of these militarily active between 1919 and 1921.[77] Kathleen Connolly (later Barrett, sister of Seán Connolly killed at the opening of the Rising) was one of a small number of ICA women who joined Cumann na Ban after 1916. She was in City Hall during Easter week, was arrested there, and on her release distributed funds collected by the Irish National Aid Association and Volunteers Dependents' Fund. From late 1916 until the end of the Civil War, she was a member of the ard craobh branch of Cumann na Ban (though her War of Independence service was later rejected by the military service pensions board).[78]

There was also a significant structural reorganization of the Irish Volunteers in Dublin between 1917 and 1919. Eventually, there were five battalions in the Dublin Brigade: 1st and 2nd on the north side of the Liffey, 3rd and 4th on the south side, and a separate 5th Battalion of 'Engineers'.[79] The latter were men with 'craft and experience' deemed useful for the disruption of communications, munitions development and bomb making; their first commandant, Liam Archer, worked in the GPO.[80] City IRA units occupied a much larger area than the metropolitan divisions policed by the DMP. On the north side, the 1st Battalion area extended as far west as Blanchardstown and Castleknock and the 2nd Battalion carried on east from Clontarf to Howth.[81] The 3rd and 4th Battalions initially covered the entire south of the county, but they were eventually split when new 6th and 7th Battalions were formed. This was reflective of a structure and hierarchy that was remarkably, and of necessity, adaptable. In north Dublin, the Fingal Battalion became a brigade but could no longer rely on the leaders of Ashbourne; Thomas Ashe died from a botched attempt at forced feeding while on hunger strike in 1917, Richard Mulcahy was promoted first to brigadier of Dublin and then chief of staff at GHQ, and Richard Coleman, captain of the Swords company, died in November 1918 from 'Spanish influenza' while interned in Usk in Wales.[82]

Cumann na Ban was also reorganized after 1916. It became more republican and 'more explicitly feminist, or at least its feminist members found it easier to present the organization in a more progressive light'.[83] A 'semi-military organization' was created, 'governed by a captain, first and second lieutenants, an adjutant, quartermaster, section leaders and squad leaders'.[84] Units were also organized into areas that corresponded with IRA battalions, with each branch or squad of Cumann na Ban attached to an IRA unit.[85] Fairview, for example, was paired with the 2nd Battalion and ard craobh with the 1st Battalion.[86] A nationwide executive sat in Dublin, and the city and county were under the control of a district council made up of a captain and secretary from each of the ten Dublin branches. Where branches had fallen out of existence in north County Dublin after 1916, such as at Lusk, women acted informally or were more directly connected to the IRA. Mary Adrien was director of 'all the activities in Lusk' and, in addition to a seat on Balrothery Board of Guardians ('in the republican interest'), acted as a despatch rider for the local IRA company.[87] In south Dublin, Ann McGuinness was similarly 'more associated with the Volunteers than with Cumann na mBan, and … closely associated with Andy McDonnell.'[88]

Change in Dublin was also influenced by external developments in Europe. Following Bolshevik success in the October Revolution and Russian surrender to Germany, thousands of German troops fighting in the east were freed for the Western Front. A major German offensive in spring 1918 in turn placed additional pressure on British army recruitment. Many among the war-weary British public, subject to conscription since 1916 and facing an amended military service bill that raised the age limit for conscription from forty-one to fifty, believed Ireland had shirked its military responsibilities and used the conflict to become more prosperous (a view shared to some extent by the RIC CI for Dublin). To prevent outrage at home it was thus deemed necessary to include Ireland, previously exempt from conscription, in the new bill. This was despite a recognition that there was little support for the idea in Ireland. And while opposition to compulsory military service was not necessarily the same as opposition to the war itself or its ultimate aims, it had long been clear that large sections of Dublin society would oppose any such measure.[89]

When conscription was introduced in Britain in January 1916 Ireland remained exempt, but the 'reprieve' appeared increasingly anomalous and as the war dragged on there was a growing apprehension across the island that Ireland would eventually be brought into line with the rest of the United Kingdom.[90] In October 1916, Dublin Corporation passed a resolution condemning conscription, which it believed could only be implemented by an Irish parliament.[91] The labour movement in Dublin, meanwhile, had almost universally opposed the war from the outset and the fear of conscription was already 'a growing weapon in the nationalist arsenal'.[92] When the British government introduced its Military Service bill in March 1918, the IPP voted against it but it was passed by a large majority; the clause allowing for conscription in Ireland passed by 296 votes to

123.[93] IPP MPs, under new leader John Dillon (Redmond had died in March), then resolved to remain in Ireland and focus attention on opposing compulsory military service. Wider opposition to conscription was manifested in a national anti-conscription conference, choreographed in Dublin, chaired by the lord mayor, and held in the Mansion House on 18 April. The conference included representatives from SF, the IPP and Labour. On the same day, a separate meeting of the Catholic hierarchy discussed a mass movement to resist conscription. A delegation from the Mansion House then met the bishops at Maynooth and it was agreed that an anti-conscription pledge would be circulated, with public meetings (announced at Masses around the country) and collections for an anti-conscription fund. Accompanied by a one-day strike, this was a rare display of nationalist unity not rivalled since Daniel O'Connell's emancipation movement, and it succeeded in bringing about a government climb-down and an effective end to the conscription threat.[94]

In his monthly reports, A.A. Roberts was inclined to assign selfish motives to supporters of the anti-conscription movement in his jurisdiction. In his report for April 1918, he suggested that the large farmers would subscribe to the anti-conscription fund as 'they want to keep the young men to work their farms & bring grist to their own mill & scoop in even larger profits over the war than last year'.[95] In September 1918, by which time the wider anti-conscription campaign had begun to peter out, Roberts reported that the attitude of the lower and middle classes to the war was one of 'indifference': 'All they care about is to escape the risks of fighting the Germans'.[96] While a DI in Balbriggan believed that efforts to enforce conscription would be rigorously boycotted, Roberts, perhaps naively, suggested that this could be overcome by speedy and determined action by the police and military. By October 1918, he believed the issue was attracting little interest as it was becoming widely accepted that conscription was unlikely to be implemented.[97]

Notwithstanding the enthusiasm for the anti-conscription movement, Catholic support for the war effort remained strong in Dublin until the end – again highlighting the extent to which its citizens were willing to differentiate between voluntary support for an Allied victory and impositions enforced on Ireland from Westminster. After Major Willie Redmond, brother of John, was killed at Messines in June 1917, Archbishop Walsh – a firm opponent of recruitment efforts in Dublin, a key figure in the anti-conscription campaign, and a patron of the Irish National Aid Association and Volunteer Dependents' Fund – presided at a pontifical high requiem Mass in the Pro Cathedral. Among the organizers of the service were Walsh, Lord Mayor Laurence O'Neill and Attorney General James O'Connor. Journalist Katherine Tynan was convinced that 'Everybody who is anybody in the life of Dublin' had been there.[98]

It also appears that, as the war progressed, support was increasing in terms of time and money rather than volunteering to fight. War work on the home front – fundraising, supporting Belgian refugees, treating wounded soldiers and sphagnum moss collection – all survived the political shifts that followed the Easter Rising. In late 1916 and early 1917, submarine activities and fears that a German blockade might lead to food shortages had the same effect. The latter fear was particularly vivid when the Great Famine of the 1840s remained in living memory. While the majority of ships sunk by German submarines off the Irish coast were concentrated to the south, most infamously the *Lusitania* in May 1915, the sinking of the Dublin Steam Packet Company's RMS *Leinster* on 10 October 1918 'brought the horror of war' to Dublin doors. Three torpedoes struck the ship as it steamed from Kingstown to Holyhead, resulting in the deaths of around 500 passengers (there had been between 700 and 800 on board; most were military personnel). This forced the people of Dublin to confront mass death in the way Cork had in 1915 and was vividly demonstrated in a coffin shortage prompted by the recovery of 149 bodies. Within days, a dependants' fund was established. Even after the demands of four years of war, and large collections in Dublin for Easter Rising dependants and the anti-conscription fund, the *Leinster* appeal raised over £5,000. Among the contributors was Archbishop Walsh. The tragedy also united the *Irish Independent* and *Irish Times* in condemning German barbarism.[99] It did not, however, stimulate recruitment as some commentators hoped it might. Meetings were held in Balbriggan and Howth soon after the sinking, but, as CI Roberts reported, 'results were distinctly disappointing' and the 'hostile views of a section were made manifest'.[100]

There was some reluctance among Unionist councillors to support conscription, notwithstanding the claim of an independent alderman on Dublin Corporation, representing the Drumcondra ward where there was a large number of Protestant ratepayers, that a campaign to resist conscription would bring 'the contempt of all the nations of the world'.[101] But the willing support of Dublin unionists for the Allied cause remained clear. A few days before the sinking of the *Leinster*, the Mansion House – venue of the great anti-conscription event in April – hosted a mammoth auction to raise funds for the RDF prisoner of war fund, beginning on 5 October. By 12 October some £15,000 was raised from the sale (and re-sale) of between 400 and 500 lots of jewellery, furniture, silver and memorabilia. Among the patrons were Sir Maurice Dockrell and Henry Hanna, soon to run as Unionist candidates in the general election, and James Campbell, the lord chancellor and former Unionist MP for Dublin University. While there was no obvious representation from nationalist Dublin, Lord Mayor Laurence O'Neill had readily made the Mansion House available when tents erected on Fitzwilliam Square for the auction were blown down by strong winds.[102] Dublin's continuing interaction with the war was further demonstrated in the *Irish Independent*. Directly above the paper's advertisement for the first day of the mammoth auction was an advertisement for the last day of the Rotunda's showing of the American propaganda film 'The Kaiser, Beast of Berlin': 'Enormous Success. Hundreds Turned Away Daily'. Patrons could also watch a showing of a newsreel titled: 'Our Boys in France'.[103]

The mixed loyalties of Dubliners were again evident on the day the First World War ended. While students of Trinity and the Royal College of Surgeons celebrated in the streets, their UCD counterparts tore down the Union Jack that flew at the National University headquarters.[104] Bernard McAllister, a member of the Fingal Volunteers, remembered that 'Grafton Street became bedecked by Union Jacks'. Crowds of so-called 'separation women', the wives of men who had enlisted in the British forces and were in receipt of separation allowances, 'poured into the streets and formed processions headed by the Union Jack' – 'less an expression of thankfulness for peace than a jingo demonstration against Sinn Féin Dublin'. McAllister recalled a subsequent effort to burn SF headquarters at 6 Harcourt Street. The hostility with which many republicans remembered these 'separation women' and the pejorative associations the term created with drunkenness and irresponsibility further demonstrate the ways in which class prejudice – these women were usually working class – mixed with allegiances and identities.[105] Street fights carried on into the night on both sides of the river.[106] In Blanchardstown in late November, 'loyal emblems displayed by two children' were 'roughly destroyed'. The perpetrator was described by the CI as 'an ill-conditioned Sinn Feiner of the labouring class'.[107]

As the war came to an end, Dublin was faced with another mass killer. What was commonly known as 'Spanish influenza' was first mentioned in the monthly RIC report for October 1918. Compiled by a DI, the report noted the belief that the disease had its origins at Howth but also that 'Deaths have been many, medical resources much strained & general work has been much materially retarded.'[108] This was the beginning of the second and most deadly of three waves of influenza; the first had come between June and July 1918, the second from mid-October to December, and the final wave between February and April 1919. Precise statistics are difficult to establish, but it has been estimated that about 900,000 people were infected on the island between 1918 and 1919. Some 20,000 succumbed to the disease or related effects. Dublin, along with the east coast of Leinster and north-east Ulster, witnessed some of the highest death rates (between 3 and 4 per 1,000 people in each year). The spread of the disease in the capital was facilitated by its ports and the rail networks that terminated in the city. Those who worked with the public, in shops, in the medical profession, or as police, postal workers, bank officials and clergy, were most exposed to the disease and thus most likely to die. Some unlucky Dublin homes were visited by both influenza and the First World War. When 24-year-old Catherine Moran Heatley died of 'influenzal pneumonia' at Nicholas Street, her three young children were orphaned. Their father Charles was a lance corporal in the RDF

1 'The Six Members of Parliament for Dublin', taken by Sir John Benjamin Stone in May 1911 at the members' entrance to the Terrace at Westminster. *Left to right*: P.J. Brady (St Stephen's Green), William Francis Cotton (County South), Joseph Nannetti (College Green), William Field (St Patrick's), William Abraham (Harbour), J.J. Clancy (County North).

2 King George V and Queen Mary visit Lord Iveagh's Play Centre on Francis Street during the royal visit, 8 July 1911. The London *Times* considered the 'throng of bare footed children' that gathered around the king to be an encouraging sign for the future.

3 The interior of a tenement room in No. 38 Francis Street, 1913.

4 Protest march by followers of James Larkin regarding the detention of Mary Ellen Murphy, locked out of work at Jacob's biscuit factory and convicted of assault during the lockout, at High Park Convent, 30 November 1913.

5 Seán T. O'Kelly (1882–1966), Sinn Féin member of Dublin Corporation, 1915–24, TD for Dublin College Green, 1918–21 and for Dublin Mid, 1921–3.

6 Members of the Fairview branch of Cumann na mBan, *c.*1914.

7 Irish Volunteers in formation on bicycles outside Butson's Hotel in Howth during the gun-running in July 1914.

8 John Henry Bernard (1860–1927), Church of Ireland archbishop of Dublin, 1915–19, and provost of Trinity College Dublin, 1919–27.

9 'Prevention of Epidemic' poster issued in the aftermath of the 1916 Rising.

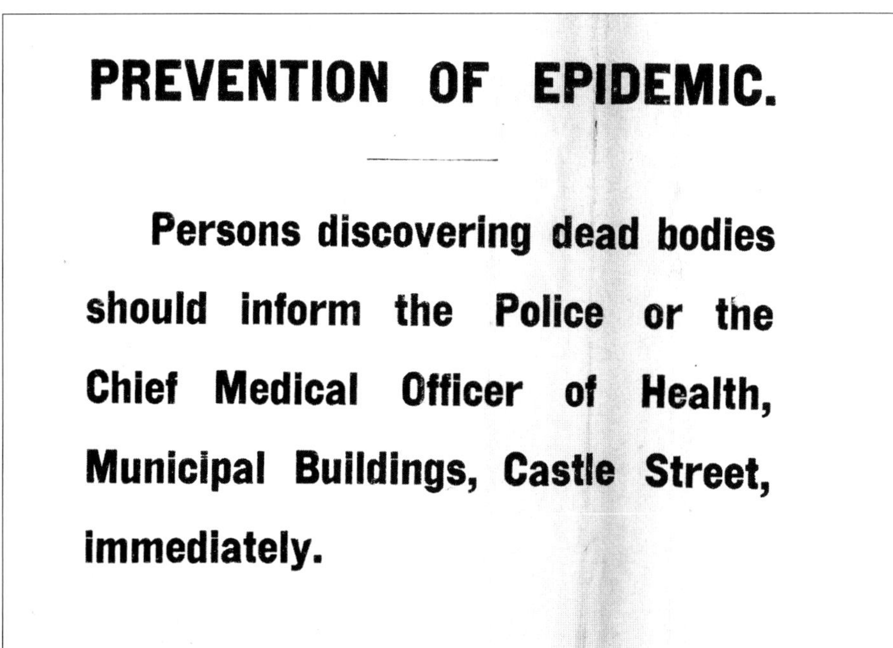

PREVENTION OF EPIDEMIC.

Persons discovering dead bodies should inform the Police or the Chief Medical Officer of Health, Municipal Buildings, Castle Street, immediately.

10 Rebuilding Clery's department store on Sackville (now O'Connell) Street after the 1916 Rising. Clery's reopened at the site in 1922.

11 A crowd at Westland Row greeting 1916 Rising prisoners released under the general amnesty, 18 June 1917. This was one of many large gatherings in Dublin to meet returning prisoners and internees.

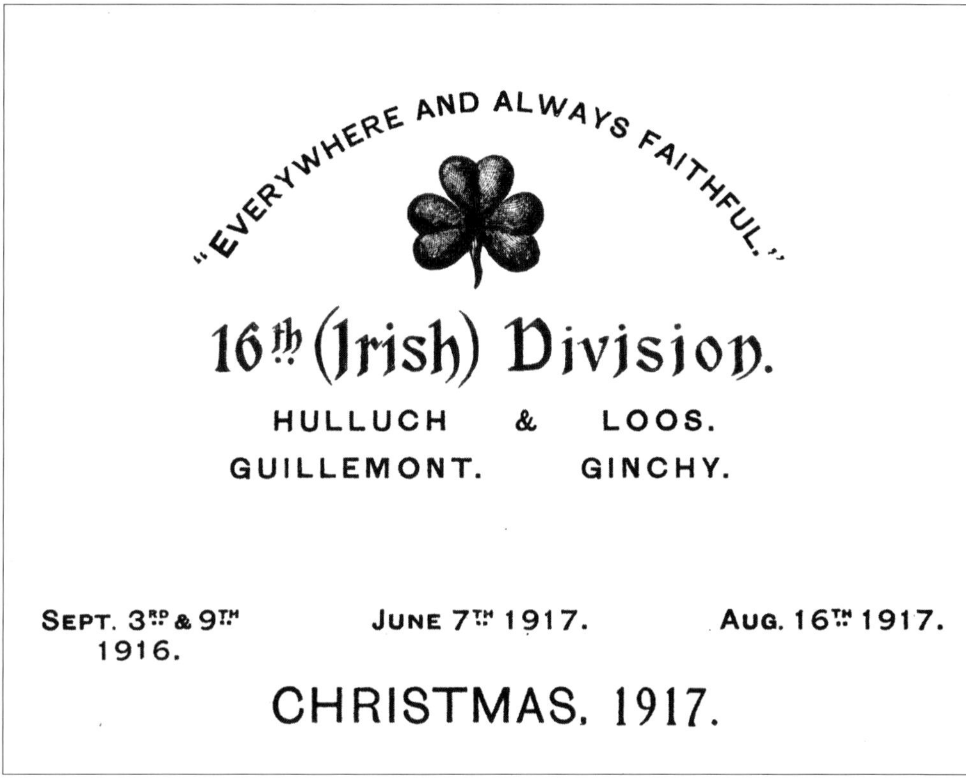

12 Card sent to Monica Roberts by Christy Fox of the 2nd Royal Dublin Fusiliers, Christmas 1917. Roberts kept up a regular correspondence with soldiers during the war.

13 A group gathered at the grave of Seán Doyle in Esker Cemetery, Lucan. From Inchicore, Doyle was killed in Kilmashogue in September 1920 and the cross was erected 'by a few friends' in September 1922. Doyle's father, Peadar, was later a TD for Dublin South and Dublin South West and lord mayor of Dublin.

14 The American Committee for Relief in Ireland, formed in 1920 to provide relief to civilians who had suffered loss or hardship as a result of the War of Independence, inspecting the ruins of the Deeds, Templar & Co. hosiery factory in Balbriggan, 14 February 1921.

15 Auxiliaries bring in a captured prisoner after a raid in Dublin, December 1920.

16 Women march outside Mountjoy Prison, 13 March 1921. Six members of the Dublin Brigade were executed there the following day.

17 Thomas and Annie Bryan. Married in November 1920, Bryan was one of the men executed in Mountjoy on 14 March 1921.

18 Children watch as smoke billows from the Custom House, May 1921, following the IRA's attack on the building.

19 *Left to right*: Rory O'Connor, Oscar Traynor, Constance Markievicz and Muriel MacSwiney, at the Wolfe Tone commemoration in Bodenstown, Co. Kildare, on 20 June 1922, just over a week before the bombardment of the Four Courts and the opening of the Civil War.

20 National army recruiting office on Great Brunswick (now Pearse) Street, 1922.

21 View of the Four Courts with smoke billowing from the Public Record Office during the Battle for Dublin, June 1922.

22 Evacuation of the Edinburgh Hotel during the Battle for Dublin, 5 July 1922.

In Ever Loving Memory
OF OUR BRAVE SOLDIER
JOHN GAFFNEY,
Irish Republican Army,
WHO DIED FOR IRELAND
on the 17th November, 1922,
AGED 20 YEARS.
R. I. P.

Dearest PETER and JOHN you have left us,
In this weary world of pain,
Praying for the Irish freedom
Which your Irish blood was slain,
We do not know the pain they suffered
Nor did we see them die.

23 Memorial card for ATIRA volunteer John Gaffney, executed in Kilmainham Gaol on 17 November 1922. Peter Cassidy, mentioned on the card, was executed on the same day. Both were from Usher's Quay.

24 Seán Lemass after his victory in the Dáil by-election for South Dublin, 1924.

and had been killed on the opening day of the Battle of the Somme in July 1916.[109] Nevertheless, alongside the ordinary challenges of daily life in the city and county, activism, electoral politics, and ultimately military activity carried on despite a pandemic that interrupted daily life, stretched medical and other resources, and confined or killed large numbers of Dublin's population.

The 1918 general election, called by David Lloyd George at the end of the war, was the first parliamentary vote since 1910. Polling day was 14 December 1918, with results delivered two weeks later. While 25 of the 103 constituencies around the country were uncontested and taken by SF (leaving large numbers of newly enfranchised men and women without a chance to vote), all Dublin constituencies were contested.[110] SF's success was built on the changes of the previous two-and-a-half years, but also on effective electioneering machinery. In early November 1918, just before the war ended, the DMP estimated that there were twenty-three SF clubs in the city with a membership of 4,640. SF activity in the capital the previous month, which included the annual convention on 29 October attended by some 500 members, was 'mainly confined to electioneering work' and several meetings were held at 6 Harcourt Street by the SF executive that focused mainly on preparing for an impending election.[111] SF candidates were selected – as were those of the IPP – centrally, principally by Harry Boland. In the selection of candidates in Dublin, as elsewhere, it was the more radical elements of the broader movement that won out. The commitment to securing the republic also took precedence over the priorities of the labour movement. In spite of some complaints that the SF programme was not radical enough, Thomas Johnson eventually convinced a Labour conference in November 1918 that its interests were best served by stepping aside to allow national unity in favour of achieving self-determination. The Irish Volunteers and Cumann na mBan acted as election agents, organizers, canvassers and 'peace patrols' to prevent interference with polling stations.[112] But there was also disappointment among some suffrage activists that only one woman, Constance Markievicz, ultimately ran as a SF candidate in the capital. Hanna Sheehy-Skeffington was nominated for the Harbour constituency but, perhaps believing Alfie Byrne was not likely to be beaten, did not run.[113]

As in other counties, SF ultimately usurped the IPP but a strong Unionist challenge in some constituencies set Dublin apart from the rest of the south and west. There were seven new city constituencies (see map 3) and SF ultimately secured 66.7 per cent of the votes cast and won all of the available seats. In the suburbs and county, the result was a little less decisive and the party took three of the four available seats with just under 48 per cent.[114] In the St Patrick's constituency, Constance Markievicz became the first woman elected to Westminster when she won a three-way contest with the IPP's incumbent William Field and independent nationalist J.J. Kelly (a Unionist candidate had been selected but later withdrew). Her vote was almost double the combined tally

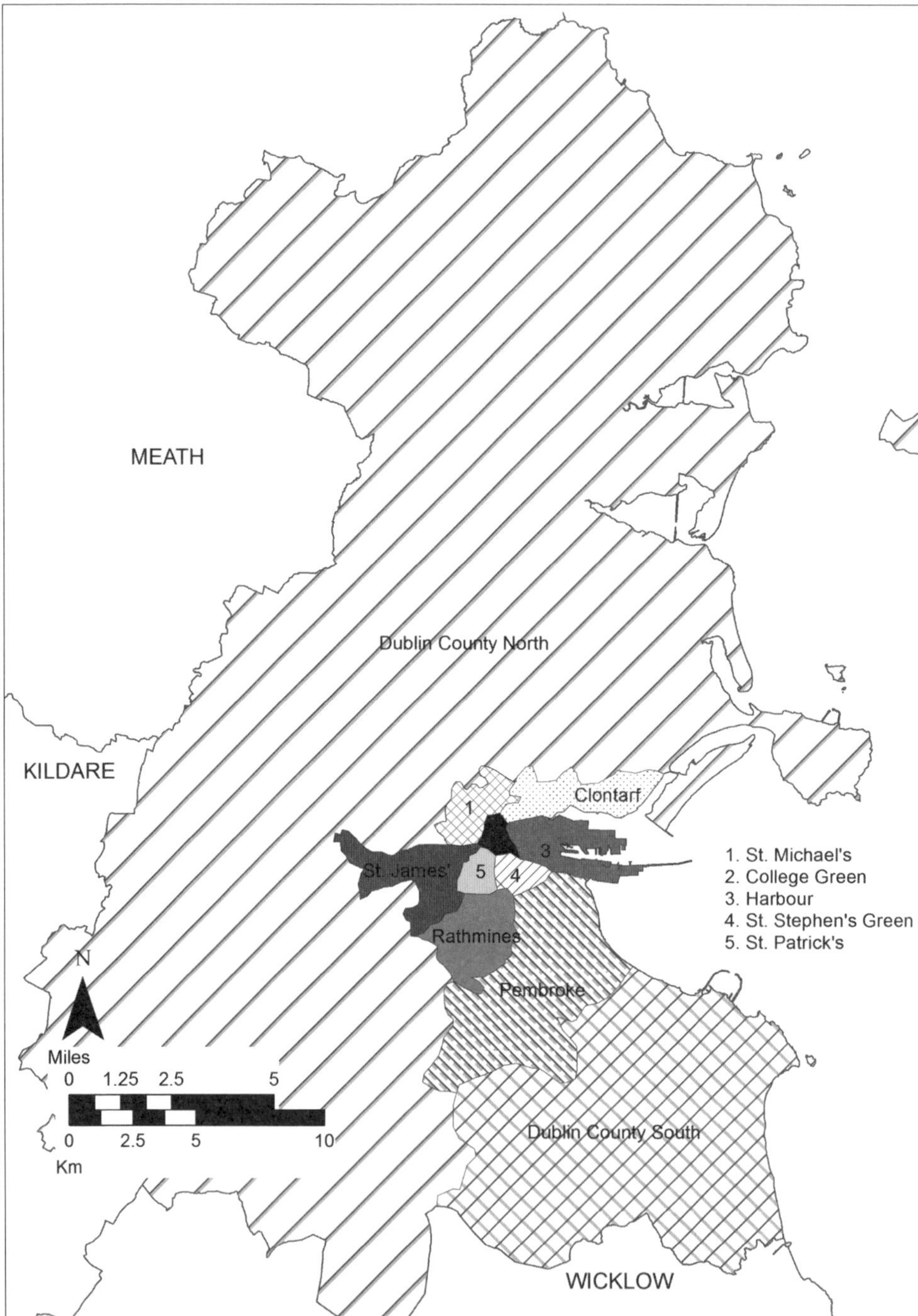

3 Parliamentary constituencies in 1918

of her rivals, while elsewhere Alfie Byrne suffered his only election defeat in twenty-seven contests across a long political career. Notwithstanding Byrne's personal popularity and vocal advocacy in parliament for Easter Rising prisoners, he lost out to Phil Shanahan's call to 'strike a blow for complete independence' – a particularly noteworthy sign of SF's support.[115] SF candidates won the remaining five city seats by large margins in contests with IPP or nationalist candidates, though Unionist Henry Hanna polled a respectable 2,755 votes in St Stephen's Green and was less than 200 votes behind second-placed P.J. Brady, the incumbent and IPP candidate; SF councillor Thomas Kelly topped the poll on 8,461 votes. Arthur Samuels and Sir Robert Woods took the traditionally Unionist Dublin University seats, defeating the diehard Unionist William Jellett and Nationalist Stephen Gwynn. When Samuels died in 1919, Jellett won the resulting by-election.[116]

SF was also victorious in County North and County South – with Frank Lawless and George Gavan Duffy respectively taking those seats. These constituencies had rather different demographics and voting histories, and the candidates were likewise from backgrounds that might initially appear to have little in common. Lawless ran a successful farm in Saucerstown in Swords and was the patriarch of a strong advanced nationalist network in the area.[117] Gavan Duffy was born in England and had first come to public notice as Roger Casement's solicitor during the latter's trial for treason, and thereafter moved to Ireland where he was called to the bar.[118] Gavan Duffy appealed to voters on the promise of having Ireland's right to self-determination heard at upcoming peace negotiations in Paris. He also asked that they remember the 'humiliating record of the "Irish Party" in recent years', examine the party's record on issues like 'conscription and the war, and its record on the executions … and thereby take the measure of the men whom the overwhelming voice of your people consign to oblivion at last'.[119] This was evidently successful, though there was a strong Unionist showing in the constituency as Sir Thomas Robinson got within 800 votes of Gavan Duffy's total of 5,133.

Desmond FitzGerald won comfortably in Pembroke, where he largely matched the combined tallies of his Unionist and IPP rivals, but Sir Maurice Dockrell topped the poll for the new constituency of Rathmines to secure the only non-university Unionist seat outside of Ulster.[120] Dockrell thus considered himself 'the sole representative in this House of about 350,000 Unionists'.[121] The nationalist vote in the constituency was split, as the IPP and SF also ran candidates. Barrister George Moonan, a prominent Gaelic League organizer and first-time IPP candidate, had attempted to appeal to unionists in the constituency and urged voters to reject 'Carson, Partition and Dockrell', 'Partition and Sinn Fein', and vote for 'Moonan and Home Rule for the whole of Ireland'.[122] This appears to have had limited success, while Dockrell appealed directly to new women voters and was supported by the electorally experienced and popular Lady Dockrell. Interventions by the *Independent* and Archbishop Walsh against what they saw as the IPP's acceptance of partition probably undermined Moonan's message further and he finished with 12 per cent of the vote (to Dockrell's 50 per cent). Nationalists tried to see Dockrell's win not as a victory for unionism, but instead as a personal victory. The *Irish Independent* consoled itself in noting that 'if a Unionist was to be returned for any seat, we, in common with most of the citizens, would prefer Sir Maurice Dockrell to any other unionist'.[123] Defeated SF candidate Patrick Little went further, claiming 'nothing pleased him more than the contrast that existed between the Unionists in general and Sir Maurice Dockrell'.[124]

The *Independent* suggested that, outside of Rathmines, Unionists had 'fared badly', and would have hoped to win the seats in Pembroke and South County.[125] Yet, Unionists secured over 18,600 votes across four non-university Dublin constituencies, about a quarter of the electorate, only coming third behind a Nationalist candidate in Stephen's Green. While this was not near enough to dampen the SF victory, it demonstrated that for a significant minority of Dubliners the battle in 1918 was not for the future of an independent Ireland, but for maintenance of the Union.[126] They had access to the *Irish Times* and *Daily Express* to mobilize support. Opportunities for public displays were more limited than for their Ulster brethren or nationalist and republican rivals, but unionist men and women in Dublin had raised funds for the campaign, canvassed and organized public speeches.[127] There was, though, little they could do as the SF members elected to Westminster instead formed their own government in Dublin, as Dáil Éireann, and a physical force campaign for independence began.

6. The IRA at war in Dublin, 1919–21

In April 1921 an IRA GHQ staff memorandum noted that

> In one vital respect the present struggle differs from any other Military attempts to obtain the Independence of the Country – for the first time the National Military Command is securely established in Dublin. On every former occasion from King Edward Bruce onward the English hold on Dublin was never seriously challenged, and in the long run this hold on the Capital turned the scale. Therefore, the grip of our forces on Dublin must be maintained and strengthened at all costs … The precise measures to be adopted for strengthening Dublin require detailed consideration, but it cannot be too clearly stated that no number nor any magnitude of victories in any distant provincial areas have any value if Dublin is lost in a military sense.[1]

After a slow start, the War of Independence in Dublin had, by then, intensified significantly as the capital witnessed some of the most famous – or infamous – events of the conflict. The city's perceived centrality to Ireland's revolution, as outlined in the GHQ memorandum, has been reflected in popular memory ever since: through the telling and retelling of the activities of the 'Squad', daring escapes by Michael Collins, 'Bloody Sunday', or the execution of Kevin Barry. But ultimately, as GHQ recognized, the key to the war in Dublin city was survival. The war in the county, by contrast, has received much less attention. This too reflects Dublin county's place in the war as it was judged at the time. In late 1919, for instance, the Cork-born RIC CI for Dublin, A.A. Roberts, informed his superiors that the police had 'much more to fear from the revolutionaries of the City than of the County'.[2] If there was some truth in this, it ignored the extent to which the county IRA – especially in Fingal – was led by locals. Roberts also failed to predict the pockets of more intense violence that would follow in late 1920.

There were thus at least two, if not more, distinct conflicts in Dublin. Urban guerrilla warfare in the city could overlap with the county, but the fighting in rural Dublin was inevitably substantively different. Moreover, north and south county Dublin could be at once connected to the city and independent of each other as the conflict regularly ignored administrative boundaries. The Fingal Brigade area crossed into County Meath and the 6th and 7th Battalions (formed during the conflict) included companies on the Dublin/Wicklow border and in Bray and Blessington. By the standards of Cork, or Tipperary, or Belfast, or even Dublin city, the war in the county may indeed have been relatively 'passive'.[3] But much of the early IRA activity of 1919 was in the county rather than the city given that a raid on Collinstown Aerodrome was followed by a failed attempt to assassinate the lord lieutenant at Ashtown in December 1919 – the first major operation in Dublin since 1916.[4] GHQ later forbade 'offensive operations against British forces and establishments in Fingal' for a period, with the district apparently deemed too important as a line of communications or escape to risk the imposition of martial law.[5] Howth and Sutton were likewise deemed more suitable as 'a place of quiet retreat for IRA personnel'.[6] Individual operations planned for the south of the county were also cancelled by GHQ where it was feared they would disrupt larger actions planned for the city.[7]

GHQ's close relationship with the Dublin Brigade was a defining feature of the war in the city. The famous Squad was a GHQ unit drawn from the Dublin Brigade, and the Brigade was also called on by headquarters to carry out specific operations. The brigade commandant's seat at army council meetings, meanwhile, did little to discourage complaints about central interference.[8] But Dick McKee and Peadar Clancy, O/C and vice-O/C respectively until November 1920, were also responsible for curtailing initial activity in the city. In early 1919 the Volunteers 'had definite orders not to attack British soldiers', and an attempt to take on 'the full might of the British army' during the Victory Parade in July 1919 was cancelled when brigade headquarters decided – logically enough – that small calibre automatic pistols would be ineffective against tanks.[9]

Most shooting in Dublin city before 1921 was carried out by a small group of gunmen, peaking on 'Bloody Sunday', 21 November 1920. Fourteen suspected British intelligence officers were shot that morning and another fourteen civilians killed by Crown forces at Croke Park in the afternoon. The Dublin Brigade also lost McKee and Clancy, shot out of hand at Dublin Castle. The scale of violence in the city and the range of participants increased significantly thereafter. By January 1921, just as an active service unit (ASU) (the city's 'flying column') was belatedly becoming operational, individual companies were encouraged to engage in patrols and ambushes. In one of these actions, at Kenilworth Road, Todd Andrews finally achieved his 'burning ambition to fire a shot for Ireland' – something which, he later recalled, 'produced in me a state bordering on ecstasy'. It was also an example of what became a familiar template: Andrews and his colleagues attacked a British lorry with grenades (or 'bombs') and Webley revolvers (their 'dogs') before using the cover of the city to escape, handing over the guns for deposit in the company arms dump.[10] Rifles, prized by the IRA in the countryside, were of little use in the city and were sometimes given away in favour of automatic pistols, revolvers, grenades and mines.[11] Engagements were often brief, but their value lay in repetition and by February 1921 it seemed to Nevil Macready, the British army general officer commanding in Ireland, that the 'bombing of Military or Police vehicles is now almost of daily occurrence'.[12] The largest engagement in the city after Bloody Sunday, however, abandoned that formula with an ambitious but costly raid on the Custom House in May 1921.

If there was a typical militant in Dublin after 1916, then he or she was young and single, neither very wealthy nor very poor, and Catholic. Oscar Traynor later described the Dublin Brigade as 'made up in the main of Dublin artisans, with a sprinkling of students from the National University as well as a few from Trinity College, and almost all the professions were represented'.[13] The Dublin Brigade, therefore, both reflected and was shaped by the employment environment in the city. There were over 8,500 merchants and agents in 1911, for instance, and while these men are hard to find in the IRA their businesses attracted the shop assistants and managers who made up almost one-third of officers and nearly 20 per cent of the active rank and file.[14] Five grocer's assistants and two grocer's managers were killed in the city between 1919 and 1921 while members of the IRA; all had been born outside Dublin. The largest group of Dublin Brigade fatalities were skilled tradesman or apprentices, accounting for twelve from a total of forty-one, and roughly matching their proportion of the working population. Students, meanwhile, were over-represented among the IRA and its fatalities.[15]

Unmentioned by Traynor were the significant numbers of unskilled workers, particularly those with more secure labouring jobs with the corporation or the larger industrial firms. Guinness – owned by a family well-known as unionists – was a place of work for both republicans and their enemies: a 1920 IRA intelligence note recorded that a man who was 'suspected by our local people' had worked for Guinness 'three or four years ago, and might be known to some of our people there'.[16] At least 151 of the men and women 'out' in 1916 worked for Dublin Corporation at some point in their careers, and the corporation remained a prominent employer among members of the Dublin Brigade.[17] Individual units were in turn shaped by the working environment in their area. The railway works was the major employer in Inchicore, for instance, and the 4th Battalion 'had a good deal of men' who worked there.[18] Many units attracted members from a mix of backgrounds, but men from the same professions could cluster in the Dublin IRA just as they did within the general population. One company was made up primarily of workers in the licensed trade and another was formed from a large group of grocers' assistants who had late shifts. University students – many with no home ties to Dublin – were particularly noticeable in the 3rd Battalion's 'C' Company and in the Engineers' Battalion.[19]

Inward migration meant that the Dublin IRA and Cumann na mBan were heavily populated with outsiders. Traynor later suggested that 'every county in Ireland was represented by one or more members and many of these men found death on the streets of the capital fighting for the nation's freedom'.[20] Francis Gleeson, raised in the affluent West Derby suburb of Liverpool by Tipperary parents, had been studying at Liverpool University to become a secondary school teacher but came to Dublin to avoid military service. Once there he took on a job as a clerk, adopted a pseudonym ('Aedan Redmond'), and joined two older brothers in the movement.[21] Work was a more common draw, though, and Peadar Clancy, for instance, first came to Dublin to work as an outfitter.[22] Martin Savage, killed at Ashtown in December 1919, grew up in a thatched cottage in Sligo, one of fourteen children born to a farmer who worked twelve statute acres of marshy land.[23] In Dublin he was said to have been earning 'a very good salary' as a shop assistant.[24] Thomas Whelan was a Galway-born labourer and one of six Dublin Brigade men hanged on 14 May 1920. Whelan's mother later wrote that 'he went to Dublin in 1917 to earn for me & his Brothers & Sisters & father & every one in Dublin knows that I am a Poor woman back here in the Poorest Part of connemara [*sic*]'.[25]

The Fingal IRA likewise reflected the nature of work in the county, where about a third of employed males aged over twelve worked in agriculture in the 1920s and farmers' sons and agricultural labourers were prominent among brigade, battalion and company officers.[26] In this regard, the Fingal IRA stands apart from its country counterparts where farmers and agricultural labourers were significantly underrepresented.[27] Much of the republican network in the Swords area revolved around the Lawless farm in Saucerstown, owned by 1916 veteran and TD Frank Lawless. His eldest son, Joseph, was a brigade officer in Fingal and at least one of his brothers – Colm, a farmer – was in the local IRA. Two younger siblings, Kathleen and Eveleen, were members of Cumann na Ban. In 1922, Joseph Lawless married Monica 'Dot' Fleming, a member of the ard craobh branch of Cumann na mBan who also had siblings in the movement. Kathleen Lawless married Bernard McAllister in 1929. He had been a battalion intelligence officer in Fingal and was from a large farming family in Donabate. James Crenigan, another member of the Fingal Brigade, worked as an agricultural labourer at Saucerstown. His brother John, and Peter Wilson, both killed at Ashbourne in 1916, had also worked there. The influence of other significant demographic groups in the county is seen in the Westons in Lusk, who were masons and dressmakers rather than agricultural labourers. Another prominent republican family, the Taylors in Swords, were the sons of a publican.[28]

Most IRA officers in Fingal were natives of the area in which they operated (including companies that crossed the border into County Meath). The adjutant of the brigade's 1st Battalion, Daniel Killian, was an exception as he was born in Roscommon. Thomas Peppard, the brigade intelligence officer, was born in Brunswick Street in the city but raised in Lusk.[29] Michael Lynch, Fingal O/C, was a corporation abattoir superintendent. He was later denounced by Joseph Lawless as 'a City man' who continued to live in the city and paid only periodic visits to local units and presided over infrequent and unsatisfactory brigade council meetings.[30] Key officers in south county Dublin, meanwhile, were drawn from the skilled workers and clerks of the city and suburbs. Andy McDonnell grew up in Ballsbridge and Rathmines and admitted that he was initially considered an 'outsider' and 'a city man' when sent out to organize in Ticknock and Barnacullia in 1917. Unlike Lynch in Fingal, whom he considered 'very weak', McDonnell eventually won over the 'mountainy men' – stone cutters and blacksmiths – that he trained.[31] The other staff officers in the 6th Battalion were also from the townships: Michael Chadwick was living in Rathmines in 1918 and Brian and Niall MacNeill, sons of Eoin, in Herbert Park and later Booterstown.[32] Patrick Kavanagh 'came home to the country' in 1919 as he 'was not getting good health in the city.' He joined a local company in 1920 and was second in command of the 7th Battalion by July 1921.[33] The captain of the Bray company, Larry O'Brien, had been in the South Dublin Union in 1916 before moving out to Bray for work.[34]

Those who fought for the republic only ever comprised a tiny proportion of the population. Nominal rolls compiled in the 1930s (an imperfect but useful gauge) indicate a strength of 5,326 men across the Dublin Brigade by the time the truce came into effect. The size of individual companies, the brigade's smallest unit, ranged from 75 to 140 members.[35] More important was the 'fighting strength' which Oscar Traynor estimated at about 1,150 by early 1921, with only a fraction of the men in any battalion deemed 'active'.[36] The Fingal nominal rolls list 614 men in four battalions in July 1921 with an average company of 31 members – much smaller than those in the Dublin Brigade.[37] This was about average when compared to its country neighbours. The 1st Meath Brigade (covering parts of Meath and Kildare on the Dublin border) listed 408 men on its own nominal rolls for July 1921; the 3rd Meath Brigade, the largest of the four Meath Brigades, listed 796.[38]

Following the reorganization of the IRA between 1916 and 1918, further restructuring took place during the conflict. These changes were, in essence, a recognition of the very different wars that took place in Dublin. When a divisional structure was adopted across the IRA in 1920, Fingal was included in the 1st Eastern Division with a headquarters in Dunboyne, County Meath, and was separate to the Dublin Brigade's 2nd Eastern Division.[39] The splitting of the Dublin Brigade's 3rd Battalion in October 1920 similarly reflected the very different requirements of the war in the south county's more rural districts. The new 6th Battalion had 876 men on its nominal roll for July 1921 (though, as with the other Dublin battalions, only a fraction of these were 'active' men). Andy McDonnell – considered 'an outstanding man' – was promoted to O/C.[40] In May 1921 Gerry Boland, older brother of Harry, was appointed O/C of a new 7th Battalion, separated from the 4th after further reorganization in south Dublin.[41] The 6th and 7th Battalions were divided by the Dublin and Wicklow mountains and Boland's command area stretched south in a more-or-less straight line from Clondalkin and Tallaght in south-west Dublin to Valleymount in Wicklow. It was by far the smallest Dublin battalion and had 248 men in six companies in July 1921, with an additional 41 in an ASU that included men from a column disbanded in bordering parts of Kildare and Wicklow.[42]

Cumann na mBan nominal rolls, meanwhile, list 669 members in nine Dublin City Council branches. These ranged in size from 32 named members in Fairview to 165 members in the ard craobh (or central branch).[43] Some republican women also operated outside of the formal organization, particularly when it afforded additional immunity from suspicion.[44] Cumann na mBan had relatively small numbers in Dublin county, but even these were woefully underestimated by the RIC which consistently recorded only one branch with thirty members.[45] Nominal rolls for North Dublin (or Fingal) District Council list 131 members across seven branches, ranging in size from 10 members (Artane) to 29 (Skerries) in July 1921.[46] But only four branches – Howth, Blanchardstown, Balbriggan and a newly formed company in Donabate – were considered 'in operation' between 1919 and 1921.[47] As late as June 1921, the Fingal Brigade quartermaster informed member Brigid Connolly that he had not been aware of 'the existence of Cumann-na-mBan in our (Fingal) area', even though Connolly had been in contact with a battalion O/C. The quartermaster noted that had he known he would have been in touch as 'our men were very badly in need of assistance,' and enquired about new shirts, socks, home-made cakes ('a treat to us'), and weekly washing.[48] When Theresa Redmond (née Kehoe), captain of the Dún Laoghaire branch, made up a list of members in south County Dublin she came up with similarly small numbers: thirty-one names for five branches attached to the 6th IRA Battalion. This was again an underestimate as Redmond was able to remember sixteen members from her own company but only three each from Deansgrange and Bray and two from Dundrum.[49] A more recent list names ninety-nine women who were 'actively involved to some extent or other in the struggle for independence in Dún Laoghaire and surrounding areas', though not all were necessarily members of Cumann na mBan.[50]

When asked what a member of the executive was doing when 'things got hot in Dublin in 1921', Lily O'Brennan responded:

> In Dublin nearly every member of the executive was a member of a local branch. I was a member of the Executive and was also Secretary. I was also in the Ranelagh Branch. I was always there for the various things that I was required to do … The District Council was composed of the Captain and the Secretary from every branch. They met once a week and considered anything that was necessary to be done – putting up posters, etc. The Captain went back and saw that her unit was trained and ready at a moments' notice to do anything.[51]

In one sense, this was a neat summary of the consistent and often understated activity carried out by the most committed republican women.[52] But it also undersold women's contributions to the military conflict and the now famous intelligence war. Waterford-born Lily Mernin was a shorthand typist in Dublin Castle and smuggled out reports on the movement and distribution of Crown forces, or lists of names and addresses of intelligence operatives. She also passed on gossip overheard within the Castle and used social functions to identify British agents and prominent Auxiliaries, walking Dame Street with Squad member Tom Cullen and accompanying him to sports galas and race meetings to point them out – 'a still more dangerous task'. Mernin's information fed directly into the list of names used for Bloody Sunday and Frank Saurin acknowledged that it contributed to the 'success attending a number of "jobs"'.[53] Annie Brennan elicited information on government telegraph and communication systems from a friend who ran a canteen in the Lower Castle Yard.[54]

Eilís McNamara's war is an example of the sort of work that made it possible for men to attack Crown forces in an urban area. She was in charge of an arms dump in Mount Argus; carried guns and grenades to ambushes in Bluebell, Blackrock and Ranelagh; tended to wounded men; secured and delivered two additional revolvers for use on Bloody Sunday when they 'were short'; brought petrol for use in the burning of the Custom House in 1921; and was a 'courier' assigned to the ASU.[55] Similarly, in Dún Laoghaire, Teresa Kehoe carried revolvers and grenades to the 'scenes of operations or intended operations'.[56] Women repeatedly took advantage of perceived social norms to hide their activities and blend into ordinary life, posing with IRA men as courting couples, carrying despatches to avoid male searchers, and using prams and long skirts to transport arms.[57] Catherine Rooney (née Byrne), a 1916 veteran, remembered bringing guns to a dump in 'a shopping bag containing cabbage'.[58] Rose McNamara 'had to arrange for the allocation of girls to the different First Aid Stations during the ambushing period'.[59] This was vital for wounded men in a built-up area who could not immediately attend hospital, though credit was not always forthcoming. Maureen Beaumont (McGavock in 1920) recalled how Ernie O'Malley was brought to 51 Lower Beechwood Avenue 'with an ugly wound in his leg', which was dressed 'every afternoon' by Josephine Aherne: 'I notice she gets no credit for that in his book *On another man's wound*.'[60]

Women in the county transported arms and ammunition, carried despatches, collected money, arranged 'safe houses' and generally looked after 'the needs of the fighting units'. In north Dublin, members described tending to men 'in whom the enemy had an interest', but also the 'observation of the movements of hostile forces', 'compiling lists', and 'Abstracting information of use to the IRA'.[61] Women provided a regular line of communication between city and county, and between the townships and the south county.[62] They also appear to have been the primary fundraisers in Fingal, engaging in seemingly open 'house to house collections' and 'concerts and Aeridheachta and things like that to make money'.[63] Nominal rolls list Dr Eleonora Fleury, the first recognized female psychiatrist in Britain and Ireland, as captain of the company in Donabate.[64] In 1920 the Donabate company 'collected a good deal of money' for active Volunteers.'[65] Sourcing sympathetic dentists and barbers and organizing funerals of deceased Volunteers were other necessary but easily forgotten contributions to the struggle.[66] Indeed, as far as the RIC was concerned, Cumann na mBan was 'Not Active' for almost all of the conflict.[67]

From IRA GHQ's perspective, much of the war outside the city was a disappointment and personality clashes seem to have hampered the Fingal Brigade. Daniel Brophy stepped aside as Fingal O/C and returned to the ranks during the War of Independence, apparently due to some unexplained 'little differences'. His desire to engage in military action was apparently scuppered by GHQ and later by his own commanding officer.[68] While Joseph Lawless was willing to admit that 'all the members of the staff were equally to blame' for being too cautious, he was particularly critical of Michael Lynch who was reappointed O/C in Fingal after a period in the city.[69] For his part, Lynch insisted that Richard Mulcahy 'forbade him to adopt a fighting policy in Fingal' until 'the members were sufficiently trained'. When he arranged for machine-guns for an attack at Hedgestown, failure was the fault of the 'expert' machine-gunner brought out from the city.[70] Lawless later claimed that Brophy and James Derham were 'actively engaged with some others at the latter part of 1920 in trying to force the Brigade into activity against the wishes of the Brigade O/C'. Their work 'to bring off a big coup at Balbriggan' was 'hampered by our OC' and ultimately came to an end when they were arrested in December 1920.[71] Lawless was also 'dumfounded' to learn that Lynch had taken off to England with his wife 'for a few days' holidays' in early December. After Lawless failed to have Lynch replaced, their relationship became 'strained'.[72]

Lynch's difficult relationship with GHQ was evident in disagreements over armaments in early 1921. In a March report, Lynch noted that there was a 'willingness to do any job' among the men, but their most significant difficulty was 'the urgent need' of 'grenades and revolvers'.[73] Gearóid O'Sullivan, IRA quartermaster general, however, reported to Mulcahy that he had withheld arms from Fingal as there was not enough activity in the area and arms received had been poorly cared for, while loans from the Dublin Brigade had not been returned.[74] Mulcahy then wrote to Lynch to complain that his 'hasty and casual' report had been 'unsatisfactory in every way'. A scathing memorandum on 'Conditions in Fingal' was attached, noting the 'negligible' casualties and damage inflicted in a 'Black-and-Tan infested area'.[75] This surprised Lynch, who noted that the area had been in 'a hopeless state of disorganization' when he returned there and believed that he had 'done quite well' in achieving his aim of clearing the area of Crown force patrols 'after dark' (which in turn had made it more difficult to engage the enemy at night). Tired from pushing a bicycle around his area, Lynch admitted that on arriving at his headquarters he felt 'more like resting than doing strenuous mental work', continued to insist that more revolvers, rifles and grenades were needed before more activity could be attempted, and cautiously requested the allocation of a motorcycle.[76]

Whoever was to blame, the brigade's achievements were modest and this was perhaps exemplified by a raid on the British army remount depot in Lusk that secured £300: the depot was unguarded and all its staff were civilian.[77] The depot was later burned and this reflected a pronounced emphasis on destroying government property in the area. As late as June 1921, coastguard stations, occupied by unarmed coastguards and their families, were burned in Skerries, Rush, Loughshinney and Rogerstown.[78] By comparison, it appears that the initiative and energy of Andy McDonnell and Michael Chadwick were significant in dictating the nature of conflict in the more ambitious south Dublin units. The isolated 7th Battalion was much less active.[79] The most consequential action in the battalion's brief existence before the truce was the destruction of a military pumping station in Clondalkin.[80] The arrival of Gerry Boland as O/C may have eventually changed the dynamic, but Andy McDonnell later claimed that Boland was not originally put in charge of the 6th Battalion as Oscar Traynor feared Boland would 'weigh things up and brood over them' rather than getting them done.[81]

A comparatively small number of police barracks were abandoned in 1920 and Dublin county remained relatively well policed (see map 4). While there was a tendency to refer to all Crown forces in Dublin as 'Tans', the RIC seems to have favoured sending the more experienced policemen of the 'old RIC' to serve there. In the end, only a tiny proportion of the men who served in Dublin were Black and Tans, recruited from early 1920 to fill gaps in the strength of the force.[82] Gormanston military camp was just across the border with County Meath. It was used to train newly recruited policemen and members of the Auxiliary Division of the RIC (ADRIC), which had its own command structure. To Michael Rock, the area thus 'literally swarmed' with Crown forces and 'was not good country for guerrilla warfare'. Attempts at ambushes on the Dublin to Belfast road only saw 'a few shots', but this was because Crown forces 'always made away in great haste' and did not look for a fight.[83] Shotguns easily confiscated from local farmers in the countryside, meanwhile, were deemed useless for guerrilla warfare in the flat, open countryside.[84] South Dublin was policed by a scattering of DMP and RIC stations. Nearby were Beggars Bush Barracks, Portobello in Rathmines, Wellington Barracks on the South Circular Road, a naval base in Kingstown/Dún Laoghaire, and army barracks just over the Wicklow border in Glencree and Bray. Plenty of shots were fired at these posts, but successful captures remained elusive. Patrick Brennan later claimed this had never been the intention as they were 'stoutly built' and 'strongly garrisoned' in the face of the arms available to the attackers.[85] The naval base at

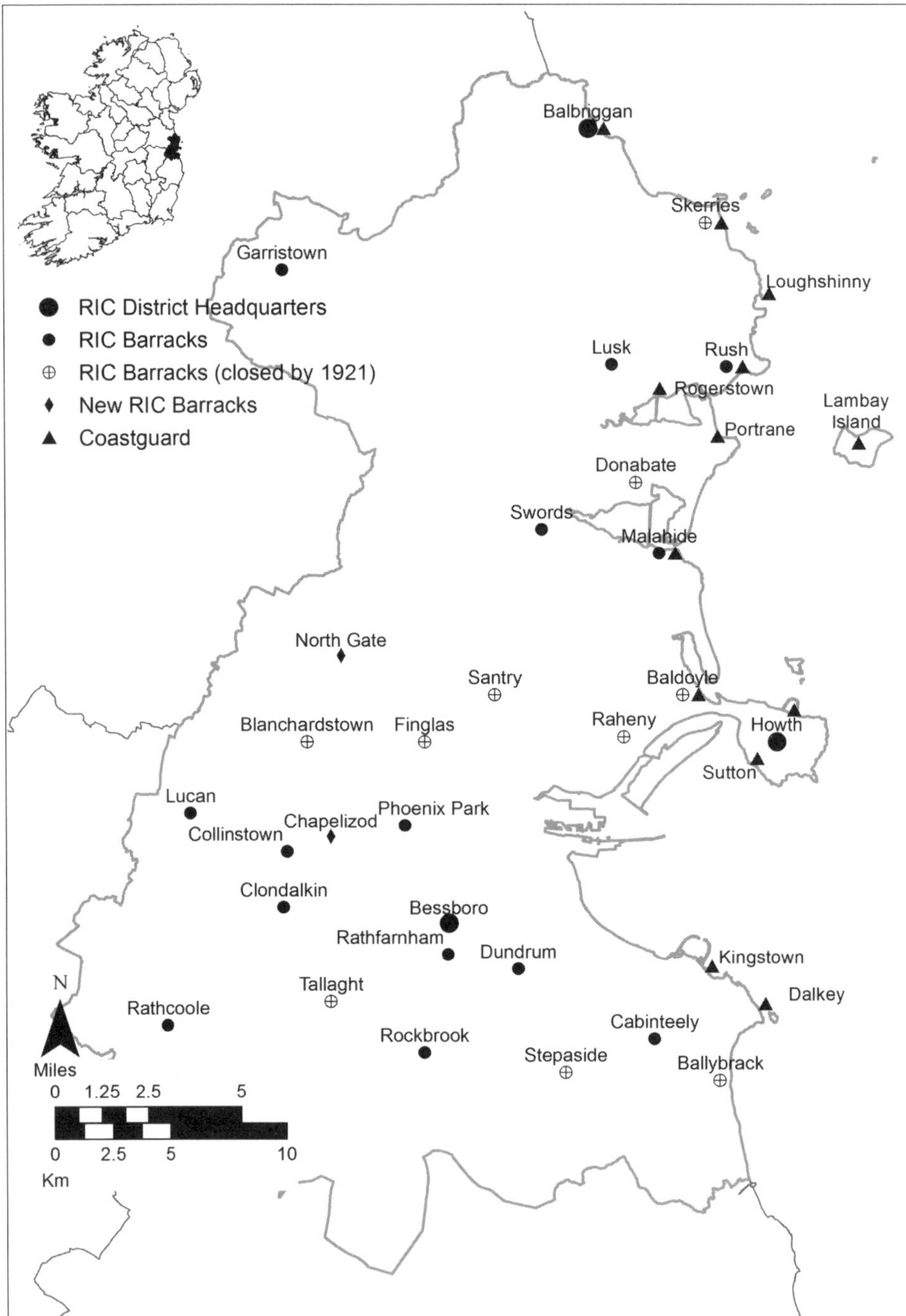

4 Distribution of the Crown forces, 1919–21

Dún Laoghaire was 'attacked several times' and shots were fired regularly at police patrols, albeit with limited results.[86] The British were accused of concealing their casualties, but this ultimately mattered less than the IRA's ability simply to keep fighting.[87]

Martial law was introduced in Dublin city in February 1920 and in June the British army began barricading roads leading into the city. According to the *Evening Herald*, Dublin gossip suggested a range of motives. These included a desire to cause 'irritation and disaffection among the inhabitants', to create the impression of a 'land of crime' that would damage trade and commerce, or as a way to frighten 'visitors and tourists from seeing things for themselves and learning the truth'.[88] In addition, the army patrolled in the county, policed the city curfew, raided suspect premises, and temporarily cordoned off smaller blocks of the city to facilitate arrests of prominent republicans.[89] Sir Nevil Macready later complained that when he arrived in Ireland in April 1920 all army units were understrength and under-armed.[90] But by June 1921, there were 499 officers and over 8,500 other ranks in Dublin barracks, an increase of over 60 officers and 1,000 men since May alone.[91] Lessons were learned from earlier failures, including the need to vary routes of travel and the value of having lorries travel in numbers and at a distance from each other, forcing the attackers to either wait for the last lorry or expose themselves early.[92] Perhaps the most significant army engagement in the city, and an example of its early errors, took place in September 1920 when the Duke of Wellington's Regiment were ambushed while collecting bread from Monk's bakery on Upper Church Street. Kevin Barry was caught at the scene, the first Volunteer captured in this way, and executed in November. He was soon immortalized in ballad as 'a lad of eighteen summers'; the youngest of the three soldiers killed was 15 years old.[93]

In the DMP area, a small number of constables were shot and killed or wounded and G Division detectives were frequent targets for the Squad. Assistant Commissioner William Redmond, shot dead on Harcourt Street in January 1920, was the highest-ranking DMP assassination in the force's history.[94] By late 1920 the metropolitan police was 'left in peace by the gunmen' and became, as Macready put it, 'mere ornaments standing about at the street corners watching the traffic and passing the time of day with casual acquaintances'.[95] ADRIC thus had a much more significant influence on the conflict in the city, with as many as five and never fewer than three companies stationed there at any time. A depot company was based at Beggars Bush from September 1920, while F Company was stationed in Dublin Castle under the operational control of the army's Dublin District. Other companies were periodically stationed at Beggars Bush, Portobello, or the London and North Western Hotel at North Wall. Much of their conduct in Ireland aligned with popular perceptions of drunkenness and cruelty, but very few Auxiliaries had criminal convictions before coming to Ireland, or afterwards, and the 'hard core of the Division' were experienced and efficient soldiers. Required to have held a commission in the British armed forces, they were generally older but not very far removed socio-economically from their enemies in the IRA.[96] Auxiliary patrols became regular targets for the Dublin Brigade and ASU, though a captured IRA report suggested that the practice by the Crown forces of bringing 'hostages' had made at least some Dublin Brigade men reluctant to fire. An unsuccessful attempt to bomb the London and North Western Hotel in April 1921, during which the IRA lost Peter Freyne, was a rare IRA attack on ADRIC quarters.[97]

Soldiers and Auxiliaries carried out daily raids in the city, with F Company ADRIC alone visiting an average of three suspected properties per day between April and July 1921. These raids were often based on limited or faulty intelligence, and frequently came to nothing beyond damaged doors or other property, but the psychological impact was clear.[98] With a propagandist's flair, Erskine Childers captured something of the widely pervasive fear they generated:

> Think of raiding a private house at dead of night in a *tank* (my own experience), in a tank, whose weird rumble and roar can be heard miles away! … A thunder of knocks: no time to dress (even for a woman alone) or the door will crash in. On opening, in charge the soldiers – literally charge – with fixed bayonets and in full war-kit.[99]

The father of William Gorman, shot dead during an ambush on South Great Brunswick Street, claimed the 13-year-old had been on his way to visit his sister who was in hospital owing to 'shock to the nerves caused by frequent military raids'. It was also claimed that a baby sibling had been 'literally frightened to death by the military'.[100] Often unreported, or commented upon in vague or evasive terms, was the threat of what Childers described as 'brutal severity to women'.[101] No clear cases of rape or serious sexual assault in the city appear to have emerged into the public domain, though it is unlikely any prosecutions would have followed had they done so and cases surely went unreported. When the commandant of ADRIC's F Company and two of its members were put on trial for murder, for instance, they were acquitted as deathbed testimony from one of the victims was disallowed. Indeed, the Dublin District military command rather selectively concluded that 'the work of the Auxiliaries in Dublin was excellent, and the happiest relations existed between them and the troops'.[102]

Perhaps less relevant in the densely populated city and suburbs, the sympathies of local communities were an important variable in the county. The inhabitants of Oldtown in north Dublin were praised for their discretion when a column of men spent a number of weeks camped there.[103] Patrick Brennan similarly made a point of expressing appreciation for 'assistance, encouragement and prayers' received in Dundrum.[104] Equally, however, Michael Chadwick, an officer in Dundrum before becoming a battalion vice-commandant, remembered that 'everyone who had money was hostile. Naturally every hostile house had some connection with the British army'.[105] An officer in Deansgrange similarly felt that their work was 'always hampered and made dangerous by the local population' and also suggested a common connection with service in the Crown forces.[106] James McSweeney insisted that finding support for any 'Irish-Ireland movement' was always difficult in Bray and the IRA had few friends. For Sweeney, the few who did gather together in Bray were deserving of as much praise as those who fought in areas with more popular support.[107]

While simple demographics are not enough to explain civilian interaction with the IRA, some of the disparity between north and south Dublin becomes clear when the Protestant minority – generally assumed to be loyal to the British administration – is considered. Deansgrange was part of the Stillorgan District Electoral Division (DED) where 65 per cent of the population were Roman Catholic in 1911, while in Bray Catholics accounted for 69 per cent, leaving large Protestant minorities. The prominence of retired police or army was also significant in perceptions about the allegiances of an area. Bray was considered 'a haven for … retired RIC men and ex-British army and navy officers'.[108] In parts of south Dublin and elsewhere the large Protestant minority could smother IRA activity.[109] Where Protestants were in a more isolated minority, the dynamics were different. Oldtown was entirely Catholic, with the surrounding Clonmethan DED 95 per cent Catholic, so is likely for that reason that a local Church of Ireland clergyman was apparently compelled to approach the IRA to ensure that 'members of his Church would not be suspected of informing on us'.[110]

Thomas Peppard admitted that the people in Fingal were generally sympathetic until asked to do something which 'endangered their lives or liberty'.[111] And while religion could never be entirely irrelevant when it was so closely linked to loyalist and unionist politics, there is little to suggest it ever became a defining feature of the war in Dublin. Even in the city and townships, where Protestants were more numerous, there is scant evidence of a desire actively to resist the IRA. The army's official history of the conflict asserted that in Dublin 'a considerable minority were professedly loyal but were so intimidated that they refused to give information even when they themselves had been the sufferers by IRA action'.[112]

Dublin city residents were also more clearly grouped by social class rather than religion – ruling out the sort of intra-communal violence witnessed in the most heavily segregated parts of Belfast. Instead, the Squad's intelligence war has dominated the popular narratives of the war in Dublin city. As Joe Leonard remembered it, the Squad developed out of the 'urgent need of vigorous action against the British executives and Detectives who were harassing Dáil Éireann and the members of our headquarters staff'.[113] The shooting of Alan Bell in March 1920 captures much of what they did. A former RIC DI and resident magistrate, Bell had been brought out of retirement in 1919 and by early 1920 was investigating and seizing republican funds. On the morning of 26 March, he boarded his usual 9.30 a.m. tram from Dalkey into the city and was followed by Paddy O'Daly and Tom Keogh. At the Aylesbury Road stop, O'Daly and Keogh signalled to Mick McDonnell, Liam Tobin, Vinnie Byrne, Jim Slattery and Joe Dolan that Bell was on board. He was bundled from the tram – 'Come on, Mr Bell, your time has come' – and was found with bullet wounds to the wrist and groin, with one behind the ear that had proved fatal.[114] The Squad's members were hand-picked but initially inexperienced and even naïve. Nerves, panic and fear made shooting more difficult – even at close range – and men fired too early, misfired, or were unable to fire at all. Slattery told Ernie O'Malley that the key was 'getting close to your man' but also admitted to having missed his target even when 'up close'; Tom Cullen was known as 'a terrible shot'.[115] Soon, however, men engaged in active service became accustomed to the dangers and the fears. This was made easier by strong bonds forged through mutual experiences within active units, and through admiration and loyalty towards direct superiors. In Dublin, this devotion was owed to Michael Collins who took personal interest in the operations of the Squad and ASU, meeting members before and after operations.[116]

A key moment was 21 November 1920, Bloody Sunday.[117] At 9.00 a.m. that morning, selected members of the Squad and individual Dublin Brigade companies entered seven lodgings on the south side of the river and the Gresham Hotel. Within fifteen minutes, fourteen men had been shot dead and five more wounded. One died eighteen days later. An auxiliary cadet, Maurice Spenle, shot himself in the head that afternoon, the morning's events 'preying on his mind', and the wife of another victim died giving birth to a still-born child. But not all of those killed were intelligence agents.[118] Several other targets escaped either because they were lucky enough to have been elsewhere that morning or the men assigned to their lodgings did not turn up. At the Eastwood Hotel on Lower Leeson Street, Christie Byrne remembered that 'Our man was gone … We searched the whole bloody house for him'.[119] Charlie Dalton later complained that in 'some instances the excuses put forward for the non-carrying out of instructions were not considered very satisfactory'.[120] Some names had been removed from the list of targets as it was being compiled and others cut by Cathal Brugha where he believed there was insufficient evidence.[121]

That afternoon, just after 3.25 p.m., Crown forces fired on players and spectators at a Gaelic football match in Croke Park between Dublin and Tipperary, attended by a clearly unperturbed crowd of about 5,000.[122] Fourteen were killed or later died of wounds. The youngest victim was probably the first, 11-year-old William Robinson from Little Britain Street (known as Perry), shot through the shoulder and back as he sat in a tree overlooking the ground. A ricochet bullet killed 14-year-old John William Scott from nearby Fitzroy

Avenue. The one female victim, Jane Boyle, was due to be married in less than a week.[123] To illustrate just how close the First World War remained, Michael Feery, a First World War veteran, bled out on Canal Street after being impaled on a spike trying to escape the crush, while the Tipperary goalkeeper was a survivor of the Somme.[124] The government line was that firing had first come from the crowd. This was contradicted by eyewitness accounts and few with nationalist or republican sympathies would have seen it as anything other than a reprisal. The *Freeman's Journal* immediately made a comparison with the infamous Amritsar massacre in India a year earlier.[125] More recently it has been suggested that Croke Park 'did not begin as a reprisal'. Rather, once they reached the ground 'the police began firing without provocation'.[126] Some of the morning's killers had gone to the match themselves but wisely fled. Unknown to those doing the shooting, or the authorities afterwards, four of the victims, Thomas Hogan, Thomas Ryan, Joseph Traynor, and Tipperary player Michael Hogan, had connections to the IRA.[127] Ryan was a company section commander in the Dublin Brigade and it was later claimed that he had been 'on all the big jobs'. The morning before he died, he was said to have been out looking for a British intelligence officer on Marlborough Road.[128] Traynor was a member of F Company, 4th Battalion, but seemingly not among the 'active' members of his unit.[129] Perceptions about what Michael Collins and his men achieved that morning ultimately became as important as the reality. While the extent to which Bloody Sunday actually crippled British intelligence in Dublin is debatable, the power of the event was clear. This was especially important given the cost: Commandant Dick McKee and Vice-Commandant Peadar Clancy were killed. Beaten and shot out of hand in Dublin Castle that evening, the authorities implausibly claimed that McKee and Clancy had been shot while trying to escape. This was immediately dismissed by republicans and contradicted by medical evidence.[130] Their deaths were considered a 'personal disaster for Michael Collins'.[131] But given the lack of significant military success before their deaths, this may have reflected personal popularity or romantic veneration of the dead more than their loss as military leaders.

In many ways, though, Bloody Sunday was unrepresentative of the war as most Dublin IRA men experienced it. Before late 1920, Dublin companies spent their time drilling or parading, with four or five men engaged in additional intelligence work.[132] The most active were drawn from a small elite and Frank Henderson told Ernie O'Malley that 'We didn't take on a lot of men'. Instead, it was preferable to rely on a small number who had been 'tested and found to be satisfactory'. For others – the 'great number of untried men in every Company' – the remainder of the war involved transporting arms or their nightly patrols.[133] Todd Andrews described a company lieutenant named Liam Murphy as 'a paradigm of the ordinary man who made up the Dublin Brigade'. 'Not much recognition has been given to the Liam Murphys', Andrews wrote, but

> These were the men, some of whom never fired a shot, who were the infrastructure on which the Columns and the Active Service Unit and General Headquarters itself rested. It was no small thing after a day's work with pick or pen to turn out in the evening to do some minor routine jobs or even to attend parades.[134]

This was remembered in 1940, when a deputation from the 1st Battalion complained to the military service pensions board on behalf of men they believed had been wrongfully 'turned down by the Board just because they did not shoot someone in 1920'.[135]

Internment was a much more common experience than shooting for Dublin guerrillas, and Bloody Sunday encouraged more vigorous British efforts to round up republican suspects.[136] Between June 1920 and July 1921 alone, the army recorded that 3,170 men and women had been arrested in the Dublin District, though only 182 were convicted and more than half were released.[137] About forty members of the 1st Battalion were captured while 'on parade' in Lourdes House on Buckingham Street, and nominal rolls later recorded that at least fifty company and battalion officers from city units were interned by 11 July 1921.[138] Active republicans could, moreover, expect capture at any time. Todd Andrews was arrested for the first time at home in the middle of the night after a cancelled operation.[139] But, as the military admitted, 'identification was difficult' and men who were never members of the IRA were arrested alongside inactive members like J.J. Devoy, who had stepped aside in 1919 but was arrested in December 1920 and held for three weeks in Mountjoy.[140]

Finding and dealing with informers was a more prominent feature of the war in some places than others. Fingal veterans uniformly told the Bureau of Military History (BMH) that 'no spies' were shot there, either suggesting that there were none in their area or that the enemy had no 'agents of value'. Watch was kept over 'individual residents whom we were suspicious of', on public houses, and on local women keeping company with soldiers or police.[141] But the brigade intelligence officer admitted that they did not have any real training and were 'left to plod along in our own way'. The 'post offices in Balbriggan and Swords were not tapped for information', he remembered, but the 'people in the post office in Duleek and Garristown were working for us wholeheartedly'.[142] Thomasina and Mary Weston had contacts with a policeman in Gormanston and thus received warning of impending raids by the Crown forces.[143] Evidence of spying, though, remained hard to come by and there seems to have been restraint in its absence. In one case, it was claimed that no action was taken when a cheque from Dublin Castle was discovered in the post of a local employee of the British authorities who was 'otherwise harmless'.[144] In another, a deserter from the British army was apparently put on a boat to England. 'We never heard from him afterwards'.[145]

City guerrillas faced significant challenges when trying to root out those regarded as 'touts'. Several Crown intelligence operatives and perhaps as many as fifteen suspected civilian informers were found and shot in the city, a large proportion of them ex-servicemen.[146] But in spite of an impressively sophisticated intelligence network, there were also misses, mistakes and cancellations. In April 1921 six suspected 'touts' were arrested by an IRA company on Richmond Road, but 'let free when found out they were alright'.[147] Attempts to take out RIC men sent from the country to patrol Dublin streets in plain clothes, named the 'Igoe gang' after Head Constable Eugene Igoe, were unsuccessful, as were efforts against the government's 'police advisor', Major General Hugh Henry Tudor: 'Every time we waited for Tudor something turned up'.[148] This could be a grizzly business. When ex-serviceman Denis 'Hoppy' Byrne survived an attempt on his life, he was dragged from Jervis Street Hospital and shot dead. Elsewhere, on the night Augustine 'Gus' Murphy and Paddy Rigney apparently left a suspected spy with several bullets in his body and two broken arms (but still alive), Rigney remembered that a young girl had been killed by a ricochet bullet, and 'Gus couldn't sleep thinking of it'.[149] When the body of a man 'having all the appearance of an ex-soldier' was found in Dundrum with 'woollen drawers' bearing a British army mark and service number, it was established that the service number did not match the deceased man and his body was never identified.[150]

In contrast to the considerable attention paid to the war in the capital, the Dublin Brigade's ASU did not acquire the fame of some other IRA flying columns. Divided into four sections of about twelve men each, two sections each side of the Liffey, they were described by veterans as 'the best fighters in the Brigade'.[151] Unlike country ASUs that developed organically as men went 'on the run', the first O/C, Paddy Flanagan, was said to have 'had a big say in the selection of men' and if 'a Volunteer was called on he had to go'.[152] Gathered together in December 1920, the ASU's first operation was an ambush on an ADRIC lorry on Bachelors Walk on 12 January 1921. There were no fatalities after this first attack, during which at least four grenades and revolver fire were directed at the lorry; one onlooker suffered a 'slight sting' as a bullet grazed her neck. But the unit soon refined its tactics and carried out raids, ambushes and assassinations thereafter. Flanagan was replaced by Paddy O'Daly in May 1921.[153] The Dublin ASU was further set apart from country counterparts by the £4 10*s*. a week they received, the same pay as the Squad and roughly the standard wage of a craftsman in the city (substantially less than the basic £7 a week earned by ADRIC cadets).[154] Members of the Fingal Brigade's ASU received 10*s*. a week in lieu of cigarettes, though the quartermaster later complained that it 'barely kept any of us going in cigarettes or tobacco'.[155] Cumann na mBan had some full-time organizers but they were 'paid very little'. Lily O'Brennan was acting secretary to the executive council and received 30*s*. a week or '£2 for a short time. It would not keep a bicycle going'.[156]

The ASU was designed to 'counter increased British activities', but another early operation highlighted the specific difficulties posed by the urban environment, and how easily mistakes could be punished.[157] On 21 January 1921, No. 1 section, under Frank Flood, was spotted by a DMP constable in position at Binn's Bridge in Drumcondra. Flood decided not to detain the policeman, who naturally reported to his colleagues, and the IRA section opened fire on an Auxiliary lorry travelling from Gormanston that passed shortly afterwards. They were met, however, by another lorry summoned from the city carrying a machine-gun. Michael Magee was shot and died the following morning. Flood, Patrick Doyle, Bernard Ryan and Thomas Bryan were captured trying to escape and hanged in Mountjoy in March; 17-year-old Dermot O'Sullivan had his sentence acquitted on account of his age, though Flood was only two years older.[158]

The British army acknowledged that Dublin was 'an ideal town for guerrilla operations', with its narrow streets and alleys, and crowded networks of slums and underground cellars.[159] However, curfews made raids and other activity near impossible after dark by removing crowds from the streets, while the use of grenades in an urban area during daytime ambushes was particularly dangerous. A house surgeon's description of the injuries sustained by Daniel Carew, one of two Volunteers mortally wounded during an ambush on Harcourt Street in April 1921, vividly illustrates the hazards of street fighting:

> I found he was bleeding from a wound over his left thigh. This was an entrance wound. About the same level behind was an exit wound – there was a compound fracture of the left ankle, the foot being almost detached. Over the centre of the abdomen was a large superficial wound; the back of the left arm was badly torn including the muscles. He had a small wound over the Scrotum. He was operated on that night but died the following day. In my opinion death was due to shock and haemorrhage following these injuries.[160]

Street ambushes also posed a real risk to civilians. Oscar Traynor later claimed that the explosion of grenades at the start of an IRA attack in the city served as a signal to bystanders to 'take cover, an art in which the citizens soon became expert, thus leaving the Volunteers, soldiers and the enemy troops shooting it out in semi-isolation'.[161] This was somewhat disingenuous, and Traynor was much more callous when speaking to Ernie O'Malley. He described to O'Malley how a 'woman dealer who had two or three children' was killed during 'a good ambush' in Camden Street. Traynor was rebuked by Brugha – 'I always got a lecture, or what seemed to be a lecture from Cathal Brugha' – who ordered ambushes not to take place on Saturdays when the streets were busy: 'The men had a joke about it: "The weekly Saturday night ambush postponed to Monday".'[162]

Brugha's policy may have limited civilian casualties, but it did not prevent them. The first fatality identified after the ambush that killed Daniel Carew and fellow republican Terence McGlynn was Michael Daly, a 26-year-old unmarried painter's foreman and vice-captain of Glasnevin Football Club. Daly easily fitted the profile of a typical Dublin Brigade man, but his 'whole ambition was racing, football and dancing' and he had simply decided on a walk with a friend rather than a game of billiards.[163] All three died from gunshot wounds but the military inquiry offered a verdict of 'justifiable homicide' by members of the Worcester Regiment for McGlynn and Carew, while Daly's death was declared 'accidental'.[164] A month earlier on Camden Street – part of a stretch that became known colloquially as 'the Dardanelles'[165] – 3-year-old William Fitzgerald was killed by a fragment from a bomb thrown at a passing military lorry.[166] In May 1921 on Grafton Street ('Dublin's most fashionable thoroughfare'), fifteen men, women and teenagers were wounded by shrapnel from a grenade attack on an Auxiliary lorry and 'as many more were trampled on in the terrible confusion'.[167]

Civilians could also be caught in the wrong place at the wrong time in the county, as demonstrated by the killing of John O'Neill and Henry Guy on the same day in March 1921. The former was a case of mistaken identity by the IRA in Malahide, whereas in the case of Guy, Auxiliaries 'opened fire somewhat hastily' on unarmed men playing pitch and toss in Sutton (both men, coincidentally, were ex-servicemen).[168] A tit-for-tat cycle of reprisals and counter-reprisals centred around Balbriggan characterized the most serious episodes of violence in Dublin county. It began with the opportunistic shooting dead of RIC Head Constable Peter Burke and the wounding of his RIC sergeant brother on 20 September 1920 in Smyth's public house and prompted one of the most infamous reprisals of the conflict.[169] Within a few hours, a party of Black and Tans, possibly accompanied by Auxiliaries, had arrived in Balbriggan from Gormanston. There, they burned John Derham's public house and by the next morning tens of thousands of pounds of damage had been done, over half accounted for by the destruction of the Deedes, Templar & Co. hosiery factory.[170] James Lawless, a 40-year-old barber and father of eight, and 29-year-old unmarried dairyman John Gibbons were also shot dead in police custody. Both were known Volunteers, though Lawless was much older and more settled than the average active Dublin guerrilla.[171] Arguably, only the burning of Cork in December 1920 matched Balbriggan for infamy, with its proximity to Dublin city contributing to wide coverage in the local, national and foreign press. While there may have been some success in frightening the local population, Balbriggan was a propaganda disaster for the British. John Derham gave a graphic account to the American Commission on Conditions in Ireland later in the year, and one of the most widely reproduced images of the conflict is of wrecked homes on Clonard Street.[172]

A month after the sack of Balbriggan, the body of a 30-year-old labourer and ex-serviceman was found in a ditch between Swords and Balbriggan with two bullet wounds in his head.[173] A week later, Volunteer John 'Terry' Sherlock was found 'riddled with bullets' in a field a short distance from his home. An *Evening Herald* reporter interviewed Sherlock's 'stricken mother as she lay by the bed of her dead son, comforted by neighbours and friends'. She described how armed men had come to the house at 2.30 a.m. and how, in spite of her pleading, Sherlock left the house with the raiders. When he had not returned by 5 a.m., his father and sister began their 'grim search', eventually finding him 'in a pool of blood inside a wall in a field'.[174] Crown forces burned one more home with republican connections in Balbriggan that night, and another the following night. They shot Jack McCann in Rush in November and then Thomas Hand in Baltrasna in December. Hand's brother and sister both declared that the men who appeared at their family home, where Thomas had spent the night, in the early hours of 5 December were wearing police uniforms. The local RIC insisted that there 'was no police patrol in the area of Baltrasna on the night in question', and the military inquiry convened in lieu of an inquest recorded that Hand had been 'wilfully murdered' by 'person or persons unknown'.[175]

The point seems not to have been to eliminate the most troublesome guerrillas, but rather blind attacks on known sympathizers – 'purely an act of blackguardism and provocation on the part of the Tans', as Michael Rock chose to describe it.[176] James Lawless was earlier identified as the ringleader of a provocative meeting on Clonard Hill to celebrate the release of hunger-strikers from Mountjoy that ended with the fatal wounding of a police sergeant.[177] But Sergeant Finnerty was actually shot by John Gaynor – who later claimed Finnerty had been 'making himself unpopular and was always looking for trouble' – and Lawless was not otherwise an important member of the IRA.[178] McCann had been at Ashbourne in 1916 but was said to have stepped aside after his marriage in 1917 and had a heavily pregnant wife.[179] Hand was 42-years-old and a father of four children. By 1920 he was apparently 'on the run', but had been 'excused active service owing to his age' and was local branch secretary of the ITGWU and a member of the GAA and Gaelic League.[180] Once again, state terror only seemed to inspire more violence. In February 1921, Middlesex-born Constable Samuel Green, just two months in the RIC, died of wounds received in the same public house in which the Burke brothers had been shot in September 1920. Ambushes on police in Lusk, Ballyboughal and Balbriggan during the first half of 1921 resulted in the deaths of a constable and two sergeants. With the exception of Green, all were policemen long before revolution had disrupted their service.[181]

The biggest single action attempted by the IRA in the city and county was the attack on the Custom House on 25 May 1921. Promoted by Éamon de Valera as a symbolic demonstration of strength and intention, it was described by Sir Henry Robinson as 'probably the stupidest thing the Sinn Fein ever did'.[182] It could perhaps fit the bill for either description. About 120 men, mostly from the 2nd Battalion but assisted by all four city battalions, the Squad and the ASU, were gathered for the attack. The ultimate aim – the burning of the building and destruction of British records – was achieved but came at a high cost as at least eighty IRA men were arrested. A smaller number, including Oscar Traynor and Tom Ennis, who had led the operation, managed to escape. Ennis was seriously injured alongside Jimmy Slattery, who lost his left hand, and Seán Doyle, whose brother Patrick had been hanged in May, died from a gunshot wound to the lung.[183] One of two teenaged IRA fatalities, Daniel Head, facilitated some of the escapees and probably inflicted most of the Crown's casualties by lobbing a grenade into a lorry of Auxiliaries.[184] The five IRA fatalities matched the number associated with the Drumcondra ambush in January 1921.

Dublin Castle immediately lamented the damage to 'one of the finest buildings in the United Kingdom' and the documents it held, and the *Evening Telegraph* published a dramatic photograph of the smoking Custom House. Early press reports conveyed a sense of panic and chaos: a 'stampede', the 'awful panic that ensued among the civilian population' once shooting broke out, and the terrifying effects on the staff of the LGB.[185] Dublin ratepayers were faced with a bill for £35,000, later reduced to a charge on the Irish Free State of just over £5,000 under the Treaty. Five other families had also lost loved ones. The caretaker of the Custom House and a temporary clerk were shot dead by the IRA. Two dockers and a resident of East Wall were also killed, probably by the Crown forces.[186] To avoid the impression of a defeat, city IRA battalions were ordered to step up their activity and the Squad and ASU merged to form the Dublin Guard.[187] Emmet Dalton later suggested that the Dublin Brigade was left in 'literally a hopeless position' with 'no fighting force left', but the impact of the losses can be exaggerated.[188] The monthly report for May 1921 for the 2nd Battalion's 'D' Company records 'Reorganization' work commencing the day after the Custom House attack, funeral arrangements for their colleagues on 27 and 28 May, and a company parade on 29 May. Even if a patrol on 31 May was 'abortive', its existence at all was telling.[189] The Dublin Brigade 'Diary of Operations' for June 1921 tells a similar story.[190] Rather than the visceral, but perhaps temporary, impact of the burning of the Custom House, it was the ability to adapt and reorganize and to keep fighting that was ultimately most important.

The War of Independence was not evenly fought throughout the country, and the same was true in Dublin. The capital witnessed periods of intense violence, but also significant lulls and periods of relative peace. The urban warfare of the city was also quite different from the less famous, but perhaps more representative, guerrilla war of the county. Ordinary Dubliners had endured some two-and-a-half years of the uncertainty, disruption and danger that followed irregular warfare. However, as GHQ had hoped, Dublin ultimately held out until the British agreed to enter negotiations with representatives of the Irish republic.

7. Labour, politics and the counter-state in Dublin, 1919–21

In her memoir composed in the 1940s and 1950s, Máire Comerford described the first meeting of Dáil Éireann at the Mansion House on 21 January 1921:

> No day that ever dawned in Ireland had been waited for, worked for, suffered for like the Tuesday in January 1919 when the First Dáil Éireann met. In the queue that curled from the entrance to Dublin's Mansion House back to Kildare Street, men and women spoke softly of the dead, from the first coming of the English to Ireland, and who had given their lives to make our nation free.

Recalling what might be seen as a subtle hint of the coming of the new order, Comerford described how 'A bazaar or some similar function in aid of British war charities had bundled up the last of its Union Jacks and, on the way out, more or less passed us on the steps as we waited to go in.'[1] In tandem with the IRA's war with the Crown forces was a separate but overlapping campaign of non-violent, or at least non-physically violent, resistance and state building. Dublin city was central to much of this, serving as the base for the Dáil, the SF executive, IRA GHQ and Cumann na mBan central council, as well as home to many of its most famous names, including Arthur Griffith, Michael Collins, Richard Mulcahy, Constance Markievicz, Kathleen Clarke and Cathal Brugha (though only Griffith and Brugha were actually born in the city).

After its first, symbolic meeting, the ability of the Dáil to survive and function – using the cover of the day-to-day business of the capital – was a key part of the success of the republican movement. By necessity, the civil and military overlapped. The former provided legitimacy for the latter, while the IRA played a part in enforcing Dáil decrees and protecting the infrastructure of the counter-state. Local elections, meanwhile, allowed SF to test its mandate and public tolerance for the physical force campaign. At the same time, labour and agrarian disputes remained a prominent part of the experience of revolution in Dublin. A series of industrial disputes at the turn of 1919 might be easily overlooked but were for many an important feature of the year's events. As the war eventually escalated in 1920, some of Dáil Éireann's most significant progress came after SF success in local elections in January and June 1920 allowed republicans to take control of local government. The underground counter-state had its fair share of success, even though suppression of Dáil departments and alternative courts by the Crown forces was not uncommon.

However, just as the IRA continued to fight in spite of a series of setbacks, the counter-state endured until the July 1921 truce.

The most pressing concern for CI Roberts was not the Irish Volunteers or IRA in January 1919, but 'Sinn Féin' and the ITGWU – sources of 'most of the mischievous & disloyal elements' in the county. In the eyes of the police the two organizations were closely linked, though the Dublin CI noted that Labour saw 'higher wages & better conditions of living as more urgent than anything else – It is more concerned with realities than ideals'.[2] The ITGWU had twenty branches in the county (with seven more in the city), but 1919 was the only year over the course of the revolution that all twenty were operational.[3] Much employment in the county was agricultural, and farming – primarily market gardening, grazing and fattening – was labour intensive. The only industry of note was in the north and west of the county, with a number of factories in Lucan and in Balbriggan. This was where the ITGWU made its first significant impact in early 1919.[4]

In January, women workers in the Smyth & Co. and Deeds, Templar & Co. hosiery factories went on strike in protest at colleagues who had refused to join the union. They were joined by their male co-workers in February and after much 'marching, bell ringing and other means to compel the non-union girls, the latter gave in'.[5] Workers in Balbriggan's coal yard had already received 7*s.* of a 10*s.* demand in wage increases.[6] Around the same time, there was a strike by men employed by Dublin County Council on road works. About 400 roadmen and quarrymen were demanding 40*s.* a week and had refused an offer of 36*s.* from county councillors (dubbed 'procrastinating shufflers' by the union's organ, *Irish Opinion*).[7] CI Roberts, generally inclined to assume that commitment to agitation was less than devotional, had heard that many of the men were trying to live on a strike allowance of 10*s.* a week and whatever they earned by odd jobs, and were anxious to accept the council's offer but were being 'held back' by the union.[8] A dispute also began at the Anna Liffey Mills in Lucan, operated by the Shackleton family, when employees joined comrades around the country in taking a general holiday to celebrate Labour Day (Thursday, 1 May) and were locked out of work on their return. The strike had been largely resolved by June 1919, but a small number of the workers were not re-employed.[9]

When the labourers on a farm at Marley Grange in Rathfarnham struck over the payment of harvest bonuses in January 1919, they pre-empted wider agitation later in the year.[10] Picketing workers were surrounded by police, while the military occupied nearby St Enda's school. 'And thus', as *Irish Opinion* caustically put it, 'khaki and dark green make Rathfarnham safe for democracy'.[11] When a conference of county rural workers met at Liberty Hall in early February and demanded improved wages, hours and conditions for carters, drovers, women workers and casual labour, it did so in the context of a countrywide wages movement.[12] In March the RIC heard rumours of a planned 'general strike', but farmers held out against what CI Roberts described as 'the extravagant demands of the labourers'. The farmers, he suggested, expected to win as 'their employees are so scattered that they cannot organize a cessation of work'.[13] Some farmers in the south of the county had accepted 40*s*. a week (of a 50*s*. demand) by April, but the remainder held out. As a 'small sectional strike' of agricultural labourers started in Malahide in June, farmers locked out over thirty labourers in Donabate who had refused to work more than a half day on Saturday.[14] On a larger scale was the action of farm workers in Meath and Kildare, which saw 2,000 men out on strike by the middle of July.[15] This spread into Dublin in the form of a sympathetic strike in Garristown, while cattle were prevented from travelling through Swords to get to Dublin markets. Police protection was also deemed necessary to ensure the free passage of cattle from Meath and Kildare towards the city.[16] In August 1919 labourers from outside the county crossed into Dublin districts to intimidate non-union men, resulting in prosecutions at Swords and Rathkeale petty sessions.[17] The significant concessions granted to farm labourers later in the month were greeted with a headline in *Irish Opinion* that exaggeratedly read: 'The Land War is Won'.[18]

The first municipal elections since 1914 were held in January 1920, providing a test for the popularity of SF policy at a local level as the military conflict intensified. While the national struggle remained dominant, the discontent among agricultural labourers and among ratepayers served as a backdrop, while the military conflict affected rates and services (local elections in June were similarly preceded by the refusal of Dublin dock workers to handle British war material and an ITGWU ban on railway drivers carrying British forces).[19] These were also the first Irish elections held under proportional representation (PR). The authorities had hoped this might damage SF, but the party had voted overwhelmingly in favour of PR at its 1919 ard fheis and remained confident the new system would reaffirm its dominance.[20] A large proportion of outgoing members decided against going forward again for Dublin Corporation, and the *Irish Independent* described it as the 'dullest election' yet experienced in the capital.[21] The 63 per cent turnout was also well below the national average of 72 per cent.[22] The results were significant enough, however, if not quite a match for SF's 1918 general election success (shaped more by the restricted electorate and the distribution of seats under PR than any obvious opposition to the military campaign).[23] The formerly dominant IPP polled reasonably well after the disastrous 1918 general election, winning a larger share of the vote than Labour. This was not, however, converted into seats on the corporation. As reported in the *Evening Herald*, Nationalists ultimately won thirteen seats, with a large proportion of the total Nationalist vote going to former lords mayor Alfie Byrne and Lorcan Sherlock; SF secured forty-one. Kathleen Clarke, elected alderman in two districts, was among thirteen SF aldermen on the new corporation and the only female alderman in the country.[24] In total, SF secured about one-third of all seats in the municipal elections on the island, its additional success in Dublin reflecting the party's origins and popularity in the city.[25] Indeed, SF's 45 per cent of first preference votes in the capital was significantly higher than its 27 per cent nationally.[26]

The next big winner in January 1920 was Labour, despite internal divisions underpinned by a power struggle between William O'Brien and P.T. Daly in the ITGWU. Labour had been expected to campaign jointly with SF, but following a row prompted by a nomination to the Labour panel there were ultimately ten 'official' Labour candidates and ten 'unofficial' or Republican Labour in the field. In total, fourteen were elected with a 12 per cent share of the vote.[27] One aspect of the result that set Dublin city apart was the extent of the vote for the new Municipal Reform Association (MRA), which ultimately made up ten councillors on the 'well-mixed' corporation – including aldermen elected in three of the ten electoral divisions.[28] Focusing its efforts on the more prosperous parts of the city, the MRA's twelve candidates were made up of an equal number of nationalists and unionists. Defecting to the MRA allowed its unionist candidates, and indeed some nationalists, to make accommodations with the new order and run on a modified platform. Though it lacked a clear identity, the MRA was able to appeal to middle-class concerns that transcended political and religious divides, take up the old unionist concern of law and order, and advocate for business interests. This reflected the extent to which the allegiances of local election candidates were notoriously changeable, not least among the many who ran as independents of various shades. But SF's victory was also clear. While the party's total of active councillors was reduced to thirty-eight – with Kathleen Clarke elected twice, Thomas Kelly and Seán O'Mahony in prison, and long-standing SF councillor Seán T. O'Kelly in Paris – a working majority was secured through cooperation with Labour and Republican Labour councillors.[29]

In its analysis of the January 1920 results, the Dáil propaganda department divided municipal councils into those that were republican, republican and nationalist, or unionist. Among the Dublin authorities only the corporation and Balbriggan UDC were considered republican, with Blackrock, Dalkey, Howth and Pembroke UDCs holding a majority when combined with nationalists, and Rathmines and Killiney remaining unionist.[30] The unionist vote had contracted and was affected by defections to the MRA and the 1919 split in the IUA. Unionists won eight seats in Kingstown, but this was not enough to control the council and potential allies in the Ratepayers' Party were not elected, nor was the independent Unionist candidate.[31] Nevertheless, the south Dublin townships remained the heartland of what was left of Unionist electoral success in the three southern provinces. A total of just sixty-six Unionists were returned to urban councils in January 1920.[32] Only one, chemist William McCarthy, was successful in the Dublin Corporation election, but twenty-eight Unionists took seats on district councils in the townships in comparison to SF's forty-three.[33] Lady Margaret Dockrell topped the poll in the Monkstown ward of Blackrock UDC as an independent Unionist. Sitting since 1898, Dockrell had become the first female chair of a UDC in 1906. All five women elected to the corporation, though, were SF candidates. With the exception of Clarke, they were largely reliant on transfers and some of the biographical descriptions provided in the *Evening Herald* – 'Widow', 'Married Woman' – were telling in their own way.[34]

As in January, the June local elections prompted relatively little excitement among the general public in the county but SF again emerged as the obvious victors. Polling for county councils, RDCs, and boards of guardians took place on 8 June 1920. SF won twelve of the nineteen seats on Dublin County Council, with Republican Labour candidates taking seats in Kingstown and Swords. Unionists ran four candidates in Kingstown, though divided between independent and 'official' Unionist. Lady Dockrell secured a second election in six months on the first count as one of the former, while Unionist Dr Patrick Merrin also won a seat and separately topped the poll for Kingstown Board of Guardians. He was joined on the council by Unionist William Beckett, who was among seven candidates elected without a contest in Rathmines. The remaining two council seats not taken by SF were also secured unopposed in Rathmines. The 'most striking result', as the *Irish Independent* put it, was the defeat of P.J. O'Neill, the dominant figure in north Dublin politics and chairman of the council since 1899. He lost his seat in Swords, where Frank Lawless topped the poll for SF – a significant blow to the IPP and a further reminder of how much had changed since 1914.[35] SF also won three of the six seats on the North Dublin RDC, all six on South Dublin RDC, and had fifty guardians elected (including Lorcan O'Toole as an independent SF candidate) from a total of sixty-six. The *Independent* pointed to the 'overwhelming vote cast' for Margaret Pearse, mother of executed 1916 leaders Patrick and Willie, in the election for Rathmines Board of Guardians. Marion Clinch, who had served as a poor law guardian for Rathmines for twenty years and topped the previous three polls, lost her seat.[36]

From its first meeting at the Mansion House in January 1919, the underground Dáil government used the cover of a busy capital city to run its counter-state – aimed at undermining, usurping and ultimately replacing British administration in Ireland. The extent to which it was able to do so was no small achievement. At the opening of its second session on 1 April, the Dáil's constitution was amended and Éamon de Valera appointed president. A number of new ministerial appointments were made (notably Michael Collins in finance and Constance Markievicz in labour) and new departments created, including local government (headed by W.T. Cosgrave) and industries (under Eoin MacNeill). One way in which the civil and military overlapped was in the use of the IRA to support the counter-state and enforce the series of Dáil decrees issued after April 1919. One of the early priorities was fundraising, and the coercive powers of the IRA were used in the collection of the Dáil's national loan. Intended to alleviate serious financial problems facing the Dáil, loan bonds were sold in Ireland alongside a separate bond drive in the United States. The domestic national loan was organized on a local level and money was collected by special collectors before being handed over to trustees. It was a huge success, raising over £370,000, and greatly surpassed its original target; Arthur Griffith described it as 'one of the most extraordinary feats in the country's history'.[37] In his 1955 memoir, Sir Ormonde Winter, who had been appointed deputy chief of police and head of the secret service in Ireland in 1920, wrote that loyalists were 'forced to contribute to the Irish Republican loan to secure immunity. If instead of subscribing to the loan they evinced sympathy with the Crown forces, they ran the risk of being shot or having their houses burnt down over their heads by the rebels'.[38] While unionists or loyalists may indeed have purchased bonds as 'insurance for the future', and among subscribers were some who were not immediately obvious supporters of the Dáil, it is unlikely that this was common.[39] There was, for instance, a much higher proportion of unionists in Dublin than in surrounding counties and this was reflected in the relatively small amounts collected in the capital. Residents of Rathmines, where a Unionist had been elected as MP in 1918, were the least likely in any Leinster constituency to contribute.[40] Paying into the loan was, though, potentially a way for some who were otherwise loyal to the Crown to keep out of trouble. When a list of subscribers was found among captured documents, Winter was surprised to find the names of some of his friends.[41]

Generally, the loan was more successful in rural areas and this may in part be explained by the increased vulnerability of rural populations to republican intimidation. An increased Crown presence in urban areas in turn created a greater feeling of safety for unionists and loyalists, while Michael Collins and Arthur Griffith acknowledged that arrests and raids by police and military hampered organization in Dublin.[42] The launch of the loan was followed by a 'ferocious propaganda war', which included a promotional film shot at St Enda's in Rathfarnham that featured Collins signing bonds on a table made – reputedly – from the block on which Robert Emmet was executed. IRA units helped to ensure that picture houses would show the film while Crown forces endeavoured to seize, tear down and paint over posters, literature and slogans daubed on walls in the city.[43] The New Ireland Assurance Company, founded by Volunteers in 1918, acted as a front for the loan and its offices on Bachelors Walk were the main depot for receiving subscriptions from across the country. It was raided in January 1920 at the same time as 6 and 76 Harcourt Street – both locations used by the Dáil Department of Finance.

Dublin city and county accounted for almost a quarter of the £87,499 2*s*. 6*d*. received for the national loan at head office by 27 September 1920 from counties in Leinster, but this contribution is less impressive when adjusted per head of population. The amounts contributed per 10,000 people in city parliamentary constituencies ranged from £223 in Rathmines to £687 in Clontarf (by way of comparison, King's County and Queen's County contributed over £1,600 and £1,800).[44] Fingal veterans were later keen to record the wide success of the loan collection in their area, even though the figure in Dublin North County was only £227 per 10,000 people. The largest contribution came, in fact, from the South County constituency where £3,445 was raised, or £957 per 10,000 people.[45] For Dublin republicans who did little or no shooting at Crown forces, there was value beyond the sums collected. Aiding collections like the national loan or enforcing Dáil edicts provided important opportunities to contribute meaningfully to the movement. Indeed, the perceived success of the loan in Fingal may have served to offset or distract from some of the military deficiencies of the Fingal IRA. Likewise, contributing to the loan offered civilians unwilling or unable to join republican organizations an opportunity to aid the cause that went beyond filling in a ballot.[46] This was a contribution only available to those with means, however, and Dublin's relatively poor offering is also explained by the poverty of many of its citizens.[47]

If not universally successful in securing subscriptions for the national loan, the wider propaganda war was among the Dáil's most obvious and valuable victories. SF's publicity section was already producing its own newspaper by January 1919 and the underground government immediately set up a propaganda department. As evidence of the ongoing battle with Crown forces, the department's first director, Laurence Ginnell, was soon arrested and replaced by Desmond FitzGerald, with Erskine Childers as deputy.[48] Initially, the chief means of distributing propaganda was by pamphlets printed and distributed in Ireland, the US and – while Dáil envoys were unsuccessfully attempting to have the Irish republic recognized at the post-First World War Peace Conference – in Paris. Newspaper correspondents were also issued with weekly lists of 'Acts of Aggression committed by the British in Ireland'.[49] FitzGerald was acutely aware of the need to contact the foreign press directly to counter news originating from British sources. In November 1919 the department began distributing the *Irish Bulletin*, a newssheet aimed primarily at foreign audiences. Initially comprised of simple and unadorned reports on actions by Crown forces, it was soon issued five times a week with contributions by Childers and Frank Gallagher. As the *Bulletin* moved its premises around Dublin, FitzGerald spent his days cycling around the city, interviewing foreign journalists, and gathering information for the next issue.[50] Máire Comerford also regularly delivered a copy to the National Library of Ireland for posterity.[51] The department's success in developing a publication with a reputation for reliable reporting was evident in failed British efforts to circulate fakes.[52] Some sense of the cost of running the counter-state is found in FitzGerald's report that his department had spent £889 17*s*. 6*d*. between November 1919 and May 1920.[53]

The value of the 'Belfast boycott' was more dubious. In August 1920 the Dáil cabinet reluctantly agreed to a limited boycott of Belfast banks and insurance companies in response to the expulsion of Catholic workers from Belfast shipyards in July. By September, possibly without Dáil sanction, the ban became general and drew much initial support from local government bodies, trade unions and Catholic clergy. An advisory committee and inspectors were appointed, and enforcement committees formed around the country to ensure the boycott was enacted. The first director was Leo Henderson, but in January 1921 the Dáil appointed Joseph MacDonagh as substitute minister for finance and Belfast boycott director. The boycott's aim was to punish Belfast economically, and to protest against both sectarian disturbances and partition. Aside from the desire to ensure the reinstatement of the expelled Catholic workers, it was hoped the boycott would provide clear evidence of the economic dependence of the north-east on the south and show unionists that the six counties could not prosper alone.[54] It was, however, ill-judged and counter-productive and ultimately did not have the desired economic impact on the Belfast shipyards it was designed to punish, nor did it secure the reinstatement of dismissed Catholics. Instead, the boycott served to cement commercial ties between the north-east and Britain and widen a sense of isolation with the rest of Ireland (as some Dáil members, like Ernest Blythe, feared it might).[55]

On the ground, the boycott was enforced in the first instance by the seizure and destruction of Belfast goods arriving in the city. On the suggestion of the O/C of the Dublin Brigade, 'two Organizers were employed and a Patrol of Volunteers' set up to monitor the arrival of Belfast goods.[56] Inchicore Volunteer Joseph Kinsella claimed that 'when we had petrol or paraffin oil we would make a display' by burning confiscated goods. In other instances, it was deemed preferable to take advantage of orders to prevent goods being distributed to the general public. Kinsella recalled that a quantity of tobacco and cigarettes that could not be destroyed were disguised and sent to men interned in Ballykinlar camp in County Down.[57] When half a tonne of Belfast tobacco was seized in April 1921, it was similarly 'stored for the use of the Flying Column'.[58] Commercial travellers and agents of Belfast firms were also prevented from doing business. One unlucky agent was 'arrested and later ducked in [the] canal' by the Dublin Brigade ASU.[59] Bill Stapleton, a member of the Squad, recalled uneven success: 'commercial travellers and others were, I understand, contacted and warned to cease … In many cases, this approach met with reasonable success, but in many cases traders persisted'. He remembered one man who refused to comply and told the men who visited him that 'they could do their damnedest'.[60] While watch was kept on railways termini in the city to uncover traders still receiving goods from Belfast, it was acknowledged that very little could be done to intercept goods at Dublin Port as they arrived 'without any trace of their Belfast origins'.[61] The SF councillors on Blackrock UDC proposed that the boycott be implemented until religious tests as a condition for employment in Belfast were removed, but the motion was ruled out of order by the Unionist chair, Robert Benson. When Benson and his Unionist colleagues left the chamber in protest at a subsequent motion by Alderman Joseph MacDonagh (soon to be appointed boycott director) to suspend the standing orders, a new chair was elected by SF members and a unanimous decision to implement the boycott recorded in the minutes. SF animosity, however, was as likely to have been directed towards perceived religious discrimination in Rathmines as it was towards Belfast.[62]

Propaganda, non-violent protest and the military campaign overlapped viscerally in events centred around Mountjoy Prison. In April 1920 about seventy internees began a hunger strike to demand the status of political prisoners. Soon there were 101 taking part, most of them members of the IRA.[63] Outside, large crowds began to gather, 'kneeling and reciting the Rosary, singing hymns and waving handkerchiefs', with the army required to clear the surrounding streets. This was combined with a two-day general strike and the pressure this brought to bear on the Irish administration meant that on 14 April over sixty prisoners were released after ten days without food; by 16 April, ninety had been released, including thirty-one who had already been convicted. This was a significant embarrassment for the government and was, as the British army's report on the conflict admitted, 'hailed as a great victory by Sinn Féin leaders and their supporters throughout England, Ireland and abroad'.[64] While Todd Andrews later insisted that the hunger strike 'had not had even the slightest adverse effect on my health or fitness', Andy McDonnell remembered it as a 'frightful experience, not just hunger but the loss of sleep during an endless night, restless, to be honest, afraid and wondering what was to be the end'.[65] Most seem to have been hospitalized for a period, with bedside visits discouraged 'owing to the serious condition of some amongst the sufferers'.[66] When Francis Gleeson died shortly after his release it was agreed that he had died of an illness accelerated by his time without food. Gleeson's funeral offered the movement another propaganda opportunity. It became, as the *Chicago Tribune* saw it, 'A Study in Contrasts'. On the same day as a 'dense mass of people packed Eccles St., Berkeley Rd., and adjoining streets' for Gleeson, the funeral procession by colleagues of RIC Sergeant John Brady to Mount Jerome Cemetery took place 'through streets practically deserted'.[67]

Crowds gathered outside Mountjoy again later in the year for a vigil in the days before Kevin Barry's execution, and the IRA made a failed attempt to rescue him. When the sentence was carried out on 1 November 1920 the prison became the setting for what were described as 'moving, thrilling, historic scenes'.[68] Even larger crowds, perhaps as large as 40,000, gathered around Mountjoy on 14 March 1921, the day that six members of the Dublin Brigade were executed. Tens of thousands more attended requiem Masses. Trams, trains and ferries stopped, and shops and pubs closed.[69] Three weeks later, prayers were heard once more outside Mountjoy on the day that Thomas Traynor was due to be hanged, with members of Cumann na mBan leading recitations of the rosary and singing 'Hail, Queen of Heaven'.[70]

After the June 1920 local elections, Dublin Corporation and Dublin County Council followed their counterparts (outside the north-east of the country) in declaring allegiance to the Dáil's Department for Local Government and renounced the British LGB. A significant – and often successful – part of the republican counter-state, the Dáil Local Government Department aimed to undermine and replace British control of local authorities, while maintaining funding and infrastructure and ensuring that the LGB was ignored. An immediate example of the practical changes that could now be enforced came in south Dublin. On 6 July 1920, Kingstown UDC voted to return the name of the township to its original Dún Laoghaire, to change the name of Queen's Road to Marine Road and the name of the Royal Victoria baths to Dún Laoghaire baths, for all stationary to be printed in Irish and English (with paying orders and cheques in Irish only), and for rolling stock to be inscribed in Irish when being repainted.[71] Name changes like this represented another revolutionary battle ground. When the change of name for the township was sanctioned by Dublin County Council later that month, a SF councillor declared it a 'great victory for his party'. It was noted that some nationalists had voted against the resolution in Kingstown, while the councillor who passed it complained to the press about the use of the spelling and pronunciation 'Dunleary' – 'the half-hearted effort of some planter to vocalize the old name' – insisting that it was 'inconsistent with National dignity for us Irish to adapt our place-names and our National system of phonetics to suit foreigners or those who ape them'.[72]

More difficult was the collection of poor rates. The resulting battle between Dáil local government and the LGB for the cooperation of rate collectors and rate payers often necessitated the persuasive powers of the IRA.[73] Eight collectors had resigned when Dublin County Council repudiated the LGB, and on 4 January 1921 the IRA carried out a series of raids on their homes. Books were seized and the collectors forced to write out a cheque for the amount they had collected which was immediately cashed while an armed guard remained in the house. Up to £11,000 was collected in total, with either £500, £1,100, or £2,000 seized in one go from Charles Sutton in Kilternan – 'loyal to the Crown, but not very dangerous otherwise' – depending on who was telling the story; £3,000 was said to have been seized in Rathgar. Raiders in Cabra were described as 'very courteous and well-behaved young men' who insisted on paying for their tea, and Andy McDonnell even sent for a doctor for Sutton's ill daughter.[74] Soon after the raid on rate collectors, Dublin County Council received letters of resignation from those whose books and money had been seized and another from the Irish Poor Rate Collectors' Association, stating that it would be impossible for them to continue to collect under the present conditions.[75]

In places where the RIC had been withdrawn and the countryside left without a police presence, the IRA, or the newly created Irish Republican Police, stepped in to keep law and order. When GHQ issued instructions for the formation of police units in May 1920, it only formalized what had already been taking place in Dublin since 1918. By the time the DMP was withdrawn from political policing on Dublin streets in mid-1919, the Dublin Brigade had appointed company and battalion police officers. The day-to-day work of the republican police included enforcing licensing laws, raiding for and retrieving stolen goods (particularly useful in winning individual support), and enforcing the Belfast boycott. Criminals were also apprehended and tried before republican courts.[76] This was not just a case of replacing British law and order. It was also about ensuring that the interests of potential supporters – such as the business community or the Catholic Church – could be protected, and preventing a descent into social chaos.[77] Several Fingal veterans framed this as a universally successful attempt to reclaim authority from the 'lawless individuals' who took advantage of unstable conditions to 'prey on their neighbours'.[78] Sometimes unconventional methods followed, but these had a very clear message. In Foxrock in June 1921, for example, some youths had allegedly been impersonating IRA men for personal gain and were 'tried and found guilty of robbery under arms in the name of the IRA'. Their punishment was to be chained to the railings of the local Catholic church with a sign that read: 'Rogues and robbers, beware. IRA.'[79]

It was more difficult to operate alternative courts in the heavily militarized city, but they did take place. Joseph Kinsella recalled how he recovered £80 stolen from an 'old lady living alone' in Crumlin. When two men were noticed 'spending money much beyond their means', they were arrested and confessions extracted by 'a little rough handling'. Most of the money had been lost and the remainder spent on a gramophone, watch and clothing. Refunds were obtained from the shopkeepers who had sold the goods and following a battalion court – 'presented as legally as we could manage' – the men were ordered to repay the balance in weekly instalments, with the appreciative victim eventually paid in full.[80] More dramatic again was the arrest of a small gang of criminals known as the 'Sons of Dawn', who had carried out a series of burglaries from January 1920. In September, Dublin republican police received word of a planned robbery on Capel Street and intercepted and arrested the culprits. A court was held in the Volunteers' Columcille hall and the four young men ordered to be deported. The *Evening Herald*, presumably on information from republican police, additionally reported that two had been sentenced to 'twelve strikes each on the bare back', though this detail was not included in Liam O'Carroll's statement to the BMH.[81] Nor was this an isolated use of flogging as a punishment.[82] The limits of what the republican police could achieve in Dublin city was evident when two of the gang were subsequently arrested and put before the Southern Police Court.[83] When efforts were made to regularize the republican police in mid-1921, with Simon Donnelly, a 1916 veteran and vice-commandant of the 3rd Battalion, appointed as chief of police, there were just six full-time, paid police officers in Dublin, assisted by 'spare time Company and battalion police'.[84]

On 27 July 1920 the *Chicago Tribune* printed a photograph taken in Skerries by the *Tribune* Foreign News Service. Under the headline 'Laborer as Sinn Fein Judge', the photograph featured a man sitting at a desk with pen and quill. The caption told its American readers that 'Thomas Hand, a County Dublin farm laborer, has been appointed a republican judge. His jurisdiction is very wide and exercised with much dignity'. Hand was 'completing a statutory declaration for a republican resident. His wife is assisting him in his judicial duties'.[85] By this point the voluntary arbitration courts set up locally after 1919 had been replaced with a supreme court, district courts and parish courts, with (Dáil-decreed) civil and criminal jurisdiction and coercive powers. Republican courts were ultimately unable to supplant the British system completely, though the disruption and inconvenience they caused the British administration was not insignificant and courts on the northside of the city, in particular, had some success. In April 1921 Austin Stack, the Dáil's minister for home affairs, wrote to Richard Mulcahy as TD for Dublin Clontarf and noted that 'the North City Justices are attending to their work fairly well. I wish things were as good all over as they are in your "Bailiwick"'.[86] Later that year Stack included 'North Dublin City' among the 'few districts which never for a day ceased to carry on their work'.[87] In other parts of Dublin and elsewhere in the country, the Crown forces had been able to suppress many republican courts by autumn 1920. In May 1921 Stack's own office on Molesworth Street had been raided and 'all papers, files and office furniture were seized', along with Stack's name stamp. The raid raised suspicion about a visitor earlier in the day who had claimed to be working for *Thom's Directory* and enquired about the office's front organization.[88] Standing orders had been issued to all departments less than two months earlier with instructions for the maintenance of documents and other items to prevent their capture during 'raids by the enemy'.[89] But Dáil secretary Diarmuid O'Hegarty's own stationary and rubber stamp were captured a fortnight later and he reported that all subsequent documents sealed or stamped from the president's office or general secretariat should be considered forgeries.[90]

In addition to enforcing Dáil policy, the non-physical harassment of local loyalists ranged from threatening letters to raids on their homes. A resident of Shankill objected when asked to rewrite an intercepted £39 cheque for car tax to be made out to 'the Republican Government', but soon relented when 'a revolver was produced and they were held up'.[91] There is no evidence in police reports of serious attempts to boycott the Dublin RIC, though policemen in Balbriggan and Dundrum were occasionally sent the sort of threatening letters that became common elsewhere.[92] In May 1920 a female barrack servant and an unsuccessful candidate for the RIC were similarly threatened, and in July a motor agent in Howth was warned by the 'Competent Military Authority, IRA' that he used his motor car to convey police or military 'at his peril'.[93] Such threats could be very effective, but appear to have had a limited impact in County Dublin when there was little sense they would be acted upon. When Balbriggan Head Constable J.E. Hunter received a letter that read: 'Beware your day has come, you are a doomed man R.I.P.', he was unperturbed. 'The Head Constable does not consider himself in danger, and is inclined to believe that it was sent with a view to annoy him.'[94]

After a major reorganization of the Irish administration in 1920, high-ranking Dublin Castle officials involved in political work, as well as English civil servants sent to Dublin, were moved with their families into Dublin Castle or given armed police escorts.[95] Despite gravitation towards a 'greening' of the Irish civil service, the top jobs remained largely the preserve of middle-class Protestants with links to the old Ascendancy.[96] This, allied to their role in implementing the British government's coercive measures, meant that higher ranking officials were deemed the most likely targets among the civil service for republican aggression. A notable example was Sir Henry Robinson, vice-president of the LGB. Though not strictly involved in politics, Robinson was, in his own words, 'regarded as a leading official of the British Government and a representative of the old British ascendancy in Ireland'. He was largely blamed for the decision to withdraw government grants from local councils who failed to submit their accounts for audit with the LGB, and his detailed knowledge of the country and constant contact with the government meant he 'was in great danger from the rebels and was protected by armed detectives & frequently had to be taken about in armoured cars'.[97] The feeling of fear experienced by these officials did not always match concerns for their safety. In his 1923 memoir, Robinson related how he eventually decided to dispense with personal protection, afforded after a threatening letter, as it was 'a challenge rather than a protection'.[98]

In August 1920 the British cabinet had discussed the situation of the English civil servants then attached to the Irish executive. It was stated that they had previously been 'immune from the attacks of Sinn Féin' but that this might change with the passage of the Restoration of Order in Ireland Act that month. The impact that the necessary step of accommodating these men in Dublin Castle would have on their usefulness was discussed, but it was argued that both the threat faced and the negative impact of being quartered in the Castle was not as great as anticipated and that the men should remain.[99] When an order came for those in the Castle to carry a pass and photograph, Mark Sturgis, a British civil servant sent to Ireland as part of the restructuring, considered it was 'more dangerous to have passes than none' (probably because it marked them out as targets) but was willing to go along with the order. Sturgis' diaries emphasize how he enjoyed himself in Ireland and suffered nothing like siege conditions after his move into Dublin Castle. Rather, Sturgis felt the benefits of landed society and hospitality, with lunch meetings, weekends in Powerscourt, horse-riding and trips to the Abbey Theatre filling the pages of his diary.[100] Similarly, George Duggan related the story of an LGB official who passed his day 'by a prolonged luncheon hour', reading in a second-hand bookshop, and watching cricket. As control of local government by his department had 'virtually ceased', 'Time glided pleasantly by'.[101]

This is a reminder of the extent to which many Dubliners carried on irrespective of the War of Independence (and Civil War that followed). In the 1940s, Donal O'Kelly wrote, rather romantically, 'The shops were open, business went on, men worked and played, made money and lost it, women went shopping, children played, young people made love and danced and went to the pictures while terror walked beside them.'[102] They might not have been expected to say any different, but the British army's report on the conflict in Ireland claimed that after 'a good deal' of initial protest, the February 1920 curfew order 'became a matter of satisfaction to law-abiding people'.[103] At the very least, most learned to work around it. The markets and the stock exchange continued to operate without a break. Censorship notwithstanding and barring a few days at Easter 1916 and a six-week closure order on the *Freeman's Journal* in 1920, newspapers were always available.[104] Those who picked up their *Evening Herald* on 22 November 1920, for instance, would have found a front page dominated by Bloody Sunday, articles about a stoppage of trains leaving Dublin termini by military order, and about Crown force reprisals in Skerries, Rush and Balbriggan. They would also have found advertisements for clothes, tobacco, kitchen appliances, German melodeons selling at a 'great reduction', and a range of medicines and proclaimed miracle cures. There were, too, notices of a full programme at the Grafton Picture House ('Where the big feature films are shown first'), the Gaiety Theatre, and the Theatre Royal, and dancing in the La Scala Ballroom, and more.[105] For the working-class poor of Dublin, in particular, earning a living remained their main priority, but the demand for entertainment also persisted, even if military restrictions made it more difficult. One British court sitting in June 1921 saw fifty-three individuals charged with staying out past curfew, including two who 'had a couple of drinks and fell asleep together'.[106]

The geography of the city was crucial to the development of the counter-state, providing the anonymity required for meetings and office spaces needed by any administration as well as the opportunity to move from place to place to avoid suppression. Away from the military campaign, the War of Independence tested allegiances in Dublin as the republican movement sought to usurp British government in Ireland. Dubliners were asked to take cases in new, locally organized (and illegal) courts, to pay their taxes to a new regime, to support Dáil fundraising efforts, and targeted with propaganda. Doing any of these things to support or engage with the republican counter-state entailed a risk, not least in the event that the whole thing came crashing down. Some were more willing participants than others. In challenging circumstances the counter-state had much success and ultimately, as with the military campaign, what mattered most was its ability to keep going.

8. From truce to Civil War, 1922–3

On 9 July 1921, following a 'momentous conference' in the Mansion House between British, unionist and republican delegates, 'Truce Terms' were announced in the Dublin evening press, officially ending the conflict between the IRA and Crown forces. All attacks by both sides would cease at noon on 11 July 1921. Military operations, manoeuvres and raids would also cease along with curfew restrictions, and the DMP would carry out normal policing duties in Dublin.[1] What followed was five months of uncertainty and anxiety, with the future unclear and the lingering threat of a return to violence. But the cessation of hostilities was also met with relief and some optimism. The *Irish Times* hoped that Dublin would 'regain some of its former glory as the Irish capital', and the paper looked ahead to the Dublin Horse Show due in August.[2] After what was officially known as the Articles of Agreement for a Treaty between Great Britain and Ireland were signed in December 1921, a cartoon entitled 'The night the Treaty was signed' made a similar point – albeit from a different perspective. The cartoon featured a large crowd of men rushing along the road from Cork to Dublin, chasing the new jobs that were presumably coming to the capital.[3] The cartoon reflected what the terms of the truce meant for Dublin – the return of the parliament that had appeared inevitable in 1912 – and also what Dublin would become for the rest of the country, the administrative and economic centre of a new independent state. Dublin's place in the period from July 1921 to June 1922 was thus much more significant than simply the site of the Dáil debates or the opening shots of the Civil War.

The path from truce to Treaty was not inevitable. When private discussions between de Valera and Lloyd George eventually culminated in the opening of another conference in October 1921, this time it was 'to ascertain how the association of Ireland with the community of nations known as the British Empire can best be reconciled with Irish national aspirations'. At that point it was unclear how exactly Irish nationalist aspirations might be shifted away from a republic, but, once negotiations began, the republic and the coercion of Northern Ireland into a new independent Irish state were never on the table.[4] The Treaty split the Dáil cabinet, the Dáil, and finally the IRA. While a majority of the general public were willing to support, or at least accept, the Treaty, the descent into civil war was complete in the capital in June 1922, when the Provisional government ordered an assault on the Four Courts – occupied by hard-line opponents of the Treaty. The long-standing consensus on the Civil War, whereby the early locus of fighting was in Dublin but that after July 1922 it was more or less over in the capital, has been shown to be 'profoundly mistaken'. Not only did fighting, and dying, continue in the city beyond July

1922, but decisions made in Dublin – by the National army military command and IRA GHQ – shaped the course of the war in the rest of the country.[5] Damage to property also spanned the entirety of the period between July 1921 and the order for the anti-Treaty IRA (ATIRA) to dump arms in May 1923. Unionists, loyalists and other enemies of the War of Independence similarly continued to suffer violence and intimidation. Nor was the Treaty the only cause of conflict in the capital. Continued unemployment drew crowds to the streets at the same time as the city was met with a large influx of refugees seeking safety and relief from violence in Northern Ireland. Vacuums in law and order also presented opportunities for ordinary crime. Meanwhile, others who had already 'lost' in the War of Independence, including unionists, loyalists, ex-policemen and ex-servicemen, were often unable to remain detached from the new, internecine conflict.

For the citizens of Dublin, one of the most obvious signs that conflict had ceased in July 1921 was the end of the city curfew. The Dublin United Tramways Company announced that it would restore its 'pre-Curfew' service, late performances resumed at the Gaiety, and the Theatre Royal and La Scala returned to showing pictures up to 11.30 p.m.[6] The final two curfew breaches put before the police courts were dismissed with a caution.[7] Writing in the *Irish Independent*, journalist Aodh de Blacam described 'the first moment of peace' in the city:

> Lorries of Crown forces ran to their destinations amid curious gazes. The 'Tans' no longer brandished weapons; they rode feet in the air, as joyous as when they first went riding through our streets – but a trifle chastened in their joy, maybe. An ice-cream cart did business under the Tricolour – not the Italian … At Nelson Pillar, fruit was retailed by the eloquent ladies who give such value (verbal) for money under the Green-White-and-Orange, and the Stars-and-Stripes. In the evening the Tricolour was everywhere – not in the mean streets only, but on proud houses in professional quarters and big places of business … As I turned unto Mary Street, at the end of which the sunset glory shone, a huge mass of people came marching up, headed by bands playing triumphant airs … Fine, straight, splendid citizens all. The road was choked with them.

De Blacam was reminded of ongoing violence in Belfast, in stark contrast to the peace in Dublin, but concluded: 'Dublin deserves its jubilation. How long it has endured the Terror as no city else could! The crowds spoke for Dublin's true spirit: thanksgiving, and yet endurance.'[8]

Up to the time of the truce, the CI for Dublin, Hugh Massy Loundes, considered the county, and particularly the area around Dundrum and the Phoenix Park, to be in an 'unsatisfactory' state. Soon afterwards, a 'decided improvement' was noticeable and Loundes reported:

> the people generally are sanguine that a settlement will be arrived at and hope that peace will be continued … The boycott of the Ulster banks is still being carried out in the Balbriggan district which is the only place in the county where these banks have branches. The attitude of the public has undergone a remarkable change, outwardly at least: things seem to be returning to the normal conditions.[9]

Within a few weeks, however, police were beginning to report minor breaches of the truce in both the city and county. A number of policemen were held up by armed men on Sackville Street and later near Amiens Street Station, as was a naval pensioner in St Stephen's Green who was accused of being a 'Black and Tan' ('he is not in the least afraid of any of these men'). Belfast boycott notices were also reported on Henry Street and in the county at Balbriggan. In November, two 'loyal subjects' on North Circular Road reported a rather polite notice requesting a £1 levy that they had been asked for in June and refused to pay. More serious were armed robberies in the city and suburbs traced to an IRA training camp.[10]

There was no deliberate lethal violence in the city or county for the remainder of 1921, but a handful of accidental deaths caused by motor cars driven by Crown forces, the accidental shooting of a member of Fianna Éireann during a training exercise in Killester, and the apparent death by suicide of an ex-serviceman and ADRIC intelligence officer.[11] The only Volunteer to die in this period was James Doyle, shot in the head at his home on Parliament Street in November. The newspapers hinted at suicide, noting that Doyle had been 'depressed' and 'despondent' owing to recent unemployment. Doyle's wife claimed that a gun had gone off during preparations to remove an arms dump, and his death was later deemed to have taken place in the course of IRA duty. Marcella Doyle was awarded a dependent's pension under the 1923 Army Pensions Act.[12]

The extent to which the IRA was on the verge of collapse in Dublin can be debated, but the truce came at a time when, as IRA officer 'Holy' Joe O'Connor put it, 'we were badly in need of a breathing space'.[13] Like units elsewhere in the country, the Dublin and Fingal IRA used the cessation of hostilities to regroup, train and prepare for a renewal of war. Training camps were held away from the city, like those in the Dublin mountains or in Mulhuddart, close to the Meath border.[14] The amalgamated ASU and Squad, renamed the HQ Guard or Dublin Guard, embarked on a training camp in late July 1921 but discipline was lacking and members proved resistant to formal training – among the graffiti chalked on a camp wall was 'The guard will not be trained'.[15] Around the same time, it had been announced in the press that all collections of levies, a common fundraiser for the IRA during the War of Independence, would cease in the Dublin Brigade area.[16] As the truce wore on, the impositions of the IRA on the public became increasingly troublesome. By January 1922, Dublin Castle official Mark Sturgis was complaining in his diary that 'Robbery with violence is by no means decreasing; the stealing of motor cars in and near Dublin is very serious'.[17] The IRA 'commandeered' bicycles, motor cars, carts and goods at will in the early months of 1922. Todd Andrews admitted that when a motor car was required for any purpose, 'there was no scruple in requisitioning the nearest at hand. In general, we treated the general population with little consideration.' On one occasion, Andrews, Ernie O'Malley and Seán MacBride crashed a car into a British tender, writing it off: 'It was not ours and we did not know or care who the owner was. Such was our frame of mind.' When meat and vegetables were taken, 'the unwilling suppliers were given chits in payment'.[18] One pro-Treaty newspaper observed that Dublin had already returned to the mood of the War of Independence, with nightly gun fire and 'insolent lorries' in the streets.[19]

After the Treaty was signed in London on 6 December, it was passed by the Dáil cabinet by a single vote before being debated across a series of public and private sessions of the Dáil at Earlsfort Terrace in December 1921 and early January 1922. Some of the tensions were reflected at local level. As the Dáil debates reached their conclusion, the chairman of the majority SF Dublin County Council called a special meeting to give members an opportunity to discuss the 'present National position'. When a vote on a proposal to 'take no action on the Treaty now under consideration by Dáil Éireann' was defeated by a single vote, it was decided that as the vote was so close there was 'no further useful purpose' in prolonging the discussion. Frank Lawless was recorded as having abstained from the vote but afterwards claimed that he had voted with the majority, while another SF councillor complained that the minutes did not reflect the reason for his absence from the meeting. He had sent a telegram stating that he considered 'discussion of the Treaty unwise. Advise reaffirmation of allegiance to An Dáil'.[20] Dublin was represented by eighteen SF members elected to the second Dáil in May 1921 under the Government of Ireland Act, which the Dáil declared as an election to its own assembly.[21] The final vote on the Treaty settlement took place on 7 January 1922, with the preferences of the eighteen Dublin TDs more heavily weighted towards the Treaty than the Dáil as a whole. The Treaty was passed by sixty-four votes to fifty-seven with eleven Dublin deputies voting in favour and six against; Thomas Kelly was too ill to attend on the day but demonstrated his support for the Treaty in a letter to the speaker. This was, however, skewed by the extent of the support for the Treaty among members elected outside of the city: the only vote against in Dublin County came from Margaret Pearse, while the representatives for Dublin Mid and Dublin City South were much more evenly split (see map 5). Three of the six women elected to the second Dáil sat for Dublin constituencies and all opposed the Treaty.[22]

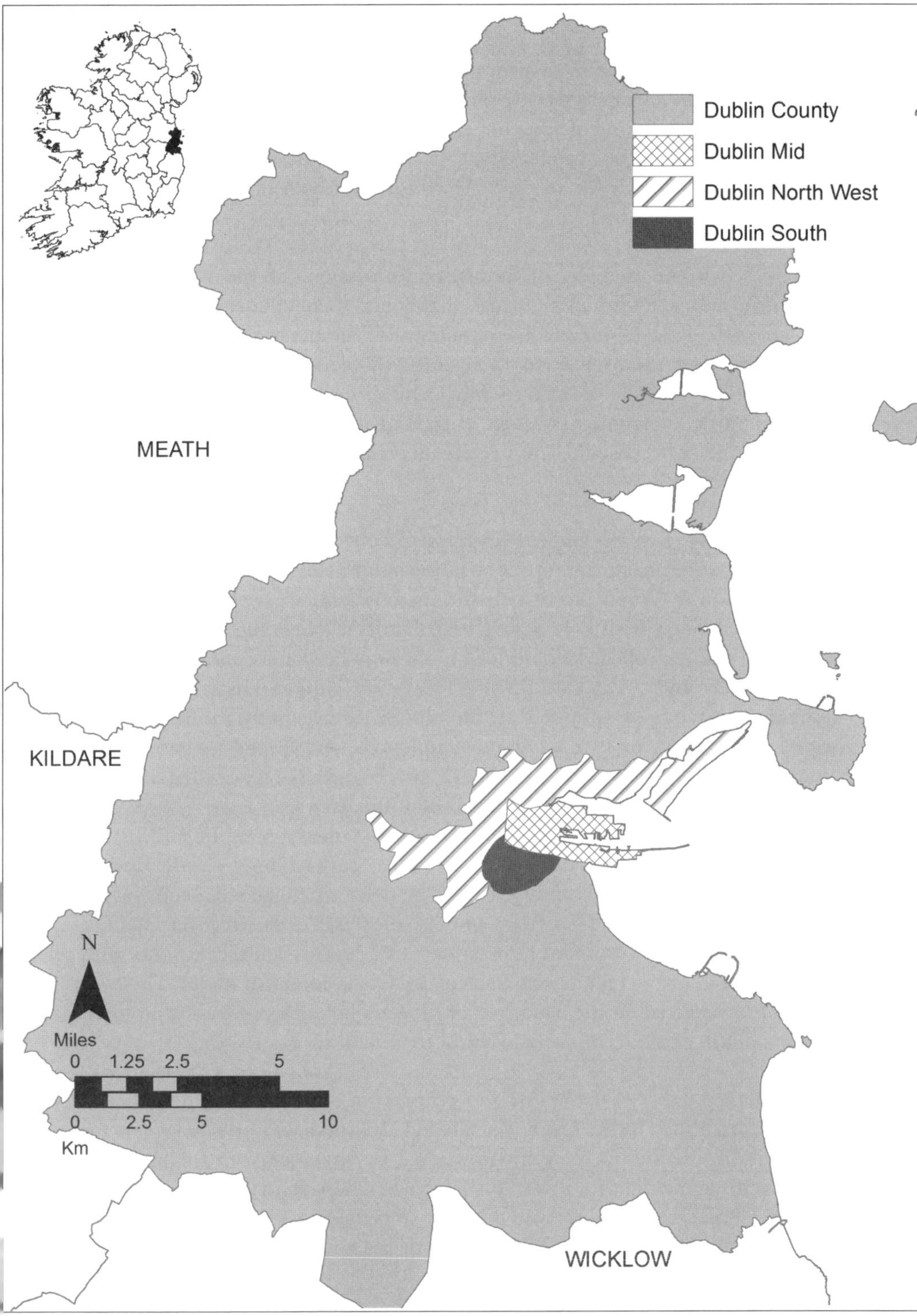

5 Parliamentary constituencies in 1922

Outside the republican movement there was wide support for the Treaty. The Dublin press, the business world, and, importantly, the Catholic Church all shared an overwhelming desire for peace and for the reconstruction and restoration of Dublin as a capital city.[23] Among the Protestant minority, it was reluctantly accepted as a *fait accompli*. An editorial in the *Irish Times* proclaimed that southern loyalists had

> watched the passage, in mournful procession, of the host of laws, institutions, traditions and ideals that bound them to Great Britain. They have embarked – not gladly, yet not afraid – on uncharted seas. They are entrusting themselves to the good-will of a majority from which, politically, they have suffered much, and with which in the past they have had little in common save love of Ireland. The Southern loyalists accept the Treaty because the country accepts it and invites their aid in making it a success.[24]

The *Church of Ireland Gazette* expressed concern for the safety of its communities, but also a commitment 'to recognize the legitimacy of the new administration'.[25] When faced with the introduction of Irish as the official language of the new Irish Free State (IFS), Trinity's *T.C.D.: a college miscellany* announced that the college had 'decided to throw in her lot unconditionally with the rest of Ireland'. A debate on the Treaty at Trinity's Historical Society highlighted a range of opinion, but the motion on accepting ratification was passed by 21 votes to two.[26] For most unionists and loyalists, therefore, it appeared as if there was nothing to do except recognize the new order, offer the state some useful service, and make the best of things.

Less than two weeks after the Dáil vote, on 16 January 1922, a Dáil Éireann delegation entered the Privy Council chamber in the Upper Castle Yard to 'accept the surrender' of Dublin Castle. The delegation handed a copy of the Treaty to the viceroy, Lord FitzAlan, and became the Provisional government of the IFS. The new government took control of a body of public servants and, three days later, forty-eight departments of the Castle administration.[27] The *Irish Independent* reflected on the handover, or 'downfall of a Bastille' as its editorial headline put it, and the nationalist view of the Castle:

> All the powers of the British Government in this country were exercised through the Castle. From it emanated all orders and proclamations for the suppression of movements started by Irishmen with the object of securing the right for this country to govern herself. In various other ways the Castle thwarted the will of the Irish people … The sinister influence and the arrogant sway of Dublin Castle are now at an end.[28]

The *Irish Times* preferred to remind readers of 'the many historic scenes and incidents associated with the great pile of buildings which has for so long been a landmark in the history of Dublin', though recent troubles meant the Castle had been 'shorn of the glory formerly associated with it'. The paper also queried the suitability of the term 'surrender' to describe what had happened.[29] Though a relatively underwhelming ceremony, and companies of RIC remained at the Castle for a number of months afterwards, this was an important symbolic moment in Dublin history given the Castle's association with British rule and its place in the minds of Dubliners.[30]

One of the early tasks facing the Provisional government was the formation of an army to replace the departing British and defend the Treaty settlement. On 31 January 1922, Beggars Bush Barracks was evacuated by ADRIC and handed over to Seán MacMahon, IRA quartermaster general. The following day, the first unit of what became the National army, the pro-Treaty Dublin Guard, marched in wearing full uniform and armed.[31] While barracks were handed over to IRA units around the country regardless of local loyalties, there were no Dublin barracks handed to anti-Treaty forces.[32] Portobello and Wellington Barracks were occupied by pro-Treaty forces in April 1922 and the British army remained in the Royal Barracks, Wellington Barracks, Richmond Barracks and the general headquarters in the Phoenix Park until December 1922.[33] But many republicans in Dublin felt they could not accept the settlement. Todd Andrews, a 19-year-old in 1922, remembered feeling 'rage and disappointment' when he read the terms of the Treaty in the press; Máire Comerford 'went home and cried on my bed'; Ernie O'Malley 'cursed long and loud' and felt a bitter sense of betrayal.[34] The Dublin Brigade had been divided in two during the truce, with a Dublin No. 1 Brigade operating under Oscar Traynor and a South Dublin Brigade under Andy McDonnell comprising a total of 5,500 men. Traynor and McDonnell were among the signatories of a letter sent to Richard Mulcahy on 11 January 1922, shortly after the vote in the Dáil, outlining their opposition to the Treaty and calling for an army convention.[35]

In March the Provisional government proscribed the planned IRA convention, but the convention went ahead with fifty-two of the seventy-three IRA brigades represented. Reconvened on 9 April, it elected an IRA executive which on 14 April ordered the Dublin Brigade to occupy the Four Courts as its headquarters. While this was only intended to be temporary, and Rory O'Connor told the press 'There is going to be no revolution' (he had earlier been unwilling to discount the prospect of a military dictatorship), for its new occupants the centre of the Irish legal system provided a valuable location for a dramatic challenge to the authority of the Provisional government. Opponents of the Treaty also occupied a number of buildings in Parnell Square, two of which had strong connections to Dublin unionism: Fowler Hall and the Kildare Street Club.[36] Meat, fish and other supplies (including £30 worth of cigarettes meant for the RIC depot) were taken from local traders and receipts were issued on behalf of the IRA or the 'Four Courts barracks'.[37] By April 1922, there were thus two rival factions – both still describing themselves as IRA – in Dublin: the pro-Treaty Beggars Bush garrison and the anti-Treaty 'IRA Executive' in the Four Courts, some 3km apart. Efforts were also still being made at compromise. There were hopes that allowing the Four Courts garrison to remain and postponing both the SF ard fheis and the general election due under the terms of the Irish Free State Agreement Act passed in March would help avoid a split. Lord Mayor Laurence O'Neill and Catholic archbishop of Dublin Edward Byrne also held a bilateral conference in the Mansion House in April, but with no result.[38] Dubliners, meanwhile, were already suffering 'increasingly from the tyranny of young men with guns'.[39]

Day to day issues remained, unemployment prominent among them. On 18 January 1922 a group of some 120 men led by Liam O'Flaherty, calling itself the Dublin Council of Unemployed, seized the Rotunda concert hall. The 'Council' included large numbers of ex-servicemen and O'Flaherty, who had earlier been among the founders of the tiny Communist Party of Ireland, told the press that local traders had committed to providing meals to the men free of charge, that they had been organized into companies and an 'iron discipline' established, and that they would offer 'no resistance' to efforts to remove them but would refuse to move or to recognize any court they were brought before. The action was described as a 'protest against the apathy of the authorities', and copies of a manifesto calling for 'work, or full maintenance' were issued around the city: 'Do the citizens of Dublin want highway robbery to be the order of the day? … If not … let them rally to the support of the Dublin Council of Unemployed and procure work for the workless and maintenance until work is secured'.[40] The Red Flag was flown and O'Flaherty declared it as the first time 'in the history of Dublin that the Red Ensign had been hoisted over a seized building'.[41] But wider opposition to what might have been perceived as a display of 'Bolshevism' was clear. After two days the occupation drew a hostile crowd, reported to be about 500, at Cavendish Row. After one youth fell and was hurt trying to reach the flag, another was successful in tearing it from its window. The Rotunda was then 'stormed and the door broken in', with 'hand to hand' fighting only ended by interventions from IRA police and DMP; the former forced the crowd back and it eventually dispersed.[42] The following day, large crowds again gathered and demonstrated their hostility to the occupation. The leaders of the council met with the IRA's chief liaison officer, appointed to oversee investigations into breaches of the truce, at the Gresham Hotel and offered to leave the Rotunda if afforded protection. Soon afterwards, they were escorted out of the building by an IRA party as the DMP 'assisted in preserving order'. Significant damage had been done to windows, doors and furniture in the Rotunda and the Red Flag had been burned.[43]

The occupation highlighted the extent of the unemployment problem in the city, and also the convergence of political and economic crises that could lead to open conflict.[44] There was much more public support when the Irish Trade Union Congress called a one-day general strike against 'militarism' for 23 April 1922. No trains, buses or trams ran in the city and a mass rally was held on O'Connell Street. Unlike the action of the Dublin Council of Unemployed, even traditional opponents of the trade union movement welcomed the strike – the *Irish Times* called it a 'people's protest against anarchy'. But this reflected widespread weariness at the growing influence of armed men acting with impunity, alarm at a sharp rise in violent crime in the city, and fears for the safety of property (not least in the context of factory seizures and the establishment of Soviets elsewhere in the country).[45]

Those in the city requiring relief grew substantially as an estimated 10,000 northern Catholic refugees sought relief in Dublin in spring and summer 1922, fleeing rioting, burning and violence. At one point in May 1922, it was claimed that well over 300 were arriving from Belfast and other northern towns each day. Ad hoc arrangements had been made to provide aid to much smaller numbers of refugees in 1920 and 1921, but these collapsed given the influx in 1922. The Provisional government largely ignored the problem, and prioritized keeping costs to the state at a minimum (in 1920 the chairman of Dublin Corporation had argued against any efforts to accommodate Belfast refugees as 'immoral' when there were thousands already on waiting lists). It was instead anti-Treaty republicans who stepped into the void. There were sectarian undertones to the relief offered to Belfast refugees, who were housed in properties confiscated from unionists while the Belfast boycott was reintroduced. Among the (unsuitable) properties into which refugees were crammed were the Fowler Memorial Hall, the Masonic headquarters on Molesworth Street, the Young Men's Christian Association on Sackville/O'Connell Street, and the Kildare Street Club. The private homes of some Protestants were also raided and seized. Ultimately, efforts to provide aid to Belfast refugees were erratic and uncoordinated. Eliciting donations proved largely unsuccessful – especially in comparison to earlier appeals for those left in need by the First World War or War of Independence – and were close to collapse by May 1922. By this stage an accommodation between the Provisional government and the IRA executive led to the 'Dáil government' (effectively the Provisional government) providing a centrally funded reception centre and accommodation. Though more organized, the building chosen, Marlborough House in Glasnevin, was too small to meet demand and men were often separated from their families; or, in the case of young, single men, simply turned away. There was more sympathy for Belfast refugees than there had been for the unemployed workers in the Rotunda – a telling example of sentiment for the national question over socialist agitation – but northern refugees were also often treated with suspicion, or as curiosities, and some had possessions stolen.

There were also accusations by Dublin republicans of ingratitude and thefts by the refugees, mirroring responses to Belgian refugees some six years earlier. By June, attention had largely turned elsewhere.[46]

The delayed general election was set for 16 June 1922. The pro- and anti-Treaty SF factions had agreed a 'pact' that would see each side run candidates from an agreed 'panel' based on their proportion of seats in each constituency in the second Dáil. Prior to the election, the British government rejected Michael Collins' efforts to pass a 'republican' constitution, insisting that the terms of the Treaty be upheld. Republicans also complained about the failure of government supporters to honour the pact in practice, and the revised constitution was only published on polling day meaning it did not become an election issue. Just before polling day, Collins also declared that the electorate should vote for the candidate of their choice.[47] More importantly, the willingness of third-party candidates to run in many constituencies meant that the profoundly undemocratic logic behind the pact was further undermined.[48] Unlike in some other constituencies, all of the non-university seats in Dublin were contested. If the election is viewed as a proxy (albeit imperfect) referendum on the Treaty, there was a clear victory for those who supported the settlement. Seán T. O'Kelly was the only anti-Treaty candidate to win a seat, and the capital was denounced in one republican newspaper for 'returning political twisters, gombeen men and Unionists at the top of the poll, while you threw out the mother of Patrick Pearse'.[49]

Anti-Treaty candidates secured less than 15 per cent of the Dublin vote, dropping as low as 9.3 per cent in Dublin County – the lowest in any contested constituency. In Dublin North West (see map 5), Richard Mulcahy and the other pro-Treaty SF candidates won 80 per cent of first preferences. As in earlier local elections, there was a notably strong minority vote for parties other than SF. This time the SF factions came off more poorly than they did anywhere else. Labour received more votes than anti-Treaty SF, and along with the Farmers' Party and independent candidates won nine seats. This was a sign of support for the Treaty, but also a clear rejection of partisan SF politics by a significant portion of the Dublin electorate. Darrell Figgis received a huge vote in Dublin County as an independent pro-Treaty candidate – having earlier been visited at his home by republicans who cut off a portion of his beard – and Laurence O'Neill and Alfie Byrne topped the poll in Dublin Mid under a similar banner. What the election actually said about popular support for the Treaty is less clear than it may initially seem, however, as the pact had somewhat hindered the anti-Treaty campaign in Dublin and the results in turn may have underrepresented support for their position among the general public. While there appears to have been less violence and intimidation against non-party candidates in Dublin than elsewhere, this was also an election carried out under the British threat of renewed war.[50]

It was ultimately the split in the IRA, rather than the political split or election results, that hastened the move to civil war. The stance of IRA veterans (and post-truce recruits) on the Treaty appears to have been most obviously based on individual loyalties and personality politics, rather than being strictly ideological. Few IRA veterans in the National army were in favour of all of its terms, or the continued connection with the British empire, and they still considered themselves republicans, but many were personally committed to Michael Collins or accepted the Treaty on his terms.[51] Even among the early core of the army, there had been indecision and prevarication. Joe McHenry resigned from the National army in March 1922 to join anti-Treaty leader Liam Mellows at the Engineers' hall on Gardiner Street.[52] McHenry recalled that before the army convention Pádraig O'Connor, promoted to colonel in the National army in 1923, had said 'he'd wash his hands of a split, as he was not definitely in favour of the Treaty'.[53] Like McHenry, others changed sides. Seán Lemass had been a training officer at Beggars Bush before leaving and joining the ATIRA. A guard detail of over thirty men at the National Bank on College Green also mutinied, with only six remaining loyal to the Provisional government.[54]

On 25 April 1922 *An tÓglach* published an article on 'the present position of the Army' and concluded that the 'vast majority' had stood by GHQ. It reported that in the Dublin No. 1 Brigade (which had five battalions and comprised the city area) 'all Brigade Staff are disloyal' and 'the majority of Battalion and Company Officers followed', but fourteen company captains remained 'loyal'. The O/C and vice-O/C of the South County (or No. 2) Brigade, Andy McDonnell and Michael Chadwick, opposed the Treaty but it was reported that several other brigade officers were loyal. In three of the five battalions, the majority of the staff were also said to have remained loyal to GHQ and in the remaining two where the staff were 'disloyal', around half of the men were considered loyal to the Provisional government. It was also reported in *An tÓglach* that full brigade, battalion and company staffs had been established in the Second Eastern Division, comprising the pro-Treaty members of the two Dublin Brigades and the Fingal Brigade, and were 'working satisfactorily'.[55]

Other figures on the split within the Dublin IRA vary and are potentially as unreliable as those in *An tÓglach*, but there were some notable variations between battalions. The majority of the city's 1st Battalion appear to have opposed the Treaty. The Dublin Brigade O/C during the War of Independence, Oscar Traynor, also opposed the Treaty but his own former unit, the 2nd Battalion, was the most obviously pro-Treaty battalion in the Dublin No. 1 Brigade. This appears to have been the result of the influence exerted by Tom Ennis and other battalion officers.[56] Traynor was dismissive of the calibre of men that joined the National army in Dublin, telling Ernie O'Malley that they 'looked like all the unemployed people in the city', though many had pre-truce service and men who had served in both 1916 and 1921 appear to have been more likely to join the

National army than remain in the ATIRA.[57] The 3rd Battalion had, indeed, trebled in size during the truce and a majority of its members were anti-Treaty.[58] Larry Nugent recalled that in K Company, 3rd Battalion, fourteen out of eighty-four joined the National army.[59] The split was more even in the 4th Battalion. In F Company, for instance, Archie Doyle remembered that between 50 and 60 per cent 'went Free State', though claimed that only about fifteen per cent of them had pre-truce service.[60]

The nature of the split could also vary significantly by company, but in the No. 2 Brigade area a majority remained in the ATIRA. The anti-Treaty Dublin No. 2 Brigade ultimately comprised of three battalions, a column from Kildare and a Wicklow (Independent) Battalion under McDonnell.[61] McDonnell was much less close to Michael Collins than others like Tom Ennis had been. While some Dublin IRA who opposed the Treaty also complained later of an 'IRB clique' exerting undue influence on the army, McDonnell recalled that 'there were very few IRB in the Dublin County' and 'very few IRA there were in the IRB.'[62] The No. 2 Brigade ultimately had a very different experience of the Civil War than their anti-Treaty comrades in the city. They fought a guerrilla war against National army troops in the sparsely populated Dublin and Wicklow mountains, but ultimately found limited popular support. Columns operating in south County Dublin were unable to inflict significant defeats on the Free State army, but did tie up considerable government resources over a number of months.[63] In north County Dublin, meanwhile, the split leaned more heavily in favour of the Treaty and there was no real violent conflict there. The anti-Treaty Fingal Brigade was said to have been reduced to a quarter of its pre-truce strength (614 members) by June 1922. Companies in Ring and Julianstown had ceased to exist along with the entire 2nd and 4th Battalions, with the exception of very small numbers of men from Rush, Oldtown and Kinsealy who were merged into or joined other battalions.[64] Neither the commandant in Fingal, Michael Lynch, nor his vice-commandant, Michael Rock, took part in the Civil War; the latter had been 'permanently disabled' when shot by Crown forces in July 1921.[65] The most active officers in the brigade during the War of Independence tended to join the National army, including Joseph Lawless, James Crenigan, Thomas Peppard and Daniel Brophy (though Lawless left for a period to concentrate on his business before re-joining).[66]

Their opponents liked to label the men who joined the army as mercenaries, motivated by money rather than a cause. If there was some truth in this, it was naturally an oversimplification and was perhaps more accurate after July 1922, when many of the experienced veterans of the War of Independence were sent elsewhere in the country and those who remained in the capital were more likely to be young and inexperienced.[67] Dublin was a significant source of recruits for the National army, drawing on a large population of unskilled and semi-skilled workers – many of whom were unemployed or underemployed. By the time a census of the army was taken in November 1922, just over 7,000 men with Dublin addresses had joined. Recruitment peaked in the immediate aftermath of the fall of the Four Courts, described below, with 1,773 men from Dublin enlisting in July 1922, though it had dipped below 400 in May and 700 in August. The vast majority had enlisted in Dublin, but almost 1,500 signed up in Kildare – principally at the Curragh. Some 281 enlisted in County Meath, and this presumably included a significant proportion from north Dublin for whom it was more convenient than the city; only seventeen enlisted in Wicklow. These were almost all very young men, with about 1,500 under the age of twenty and another 4,000 between the ages of twenty and thirty-nine. There was a much higher proportion of married men among the Dublin recruits to the National army than there had been in the pre-truce IRA. Of the November 1922 total, over 2,000 were married and another fifteen had been widowed. The key difference was likely the salary offered by the government. Only 440 held officer rank, with another 1,111 NCOs, and the remainder made up of ordinary enlisted men. A large majority also joined the infantry corps, with much smaller numbers in more specialized units where civilian trade skills would have been beneficial. Beyond the infantry, Dublin men were most likely to serve in the transport corps.[68] Dublin recruits to the National army also included a small number of men who had been 'out' in 1916, but were more-or-less inactive during the War of Independence. Again, the wage on offer was probably a deciding factor.[69]

Cumann na mBan did not split in the same way as the IRA and its executive publicly declared its opposition to the Treaty. At a convention held in early February 1922, the organization voted overwhelmingly in favour of the republic, with pro-Treaty members 'requested to resign'. While it has been suggested that a majority of the rank and file may have supported the Treaty, and almost half of Cumann na mBan branches were not represented at the convention, younger members of Dublin branches were quick to post anti-Treaty propaganda around the city. The republican women who opposed the Treaty became 'committed comrades' of the ATIRA, 'loyal, willing and incorruptible' as Ernie O'Malley described them, and were again active in arms distribution, intelligence-gathering, nursing and other auxiliary activities.[70] Among the senior resignations were Jennie Wyse Power and Min Mulcahy, both prominent in organizing an alternative to the now firmly anti-Treaty Cumann na mBan. On 12 March 1922 Cumann na Saoirse was founded at a meeting in the Mansion House attended by over 700 women. Intended to provide a platform for supporters of the Treaty, Cumann na Saoirse canvassed in the June 1922 election, engaged in significant propaganda work, and assisted government troops with intelligence work and the guarding of women prisoners as the Civil War developed. While there were branches established in several counties, Cumann na Saoirse remained a largely Dublin-centred organization and sixteen of its twenty-member executive lived in the city.[71]

The final push to civil war came when Field Marshal Sir Henry Wilson, retired as commander in chief of the imperial general staff and a recently elected MP for North Down, was shot dead on the doorstep of his London home. The assassins were two members of the London IRA. It is still unclear on whose initiative the shooting was carried out, but the British government blamed the Four Courts faction and demanded action. A few days later, on 26 June, prominent ATIRA leader Leo Henderson was arrested by pro-Treaty forces at Ferguson's garage on Lower Baggot Street. Henderson had led a party from the Four Courts to raid the Belfast firm and seize cars, enforcing the boycott renewed by the Four Courts executive. In response, General J.J. 'Ginger' O'Connell was arrested and detained in the Four Courts. Though British pressure was a significant factor in moving the Provisional government towards an assault on the Four Courts garrison, the events in Dublin were also significant – not least in allowing the government to avoid the impression of being unduly pushed by London. On 28 June 1922, fire was opened (with artillery supplied by the British army) on the Four Courts.[72] This was the moment that civil war began in Dublin.

One anti-Treaty propaganda poster produced around this time declared that 'Easter Week Repeats Itself', as republicans defended their strongholds from bombardment by British guns – this time operated by the (often inexperienced) National army.[73] Whatever the merits of the propaganda, there were clear echoes of Easter 1916 in the 1922 'Battle for Dublin'. The city centre once again came under heavy artillery fire. This time the north-east side of O'Connell Street, spared in 1916, was largely levelled. Though there was no repeat of the widespread looting that accompanied the Rising, troops occasionally deemed it necessary to fire shots to frighten groups entering abandoned shops.[74] The ATIRA also used a 'block system', occupying a series of individual buildings to create a separate 'fort of resistance'.[75] As fighting was centred near densely populated areas, civilians once more suffered significantly. At least thirty-four civilians were among a death toll of over seventy (including thirteen National army and twenty-five ATIRA). At least 150 civilians were also wounded.[76] The *Irish Times* unkindly attributed heavy civilian casualties towards the end of the Four Courts battle to the 'insatiable and utterly futile curiosity of the inveterate sensation-seeking street lounger'. However, the paper also highlighted the 'pathetic scenes' witnessed as residents were moved from their homes by National army soldiers: 'In one house two children lay dead, and owing to the conditions outside it was considered undesirable to move the bodies.'[77]

By the morning of Friday 30 June, the National army had taken the western side of the Four Courts complex and the headquarters block was on fire. As men led by Pádraig O'Connor attempted to seize the building by charging from the Public Record Office, there was a booming explosion, destroying one end of the building and a portion of the neighbouring Land Registry Office. The ornate dome of the Four Courts, which dominated the skyline along the quays, collapsed that evening. None of the attackers were killed, but a large, black mushroom cloud of smoke rose from the complex as nearby buildings and pillars shook and legal documents and other records were blown into the air, some landing over four miles away; Rosamund Jacob recalled glass breaking in one of the windows of Tara Hall almost a mile away on Gloucester Street. Within a couple of hours there were more explosions, and the Public Record Office's Record Treasury was also on fire, along with its precious collection covering several centuries of Irish history. Responsibility has been variously attributed to those who stored the mines in the complex and those who fired the shells, but it is impossible to absolve either side of blame for the loss of the records. By around 3.30 p.m., the ATIRA in the Four Courts had surrendered.[78]

Remarkably, Máire Comerford, who had remained in the Four Courts after other women were evacuated, was able to walk out during the surrender with her bicycle and cycle unimpeded to the Hammam Hotel.[79] The hotel was part of a 'block' in Sackville Street commanded by Oscar Traynor. On 4 July National army forces bombarded the block with artillery. The following morning, much of the area was on fire but Cathal Brugha ignored an order from Traynor to evacuate the Hammam. The Cumann na mBan women in the Hammam, at least thirty in number, were ordered to leave and most did so, often only very reluctantly or, in the case of the Barry sisters, by being carried out of the building. Three remained: Kathy Barry, Linda Kearns and Muriel MacSwiney, alongside a small number of men. The small contingent was then forced to retreat to the rear of the neighbouring Granville Hotel and, with their position untenable, Brugha ordered a surrender. When Brugha stepped out into the laneway, crowded with National army troops, he was shot in the left thigh (accounts vary about the exact events). The first senior republican to die in 1922, Brugha seems to have hoped that his death might bring an end to the war. Though his demise was widely mourned by friends and opponents, it did not shorten the conflict.[80] National army reports declared that 'Dublin is now completely in our hands. The county is being cleared out gradually'.[81]

Large-scale fighting ceased in Dublin city centre after ten days and there was a large semblance of normality in the capital in the late summer and autumn of 1922. The Phoenix Park races, Liffey Swim and Dublin Horse Show all went ahead without major incident in July and August.[82] On 9 August Clery's department store – 'a monument to Irish craftmanship and native skill' – opened its doors again for the first time since it was destroyed by fire at Easter 1916.[83] But the Civil War in Dublin did not end in early July 1922, however. Following the fall of Limerick to the National army in late July, the Civil War moved from its 'conventional' phase to a period of guerrilla warfare and a reversion by the ATIRA to the tactics of the War of Independence. Dublin anti-Treatyites who evaded capture after the fall of the Four Courts moved south to Blessington in County Wicklow but lacked a coherent strategy and the area was later abandoned.[84] On 31 July 1922 anti-Treaty TD Harry Boland, who had spent much of the previous two years in the US and served briefly as quartermaster of the IRA's Eastern Command, was surprised by a National army party at the Grand Hotel in Skerries and mortally wounded.[85]

In early August 1922 anti-Treaty forces made an ambitious effort to isolate the Provisional government's stronghold in Dublin city. On the nights of 5 and 6 August, over 200 Volunteers mobilized north and south of the city to dismantle and destroy bridges, roads and railway lines. Known to republicans as the 'bridges job', it was ultimately a failure. In terms of arrests, it far surpassed the attack on the Custom House in 1921. Large numbers of ATIRA were captured to the north and to the south, almost all with little or no resistance. National army officer Charlie Dalton reported that 'practically no damage was done in North County Dublin', and south of the city the anti-Treaty 3rd Battalion was said to be 'practically wiped out'. A disaster for the ATIRA, it was also seen as a missed opportunity for government forces to wipe out republican resistance in Dublin as large caches of captured documents were never adequately analysed and acted upon. Though greatly diminished, the ATIRA survived.[86]

Nor did the killing stop. On 26 August, four days after Michael Collins was killed in west Cork and two days before his state funeral in Dublin, two young men returning home from a meeting to reorganize the anti-Treaty Fianna Éireann were abducted near North Strand. The bodies of Alf Colley and Seán Cole were found dumped at Yellow Lane near Whitehall. About an hour earlier, Bernard Daly was similarly abducted on Suffolk Street and found dead in Malahide. Though the state denied any participation in the killings, suspicion ultimately fell on the army's Criminal Investigation Department (CID).[87] Based at Oriel House and Wellington Barracks, the influence of former 'Collins men' was obvious in the CID and it developed a reputation for brutality, which included the torture of prisoners. Two unsuccessful ATIRA attacks were made on (the poorly defended) Oriel House, led by Joe O'Connor. During the first in September 1922, a CID detective was shot dead before O'Connor called off the assault. Then, at the end of October, an effort was made to blow up the building but three anti-Treatyites were captured with no Free State casualties. When the ATIRA ASU, armed with a Thompson machine gun, fired on Wellington Barracks in November 1922 there were two National army fatalities, along with two civilians, killed while delivering meat to the barracks, and another hit in the crossfire. Over twenty soldiers were wounded. ATIRA Volunteer James Spain, who had been injured and captured but escaped, was followed by National army troops to a house on Donore Road before being taken out and shot five times in the head and chest. Four more of the ATIRA attackers were arrested. Joe O'Connor, perhaps the most significant ATIRA leader in Dublin, had already been arrested at work in the City Rates Department the day after the second attack on Oriel House.[88]

Along with members of military intelligence and one or two others, the CID was ultimately responsible for a series of killings in the city, perhaps as many as twenty, and were dubbed the 'murder gang' by republicans. Like Colley and Cole, other young men were suddenly bundled into cars and their bodies later found dumped on roads or lanes. This is how Éamon Hughes, Brendan Holohan and Joseph Rogers met their end in October 1922. Noel Lemass disappeared from his workplace in July 1923 and was later found shot dead and badly decomposed in the Dublin mountains.[89]

Fearing that the ATIRA campaign would bankrupt the state in its infancy, the Provisional government resolved to deal ruthlessly with those they saw as subverting the popular will. In late September 1922, the Army Emergency Powers Resolution was introduced. It allowed the trial of civilians by military court martial and the death penalty for individuals caught in possession of unauthorized firearms. Four young republicans – Peter Cassidy, James Fisher, John Gaffney and Richard Twohig – were the first executed under the resolution, in Kilmainham Gaol on 17 November. They were followed a week later by Erskine Childers, executed on a trumped up charge for possession of a miniature pistol gifted by Michael Collins.[90] On 8 December four of the leaders who surrendered in the Four Courts – Rory O'Connor, Joe McKelvey, Dick Barrett and Liam Mellows – were executed as a reprisal for the shooting dead of Brigadier-General Seán Hales and the wounding of fellow government TD Pádraig Ó Máille (probably the target of the shooting as one of the TDs who voted for the special powers resolution) on Ormond Quay. The executions, which had no obvious legal basis, were even condemned by the press, which supported the use of force and was reluctant to criticize the government openly.[91] Dublin Corporation passed a resolution of sympathy with the families.[92] The ATIRA assistant chief of staff, Ernie O'Malley, was lucky to avoid a similar fate. Having escaped from custody after the fall of the Four Courts, O'Malley was badly wounded and captured in November 1922 during a shootout on Aylesbury Road with National army troops. O'Malley had killed one soldier and wounded three others but the extent of his own injuries meant he was ultimately unfit to go before a court martial. After the loss of O'Connor and O'Malley and the attacks on Oriel House and Wellington Barracks, the National army began to get on top of the ATIRA in Dublin.[93]

The executions had their own impact on the war in the city and Labour leader Thomas Johnson told the Dáil that he was 'almost forced to say that you have killed the new state at its birth'; Kevin O'Higgins replied that 'we have no talisman except force'.[94] Though the Catholic hierarchy publicly condemned the republican campaign in a pastoral letter in October 1922, the Catholic archbishop of Dublin, Edward Byrne, privately asserted in a letter to President of the Executive Council W.T. Cosgrave that reprisal executions were 'not only unwise but entirely unjustifiable from the moral point of view'.[95] The state ultimately executed eighty-one republicans after the resolution was implemented, including four for armed robbery, more than twice the number executed by the British between 1916 and 1921. There was, though, some room for pragmatism. Arrested in Kilmainham in October and tried on 11 November 1922 for possession of a revolver, Séamus Mallin was later told by the judge advocate general that he was spared execution 'mainly because he was the son of Michael Mallin executed in 1916'.[96]

The first executions were followed by an order from anti-Treaty leader Liam Lynch against all of those who supported the 'murder bill'. Several reprisal attacks against government TDs and senators based in Dublin followed. On 10 December 1922, shortly before the first meeting of the new IFS parliament, the homes of two TDs, a civil servant and Jennie Wyse Power were attacked. Seán McGarry was not at home at Philipsburg Avenue when his house was set on fire, but his wife and three children were trapped upstairs. Tragically, 7-year-old Emmet McGarry died five days after sustaining serious burns and 'after much suffering'. J.J. Walsh, minister for posts and telegraphs, Michael McDunphy, assistant secretary to the government, and Wyse Power were much more fortunate and were unharmed. McGarry's electrical fittings business was also destroyed in January 1923.[97] That same month, Cosgrave's home in Ballyboden was burned down; his uncle, Patrick, had been shot dead during an armed raid on a public house owned by Cosgrave's mother at the end of September 1922.[98]

Those who had earlier been the shared 'enemy' of the republicans who split over the Treaty also remained potential targets, and their experiences often transcended traditional timelines of the Civil War. In January 1922 it was announced that the RIC would be disbanded. The first batch of ADRIC left Beggars Bush Barracks and took a mail boat for Holyhead on 13 January – receiving a 'hearty send-off from a number of personal friends' – and by 24 January the entire force had departed from Ireland.[99] Regular RIC men were first transferred to larger centres around the country before being released in a staggered fashion. British-born recruits generally went first, and all were reported to have left Ireland by mid-March.[100] The disbandment of all remaining Irish-born members was due to be completed at the end of March 1922, but this took several months longer. In April Major General Hugh Henry Tudor, the special 'police advisor' to the government, addressed a parade at the RIC depot in the Phoenix Park in advance of his departure to Palestine. On the same day, Tudor inspected 500 officers and men at Collinstown and was greeted there by the CI for Dublin, H.M. Loundes.[101] Another 200 men departed Ship Street Barracks around the same time, and more were due to do so before the process was suspended and then resumed at a slower pace owing to concerns about the safety and family arrangements of disbanded men. Precautionary measures were also implemented, including an army guard at the Upper Castle Yard and an armed RIC guard at the Palace Street gate to Dublin Castle.[102] A contingent remained in Dublin over the summer, at Ship Street and Dublin Castle, as Castle Guard Company and Castle Clerical Company, and at Gormanston camp.[103]

The final disbandment of the RIC was completed in late August 1922. On the morning of 17 August, the remaining members had slipped away from Ship Street Barracks in cabs and hackney cars, piles of discarded uniforms and caps left outside the barracks and taken away afterwards. That day, Michael Staines led about 380 members of the new Civic Guard (later named An Garda Síochána) through the entrance gate on Dame Street and into Dublin Castle to take over policing duties in the traditional seat of British administration in Ireland. But there was no direct handover from RIC to Civic Guard, and it was an informal and largely underwhelming affair. It was reported that only about sixty or seventy of the Civic Guard were in uniform, and by the time Staines and his men had arrived the RIC had already made their quiet exit. A small number were seen waiting around in mufti, apparently expecting a formal ceremony, but there was ultimately nothing to see. At 1.30 p.m., the Castle and barracks were handed over to the Civic Guard by assistant under-secretary Andy Cope, and a remaining guard of the Shropshire Light Infantry, which had earlier relieved the RIC guard, marched out.[104] The *Irish Times* suggested that many of the onlookers 'regarded the proceedings with a feeling of regret at the passing of what was admittedly the finest police force in the world.' An editorial in the paper declared – reflecting its own readership, perhaps, more so than the wider public – that 'there can be few men of Irish blood who do not feel a pang at the disappearance of this splendid force … a shining example of Irish valour'.[105] An order of council, signed by the lord lieutenant of Ireland, announced 31 August 1922 as the official date of disbandment and the last remaining men left Gormanston that day.[106] The unarmed DMP survived until 1925, rebranded with new cap badges, when it was folded into An Garda Síochána.[107] The last British army troops left Dublin Port for Holyhead on 17 December 1922, the departure completed without any interference.[108]

As disbanded members of the RIC filtered out of the force over the course of 1922, Ireland was 'confronted with the problem of the release into civil life of some 13,000 men', many unable to support themselves or their families indefinitely and with few prospects (including about 8,000 Irish-born, and about 1,500 Auxiliaries).[109] Fears for their safety were expressed by Sir Hamar Greenwood, the former 'police advisor' in Ireland Sir Henry Hugh Tudor, and by some of the men themselves.[110] Between December 1921 and February 1922 alone, there had been eighty-two recorded attacks on serving RIC, resulting in twelve deaths and twenty-seven serious injuries.[111] Among fourteen serving RIC killed in the twenty-six counties that became the IFS over the course of 1922 was Sergeant John Cotter, stationed at the Phoenix Park depot. He died of gunshot wounds inflicted on 2 March 1922 in Phibsborough, near his home in Cabra Park. On 28 May Sergeant William Leech, who had been assigned to the

Dublin Castle Clerical Company having previously served in Limerick, was shot and killed after leaving Westland Row (now Pearse) Station. At least fifteen disbanded RIC men were also killed in southern Ireland in 1922, none in Dublin.[112] Two British soldiers were killed by ATIRA in the city in April and May 1922, and another in Dún Laoghaire – possibly with the aim of provoking a British response (though Rory O'Connor called it 'murder pure and simple').[113]

There were some 300 violent deaths in Dublin across 1922 and 1923, made up of 129 National army, 85 ATIRA or Fianna Éireann, 76 civilians and ten Crown forces. The majority of fatalities came in two waves: during the assault on the Four Courts in July 1922 and between September and December 1922. The lethality of the conflict in the capital, however, can be overstated as among the Dublin casualties were those who died in Dublin hospitals having been wounded elsewhere and a significant number of accidents – the latter in its own way telling of the nature of the conflict. Over 500 more people were wounded.[114] Although most of the fighting and the brutality occurred in Munster for the remainder of the conflict, Dubliners played their own part there as the Dublin Guard was sent to serve in County Kerry. Non-participants living in Dublin also experienced unemployment, poverty and problems caused by a severe shortage of housing. Many remained in dirty, unsanitary and unsafe tenements. The cost of living in Dublin city was also significantly higher than elsewhere in the country. The government price for a quart of milk, for instance, based on average prices in a number of Irish towns, was 4¾*d.* in September 1922. In Dublin it was 6*d.* The price of butter was 2*s.* 6*d.* per lb in Dublin, compared to a government price of 1*s.* 6¾*d.*[115] These were all issues exacerbated by the post-Treaty conflict. The government of the IFS, no longer provisional from December 1922, finally emerged victorious when a dump arms order was issued after the death of Liam Lynch. The survival of the new (partitioned) state had been secured, but at significant political, economic, personal and spiritual cost.

9. Legacies of Dublin's revolution

In April 1955 Joe Leonard delivered a speech in tribute to Paddy O'Daly in front of the lord mayor of Dublin and cabinet minister and former IRA chief of staff Richard Mulcahy. O'Daly – 'our Leader' – had been O/C of the Squad and later of the Dublin Guard, serving with the National army in Dublin and Kerry.[1] Leonard had been with O'Daly at Ashtown in 1919, when they had unsuccessfully tried to assassinate the lord lieutenant, in the Squad and in the Dublin Guard.[2] The typed version of Leonard's speech ends with the Custom House attack in May 1921 and a terse reference to 'incidental attacks on the British Forces after the Custom House and so on to the truce'.[3] The silence over thirty years later on what followed the truce, and their shared experiences in 1922 and 1923, says something of the impact of that conflict on those who endured it. It is a silence that many, though by no means all, of its veterans preferred to keep – publicly at least. It captures the trauma of a short, bitter war that pitted former comrades against each other. But it might also speak to O'Daly's own Civil War record and some of its brutal, interpersonal violence. Paying tribute to 'The Leader, The Soldier and the Man' now sits uneasily with knowledge of his time in County Kerry, in particular.

On 6 March 1923, at Knocknagoshel, County Kerry, five soldiers were killed when a booby-trap mine exploded at what they believed was an IRA arms dump. Two were from Dublin, Michael Dunne from Lower Mount Street and Edward Stapleton from Lower Gloucester Street. The only survivor, Joseph O'Brien, was from Church Street in North Wall and lost both his legs below the knee and suffered significant blindness in each eye.[4] This was the worst single death toll for the National army in six months, and O'Daly ordered that in future ATIRA prisoners would be used to clear barricades in case of potential mine explosions. A day later, nine republican prisoners were taken from their cells and tied to a mine at Ballyseedy. The mine exploded and eight were killed, 'portions of their limbs and flesh, with pieces of clothing, were found adhering to trees and strewn along the road'. Remarkably, one of the men, Stephen Fuller, survived and escaped. Similar killings followed at Countess Bridge near Killarney and at Cahirciveen. There was no inquest and O'Daly led the army inquiry into the conduct of his own men at Ballyseedy, presenting a completely false account of events, praising the army and blaming the IRA for placing the mine. It was read into the Dáil record by Richard Mulcahy.[5] Though the Civil War officially ended in May 1923, the brutality did not cease. In June O'Daly was among a group of three National army soldiers who brutally flogged and sexually assaulted two young women, Flossie and Jessie McCarthy, daughters of a local (pro-Treaty) doctor in Kenmare, and covered their heads and hair in motor oil. In spite of the recommendation of Judge Advocate General Cahir Davitt, and the fury of Minister for Justice Kevin O'Higgins, the attacks were hushed up and only one of the men was found guilty by a court of inquiry. Two others, including O'Daly, were cleared in a case strongly characterized by victim-shaming and misogyny.[6]

On 30 November 1923, Barnet Goldberg, a Jewish man who had come to Dublin from his home in Manchester on one of his regular visits to his brother, Samuel, was taken away from outside 95 St Stephen's Green and later died in hospital of gunshot wounds. Two weeks later, Emmanuel 'Ernest' Kahn and David Miller were stopped on their way home from the Jewish Social Club on Harrington Street and asked their names and religion. Having been told to 'run for it', Millar was shot in the arm and Kahn mortally wounded. In 1924, the DMP identified James Conroy as one of the killers of Goldberg and Kahn but he had fled to Mexico before he could be arrested, following Fred Laffan who was also suspected of involvement. Laffan's brother Ralph was charged with wilful murder but acquitted. Conroy had joined the Squad in 1920, was arrested after the Custom House attack, and was later an officer in the National army. Both men travelled to the United States and while Conroy returned to Ireland in 1932 and claimed his military service pension, he was never charged and died in California in 1981. Considered the worst outbreak of anti-Semitic violence in the history of the state, the killings are also suggestive of the extent to which some of those who perpetrated the most challenging interpersonal violence of the War of Independence could apply the methods of the War of Independence or Civil War to settle personal scores. As with O'Daly in Kerry, they point further to efforts to cover up the violence of soldiers of the National army and a willingness to forgive excesses and protect men with good military records.[7]

The 'Kenmare incident' and the killings of Goldberg and Kahn cannot thus be divorced from the years of conflict that preceded them. They are also a part of a wider sequence of events intrinsically linked with the revolution that went beyond the 'dump arms' order in May 1923. While the general election in 1922 could be seen as an imperfect sign of support for the Treaty, a different picture emerged from the Dublin electorate the following year. The general election held in August 1923 proved something of a disappointment for the new Cumann na nGaedheal party, formed after the official foundation of the IFS in December 1922 from the pro-Treaty SF faction in government. Though the number of seats in the Dáil was increased from 128 to 153, Cumann na nGaedheal only won five extra seats. Some of its standout performances were in Dublin, where the party won eleven of the twenty-three seats in the three new non-university Dublin constituencies. Kevin O'Higgins, Richard Mulcahy and Philip Cosgrave each topped the poll in their constituencies with over thirty per cent of first preferences. A significant number of voters, albeit still a minority, voted for opponents of the Treaty in the city and county. Anti-Treaty SF increased its share in Dublin as Seán T. O'Kelly retained his seat, while two other anti-Treaty candidates from the second Dáil, Constance Markievicz and Charles Murphy, were re-elected and joined by Kathleen Lynn and Ernie O'Malley (still recovering from wounds suffered in December 1922). This may in part have been a judgement on the harsh measures used by the government to win the Civil War, but Labour, whose leader Thomas Johnson had condemned executions ordered by the government, also fared particularly poorly in Dublin and lost much of the ground gained in 1922.[8]

Dublin republicans were among the thousands of ATIRA prisoners who, demanding immediate release, commenced a hunger strike in mid-October 1923 that lasted until 23 November. Most dropped out of the IRA after release in December 1923.[9] The government was also forced to confront the fact that in late 1923 the army that had won the Civil War was now vastly oversized for peacetime. However, efforts to demobilize posed a significant challenge for the government, risked destabilizing the new state, and highlighted the immediate challenges of moving from war to statehood.[10] In March 1924 an influential group of army officers, believing they were being sidelined in favour of 'ex-Britishers' in the army and calling themselves the Irish Republican Army Organization, issued an ultimatum with a series of demands, including suspension of the government's demobilization scheme and a more 'republican' form of government. About fifty officers absconded from their posts with weapons and contact was made with the ATIRA about a joint assault on the state and on Northern Ireland. The mutiny revolved around some of the most active Dublin Brigade veterans, and its leaders were Colonel Charles Dalton and Major General Liam Tobin – former members of the Squad. The government ultimately lost nine TDs in sympathy with the mutineers, and internal divisions in Cumann na nGaedheal meant that attitudes towards the mutiny quickly softened. Cosgrave committed to an inquiry into the management of the army and an amnesty was negotiated. When the amnesty was broken by a military raid and the arrest of leaders of the mutiny at Parnell Street, the government demanded and secured the resignation of Chief of Staff Mulcahy and the army council. Perhaps more important than the events themselves, was the confirmation of civilian and democratic control over the army that resulted – though this was not inevitable. Those who were demobilized also suffered significantly, many of them veterans of several years of the struggle. The army was downsized by some 37,000 members, with only 9,000 securing immediate employment.[11] As the most important recruiting ground for the army, a large proportion were inevitably Dubliners.

Other challenges to the state came in successive by-elections in Dublin constituencies. There were eight vacancies in total over the life of the fourth Dáil from 1923 to 1926. In all bar one, Darrell Figgis' death by suicide in 1926, the seats were vacated by Cumann na nGaedheal TDs. Two were subsequently won by republicans. In November 1924 an election was held in Dublin South to replace Hugh Kennedy (who had won a by-election in 1923) following Kennedy's appointment as the state's first chief justice. Seán Lemass pipped the Cumann na nGaedheal candidate to the seat. Disillusioned by the government's handling of the army mutiny, two TDs in the Cumann na nGaedheal stronghold of Dublin North, Frank Cahill and Seán McGarry, resigned in October 1924. Patrick Leonard topped the poll for Cumann na nGaedheal in the resulting by-election in May 1925, but Oscar Traynor took the other seat. McGarry and Cahill joined Joseph McGrath's short-lived National Party – McGrath had been the leading government supporter of the mutineers.[12] Lemass and Traynor – two men who would become senior figures in Fianna Fáil, founded in 1926 – had tasted their first national election victories. Initially running as abstentionists, they finally entered the Dáil chamber with the rest of the Fianna Fáil deputies in August 1927.

Whatever its end point, the series of political, military, labour and agrarian conflicts that took up much of the early twentieth century left a lasting legacy. The Union was broken and new governments formed in Dublin and Belfast on a partitioned island, while there had been earlier sweeping changes to land ownership and Protestant 'ascendancy' was irrevocably diminished. Some did well out of revolution, or at least found themselves in comfortable circumstances in the years that followed. In the 1960s, *Dublin Opinion* republished its 1922 'The Night the Treaty was Signed' cartoon. It joked that one of the figures in the cartoon, rushing from Cork to Dublin, was 'now a principal officer in the Department of F——ce on a salary of £815 to £915 a year, exclusive of bonus.' Another who had been third in the race but 'dropped back to almost last after passing Monasterevan' had to be content with 'a clerical officership in the Department of Posts of Telegraphs.' A third figure had secured a '£900 to £975 position in the Land Commission, and five hours after his appointment, sent home for his brother', only to find that the latter had 'already established himself in the Office of Public Works.' The leader of the race in the original (a man with a long beard and crutches) had kept up 'a rare bat all the way till coming into Lucan when his wooden leg and the wind resistance to his nightgown began to tell against him. However, he finished a creditable sixth and secured a Junior Administrative post shortly after the abolition of the Entrance Exam for the position.'[13] This retrospective caption, reflecting some forty years after the signing of the Treaty, wryly pointed to the new opportunities that an Irish administration had brought – for some – and to the centralization of those opportunities in the capital.

Paddy O'Daly resigned his army commission in 1924 to return to his business as a building contractor. Later, he received accommodation in the Phoenix Park – in the former residence of the governor general – as overseer for the Office of Public Works. O'Daly was awarded a military service pension of £280 per annum, and in 1928 was earning £120 per annum alongside a bonus of

£198 and a free residence.[14] By contrast, in 1925 the Association of Ex-Officers and Men, National army, informed Archbishop Byrne of Dublin that the circumstances of many of its members were 'so pitiable' that between eighty and one hundred of them were forced to find a night's shelter in the Phoenix Park and other public parks in the city; 'many of them find no other means of sustenance for their wives and families but to resort to the South Dublin Union'.[15] Todd Andrews insisted that he could 'vouch on behalf of my comrades in 'E' Company of the Fourth Battalion, Dublin Brigade, that with a handful of exceptions, none of them were better off, socially or economically, as a result of the revolution'.[16] When Andrews, who had been arrested as part of the ATIRA, was released from prison in 1924 he was able to resume and complete his studies in UCD. He retired in 1966 as executive chairman of the transport authority, Coras Iompar Éireann.[17]

Many of the relatives of those who had died for Ireland, meanwhile, appeared none the better for the sacrifice their families had made. Several had gone to Dublin or been sent there to earn a better living or pursue a university degree with the intention of assisting families who remained at home. Dermot O'Dwyer was an engineering student when he was killed during an ambush on Frederick Street. His father was a creamery manager in Tipperary on £500 per year with 5 acres of land and his mother owned a property on Walworth Road in Dublin when he began university. When their circumstances changed, Con O'Dwyer was 'compelled to borrow money to enable [my son] to complete his course. I hoped when he was qualified to be in a position to clear off the debt, unfortunately these hopes were shattered, and the debt remains unpaid and I see no prospect of being able to do so now':

> Had my son been spared I would not need outside financial assistance from any quarter and it is absolute necessity that compels me to fill up the attached form or seek any compensation for the loss of my dear Boy who gave up his young and promising life for Ireland.[18]

William O'Connell was 'almost finished' his apprenticeship as a mechanical engineer when he was killed in Phibsborough in November 1920. It was hoped that he 'would eventually give a reasonable share of his earnings' to his parents, estimated at £3 of the £6 a week a mechanical engineer might expect to earn.[19]

Seán Doyle, killed in the Dublin mountains in September 1920, was living with his parents and contributing 30*s.* of the 38*s.* 8*d.* he received each week as an apprentice fitter with the corporation. His father Peadar – earning £5 per week as an engineer at Dollard's printing works, and also a councillor, 1916 veteran, and later TD and lord mayor of Dublin – put the loss of his son at £2,000 in 1924.[20] These unmarried Volunteers had been an important source of income for their parents and, often, their siblings. Martin Savage, it was said, 'sent money periodically to his father', who, in the opinion of a Garda sergeant in Sligo, 'needed financial aid'.[21] Thomas Bryan's mother claimed that even after he got married he 'was very good to her and would not see them in want.'[22] The White Cross eased some of the financial impact of an IRA bereavement but Bernard O'Hanlon's father claimed they got nothing after he was killed in action in 1920, and even the funeral costs were 'borne by ourselves'.[23] Those deemed fully dependent on the deceased, usually a wife in the case of a married man, could receive a dependent's pension from the state. Where an applicant was considered to be partially dependent they received a once-off gratuity at the discretion of the minister. Michael Magee's father was given a £75 gratuity by the state but wrote to Cosgrave in February 1925 that 'what we received looks very small, he was a good son and I would give a good many seventy-five pounds to have him back again'.[24]

Disappointment could also cross the Treaty divide. In 1941 Joe Leonard, then an army officer, was willing to go before the advisory board to support the application of Brigid Breen (née Malone), a member of the ard craobh branch of Cumann na mBan, wife of former ATIRA member and then Fianna Fáil TD Dan Breen, and sister of Michael Malone killed at Mount Street Bridge in 1916, for a military service pension. Her case had first been 'thrown out' when her husband incorrectly filled out a form and she was later given the 'third degree' by the pension board and 'offered £14'. Breen's sister Annie, who had been with her when she removed guns from Mount Street after Bloody Sunday in 1920, and when she aided the escape of Ernie O'Malley and Frank Teeling from Mountjoy, was awarded £80, but Brigid Breen claimed that her award had been cut down 'rather drastically'. Tired of 'all the ferreting the Board is doing in my case', she hoped that Leonard could write a letter 'saying you know me as being genuine – telling them to go to hell, as the Referee of the Board – Judge Tom O'Donnell is an old Redmondite M.P.'[25] There was clearly some room to come together to complain about an old constitutional nationalist – another 'loser' of the revolution in his own right. By 1942 Breen's pension had been upgraded to a D (from an E, the lowest rank) after a second appeal.[26]

The fighting took its toll on many, both physically and mentally, as outlined viscerally in wound and disability pension applications. Séamus Grace survived the British army's assault on Northumberland Road during the Easter Rising; his superior, Michael Malone, the only other occupant of the house, was killed. After release from prison in December 1916, he re-joined the Irish Volunteers and was active during the War of Independence – suffering a gunshot wound to the leg – and in the ATIRA during the Civil War. Unable to carry out a civilian occupation after 1923, medical reports highlighted Grace's poor physical and mental health in the 1920s and 1930s (for periods he lived on both Mespil Road and Haddington Road, literally around the corner from his post in 1916). In the late 1930s, Grace's disability was assessed at '100%' by the army pensions board.

In a 1940 report, he complained of 'Loss of power left leg. Great weakness of left knee and ankle. Painful callosity on left heel. Loss of memory. Confused and unable to easily concentrate. Very depressed. Easily excited; severe headaches; Well marked insomnia.' An examination concluded that Grace had 'scars and wasting on left leg … very depressed and neurasthenic. Evidence of bronchitis both lungs. Heart – fast. … Tremor of hands … Has had all teeth extracted.' Having spent a period in Grangegorman mental hospital in 1944, Grace died in 1959.[27] Others, however, were able to deal with what they had seen or what they had done quietly, privately, and in a variety of ways across a range of life experiences.[28]

Ex-servicemen and others who had served the Crown between 1912 and 1923 – Dubliners, those who served in Dublin and remained there, or those who moved to Dublin – had mixed experiences in the IFS. Housing schemes for ex-servicemen, the largest of which was the estate built at Killester under the Irish Sailors' and Soldiers' Land Trust, provided good quality housing. This was, of course, another source of disappointment for those who were not so lucky. It also prompted arguments, tenant rent strikes and evictions in the years that followed.[29] Significant numbers of ex-servicemen also lived in poverty long after their military careers were finished. Several charitable organizations operated in Dublin in the 1920s for the relief of distress among ex-servicemen and their families. The largest was what became in 1925 the British Legion in Ireland (Southern Area) when the Irish Legion of Ex-Servicemen was recognized as a British Legion area with a headquarters on Mountjoy Square.[30] In early 1925, the Dublin committee of the London-based Southern Irish Loyalists Relief Association, based in what had formerly been the headquarters of the IUA, created its own 'Ex-Service Fund', drawing primarily on supporters in Britain. It regularly clashed with the Legion on policy, and the plight of ex-servicemen was highly politicized in the 1920s, but there was significant demand for the relief it offered – often as little as a meal token or a discount on groceries. Over half of their relief was distributed in Dublin, where they found the greatest concentration of ex-servicemen. In 1925 the association's Dublin relief secretary wrote: 'The poverty in Dublin is too awful, and we get much gratitude for our dinners.'[31]

The housing schemes for returning ex-servicemen were some of the only building works carried out in the country as the Civil War progressed, and revolution ultimately did little in the immediate term for Dublin's poorest. In May 1923, the month the Civil War ended, Alfie Byrne asked Ernest Blythe, minister for local government, in the Dáil if he was aware that 'many thousands of Dublin citizens are now sheltering in rat infested basements of slum property'. Blythe responded that it had not been possible to make further funds available for municipal housing schemes 'owing to the prevailing unsettled conditions and the heavy financial deficit', made worse by 'inflated' building costs and a series of strikes. By September 1923, there was a severe housing shortage across the country, with local authority rents – such as those set by Rathmines UDC at between 16*s.* and 25*s.* per week – beyond the reach of ordinary workers. New housing and building legislation were enacted in 1923 and 1924, and the corporation's first significant municipal housing scheme, the garden suburb at Marino, was an important development. But in December 1924, the *Irish Builder and Engineer* declared that 'Housing, or the lack of it, still remains the most urgent and pressing problem of the hour in the Free State, which unhappily came in for the evil heritage left by previous Governments and Corporations'.[32]

Emigration remained another persistent feature of Irish life, and among the broad cohort of emigrants were many who had participated in the fighting but by its end had found themselves defeated, disappointed or disillusioned. One RIC pensioner, James Edward Terrett, left his job as steward of a Dublin golf club after receiving a threatening letter from the IRA and went first to Australia and then England. By his own account, Terrett, who retired from the RIC in 1918, was particularly active in searches following the 1916 Rising, informed on a local doctor who had been 'out' during the rebellion, and assisted in the arrest of Éamon de Valera in Greystones in 1918. This had all, he suggested, made him 'anathema' to local republicans.[33] W.T. Cosgrave committed to protecting the Protestant minority in the IFS, and some Protestants even appear to have received preferential treatment during the Civil War. In July 1922, for instance, Lord Massy, a prominent landowner in Rathfarnham, had a prosecution for murder dropped on the instruction of Kevin O'Higgins, the minister for justice, after he shot dead a burglar who entered his house.[34] Others had very different experiences. J.C.D. Murray, a former secretary of the CDUA residing in Shankill, said to be known publicly as 'an active supporter of the Union and an out & out loyalist', was told by armed raiders that he 'was, and always had been, a British Spy'. He claimed that from the truce to the visit of the raiders in October 1922 he had been 'subjected to constant raids and intimidation' and was forced to abandon his lands in Shankill and seek accommodation in the city, where he was unable to find steady work. Murray was ultimately awarded £300 compensation by the Irish Grants Committee, a Treasury-funded compensation scheme for southern Irish loyalists that operated in the latter half of the 1920s. He died in 1928 – of 'Pneumonia and starvation', as one correspondent put it – before the award was paid out.[35] There was more anonymity in the city, but Murray's namesake Revd Robert Henry Murray was less fortunate than most. In 1922 he claimed he was forced to sell his home on Harcourt Terrace and give up his Trinity lectureship after IRA threats. He also claimed he was targeted 'because as a clergyman I pleaded in my sermons for support of the Crown & because I kept my accounts with the Ulster Bank'. After he left, the house was raided and books and manuscripts destroyed. In what might have seemed a bitter irony, Revd Murray also sought compensation for the loss of a manuscript titled: 'The growth of tolerance'. The country, he claimed, had 'broken him'.[36]

John Murphy was discharged from the RIC in May 1922 and had intended to live in Dublin 'in obscurity until such time as the country got more normal', before moving to live with his mother-in-law in Wicklow. Instead, he claimed that he was held up on a Dublin street by five armed men and told to leave Ireland 'as my presence in the country was a menace to the cause of Ireland'. Murphy moved to Liverpool with his family where he remained in the late 1920s.[37] John Egan was warned not to return to Roscommon while he was stationed in Dublin Castle. Egan claimed that his father, who had also received a warning, 'was afraid for my own safety to allow me home as two or three ex members had been taken out and shot'. He went straight to England on the day he left the Castle.[38] Disbandment could in turn have a traumatic impact on police wives. As married men travelled abroad and searched for new lodgings and work, it fell to wives to sell up property and settle affairs. This could be made more difficult by hostility to police families and, perhaps, by opportunism within local communities. Timothy Doona was discharged from Gormanston camp in May 1922. His wife and children were living in nearby Balbriggan and Doona left for Fifeshire in search of a new home there. While he was gone, he claimed, his wife received a letter ordering her to 'clear out or she would be shot'. She was then obliged to sell their furniture as best she could, 'in some cases getting 5/- for articles that cost me pounds'. Eventually settling in Newcastle, Doona claimed he was afraid to return home for his mother's funeral.[39] Others may have left without any direct threats, but instead simply believing it meant their best chance of finding secure employment.

In line with the rest of the country, the Protestant population of Dublin declined significantly between 1911 and the first census taken in the Irish Free State in 1926. The fall in Dublin city was about 40 per cent, but less dramatic in the county at about 22 per cent. Indeed, most of the decline was among the urban working-class and large minorities of Protestants remained in the middle-class townships. Some of the decline was the result of emigration during the revolutionary period, and many of those who left undoubtedly did so as a result of intimidation or violence, but the impact of the First World War and withdrawal of the British administration and armed forces played its own significant part. There is little evidence of terror in the records for the period of the exclusively Protestant City of Dublin Conservative Workingman's Club or the Association for the Relief of Distressed Protestants – apparently mostly inconvenienced by curfews.[40] Many of the Belfast refugees who arrived in Dublin in early 1922, meanwhile, had returned home by 1926.[41] Active republicans from the north, however, were more inclined to remain in Dublin – as addresses provided with Bureau of Military History witness statements in the 1950s attest.[42]

If they so wished, the Protestants who had formerly been aligned with unionist politics could also seek and even secure election in Dublin on a range of different political platforms. While Sir Maurice Dockrell played little part in public life after 1921, his son Henry Morgan Dockrell was a Cumann an nGaedheal and later Fine Gael TD between 1932 and 1948 and sat in the Seanad between 1948 and 1951. Henry Morgan's son, Maurice Edward, followed his father into the Dáil in 1951.[43] Another prominent figure in Dublin unionism before 1922, Major Bryan Ricco Cooper, sat as an independent TD for Dublin South from 1923 until his death in 1930. Former Unionist MP for Rathmines J.P. Good was returned as a Businessmen's Party TD in the same constituency from 1923 to 1937.[44] By the early 1930s, the integration of some former unionists into Cumann na nGaedheal was obvious enough to be regularly pilloried by the cartoonist in the *Irish Press*.[45] 'Ex-unionists' in Dublin continued to demonstrate their past allegiances or their 'Britishness' – and a form of what has been described as 'cultural royalism' – long after 1922.[46]

The Church of Ireland congregation continued to maintain an emotional link to Crown and empire, as seen in the cancellation in 1936 of all parish entertainments in Clontarf 'on account of the dreadful gloom everywhere felt on the death of His Majesty King George V.'[47] In his memoir, journalist Brian Inglis recalled that in Malahide, 'in everyday matters, the fact than an Irish Free State did exist was hardly noticeable'.[48] It was also still possible to spend time with like-minded people, and to ignore the less desirable elements of the new regime.[49] Leaving the theatre before the national anthem was played, listening to British radio stations, eschewing Gaelic football and hurling in favour of 'English' games like soccer, rugby or cricket, or insisting that Dún Laoghaire was still Kingstown were more subtle forms of resistance.[50] Associations, clubs and professional bodies continued to carry the 'Royal' prefix, Dublin had more streets named after Queen Victoria than London, and, though painted over in green, the post-boxes still contained the royal cipher.[51]

Displays of loyalism were not the preserve of Protestants. Service and sacrifice in the First World War provided a particularly powerful, if complex, motivation for remembering the British connection. In 1924, 20,000 veterans were joined by an estimated crowd of 50,000 in observing a two-minute silence at College Green. They included large numbers of Catholic ex-servicemen and their families. Reasons for attending were as personal as political but 'God Save the King' was sung and the Union Jack was flown while a Celtic cross was unveiled in honour of the 10th Irish Division.[52] That year, the bitter divides of civil war meant the first official state commemoration of the 1916 Easter Rising was a small, sombre affair. Agnes Mallin was the only relative of an executed leader to attend.[53] Over 250,000 poppies were sold in Dublin in 1925 alone and high sales continued into the 1930s.[54] While the size of the crowds diminished over the years, and they were moved further away from the city centre, the Union

Jack was seen and 'God Save the King' heard at armistice ceremonies in Dublin into the 1950s. None of this happened, of course, without occasionally violent protests against what were seen in other quarters as undesirable displays of 'imperialism'. Early on the morning of Armistice Day in 1928, for instance, efforts were made by republicans to blow up the statues of King William III on College Green and King George II on Stephen's Green.[55]

The contested commemoration of the Revolution in the 1920s highlights the complexity of the Revolution itself, and the failure of simplistic narratives of Irish versus British or nationalist versus unionist to stand up to scrutiny. There were many different Dublins, and in turn many different sorts of revolutions – as well as much that might not pass as revolutionary at all. Nevertheless, the events of the years between 1912 and 1923 had a profound impact on Dublin and a long afterlife. A parliament was returned to Dublin and the constitutional status of the island shifted. Many lives were changed profoundly and irrevocably – sometimes for better and sometimes for worse. Dubliners faced the Revolution and its endgame with a range of responses, from celebration to disappointment to apathy and much in between. For all of those who still wished for things to change, there were others who preferred the status quo. For others the primary focus was simply to carry on as best they could, hoping to avoid revolution and whatever it might bring, though often failing to do so. For many, there was no neat ending in 1923. Some continued the fight for the republic, or tried to right the wrongs of the Revolution, as they saw them, in their own way. The loss of loved ones, the physical and mental impacts of fighting, emigration and disappointments large and small also lingered on for decades.

Notes

CHAPTER ONE *Dublin in 1912*

1 E. MacDowel Cosgrave and Leonard R.F. Strangways, *The dictionary of Dublin: being a comprehensive guide to the city and its neighbourhood* (Dublin, 1908), p. xv.
2 *Irish Times* (hereafter *IT*), 8 July 1911.
3 Mary E. Daly, *Dublin, the deposed capital: a social and economic history* (Cork, 1984), p. 2.
4 *Weekly Irish Times*, 1 Apr. 1911; *IT*, 23 June 1911; Ciarán Wallace, 'Civil society in search of state: Dublin 1898–1922', *Urban History*, 45:3 (2018), 434–5; idem, 'Fighting for unionist home rule: competing identities in Dublin 1800–1929', *Journal of Urban History*, 38:5 (2012), 940; *Freeman's Journal* (hereafter *FJ*), 5 Apr. 1911; Catriona Crowe (ed.), *Dublin 1911* (Dublin, 2011), pp 135, 137.
5 *Irish Independent* (hereafter *II*), 8 July 1911.
6 *FJ*, 10 July 1911; *II*, 10 July 1911; *IT*, 10 July 1911.
7 *II*, 8 July 1911.
8 R.F. Foster, *Vivid faces: the revolutionary generation in Ireland, 1890–1923* (London, 2015), p. 9.
9 *Census of Ireland, 1911, Areas, houses and population; also the ages, civil condition, occupations, birthplaces, religion and educations of the people. Province of Leinster*, County of Dublin, HC, 1912 [Cd. 6049], Table I; Joseph V. O'Brien, *Dear, dirty Dublin: a city in distress, 1899–1916* (Berkeley, 1982), p. 63.
10 Séamus Ó Maitiú, *Dublin's suburban towns* (Dublin, 2003), pp 135–44.
11 Wallace, 'Competing identities', 934.
12 Robert Lynd, *Rambles in Ireland* (London, 1912), p. 267.
13 Stephen Gwynn, *The famous cities of Ireland* (Dublin, 1915), p. 231.
14 David Dickson, *Dublin: the making of a capital city* (London, 2014), p. 380.
15 Daly, *Deposed capital*, pp 2–15.
16 Ibid., pp 2, 20–47; O'Brien, *Dear, dirty Dublin*, p. 60. See also Joseph Brady, 'The heart of the city: commercial Dublin, *c.*1890–1915' in Joseph Brady and Anngret Simms (eds), *Dublin through space and time* (Dublin, 2001), pp 303–14.
17 O'Brien, *Dear, dirty Dublin*, pp 66–7.
18 Crowe (ed.), *Dublin 1911*, p. 156.
19 Daly, *Deposed capital*, p. 4.
20 Lynd, *Rambles*, pp 265–6. See also Diarmaid Ferriter, 'Lynd, Robert', *DIB*, DOI: https://doi.org/10.3318/dib.004962.v1.
21 MacDowel Cosgrave & Strangways, *The dictionary of Dublin*, pp v, xiv.
22 C.S. Andrews, *Dublin made me* (Dublin, 2001 [1979]), p. 3.
23 Lynd, *Rambles*, p. 267.
24 Wallace, 'Fighting for unionist home rule', 941.
25 Yvonne Whelan, 'The construction and destruction of a colonial landscape: monuments to British monarchs in Dublin before and after independence', *Journal of Historical Geography*, 28:4 (2002), 508–33.
26 *Census of Ireland, 1911. General report with tables and appendix*, HC, 1912 [Cd. 6663], Tables 47 and 47A.
27 *Census of Ireland, 1911, Areas, houses and population; also the ages, civil condition, occupations, birthplaces, religion and educations of the people. Province of Leinster*, County of Dublin, HC, 1912 [Cd. 6049], vi–vii; Table III.
28 *Census of Ireland, 1911. General report*, Table 48.

29 Ibid., xxvi; Table 67.
30 D.A. Chart, 'Unskilled labour in Dublin', *Journal of the Statistical and Social Inquiry Society of Ireland*, 23 (1913/14), 162.
31 *Census of Ireland, 1911, Areas, houses and population*, Table XXIX.
32 Crowe (ed.), *Dublin 1911*, p. 27.
33 *Census of Ireland, 1911*, County of Dublin, Table XXIX; Wallace, 'Fighting for unionist home rule', 933–4.
34 *Report of the departmental committee appointed by the Local Government Board for Ireland to enquire into the housing conditions of the working classes in the city of Dublin*, HC, 1914 [Cd. 7273] (hereafter Housing report), p. 2.
35 Mary E. Daly, 'Social structure of the Dublin working class, 1871–1911', *Irish Historical Studies*, 23:90 (1982), 130, 122–3, 130; eadem, *Deposed capital*, p. 26.
36 Chart, 'Unskilled labour', 161–71.
37 O'Brien, *Dear, dirty Dublin*, p. 62.
38 Daly, *Deposed capital*, pp 64–76; eadem, 'Social structure', pp 122–30; O'Brien, *Dear, dirty Dublin*, pp 199–206.
39 *Census of Ireland, 1911*, City of Dublin, Table XX, County of Dublin, Table XX. There were smaller numbers of women engaged in other work with textiles, or making or dealing in clothes, shoes and boots, in the city and county.
40 *Census of Ireland, 1911*, City of Dublin, Table XX, County of Dublin, Table XX.
41 Caitríona Clear, *Social change and everyday life in Ireland, 1850–1922* (Manchester, 2007), pp 34–5.
42 Daly, *Deposed capital*, p. 124.
43 Fergus Campbell, 'Who ruled Ireland? The Irish administration, 1879–1914', *Historical Journal*, 50:3 (2007), 623, 641–2.
44 Daly, *Deposed capital*, pp 125–7.
45 O'Brien, *Dear, dirty Dublin*, p. 311 n. 2.
46 Campbell, 'Who ruled Ireland?', 631–2.
47 Andrews, *Dublin made me*, p. 15.
48 Martin Maguire, 'A socio-economic analysis of the Dublin Protestant working class, 1870–1926', *Irish Social and Economic History*, 20 (1993), 40.
49 *Dublin dictionary*, vii; 1911 census returns, Grafton Street, Dublin (http://census.nationalarchives.ie/) (accessed 17 June 2020).
50 Brady, 'Heart of the city', p. 289.
51 Housing report, p. 2.
52 1911 census returns, The Square, Inchicore, Dublin (http://census.nationalarchives.ie/) (accessed 9 June 2020).
53 Andrews, *Dublin made me*, pp 39–40.
54 Crowe (ed.), *Dublin 1911*, p. 156.
55 Janet Moody, *The tenement dwellers of Church Street, Dublin, 1911* (Dublin, 2017), p. 32.
56 *Census of Ireland, 1911*, County of Dublin, Table XXI; Eugene A. Coyle, 'Larkinism and the 1913 County Dublin farm labourer's dispute', *Dublin Historical Record*, 58:2 (2005), 177.
57 Caitríona Clear, 'Social conditions in Ireland 1880–1914' in Thomas Bartlett (ed.), *The Cambridge history of Ireland*, iv: *1880 to the present* (Cambridge, 2018), pp 151–2; Gerard Hanley, '"Let the harvest go to blazes": farm labourers in north County Dublin and the 1913 lockout', *Studia Hibernica* 40 (2014), 138–43.
58 *Census of Ireland, 1911*, County of Dublin, Table XXII. See also Cormac Murphy, 'Revolution and radicalism in County Dublin, 1913–21' in Myrtle Hill and Sarah Barber (eds), *Aspects of Irish studies* (Belfast, 1990), p. 17.
59 Crowe (ed.), *Dublin 1911*, p. 22.

60 *Census of Ireland, 1911. General report*, xxxii; Table 24.
61 Daly, *Deposed capital*, p. 2.
62 *Emigration statistics of Ireland for the year 1912. Report and tables showing the number, ages, conjugal condition and destinations of the emigrants from each county and province in Ireland during the year 1912; Also the occupations of the emigrants, and the number of emigrants who left each port in each month of the year*, HC, 1913 [Cd. 6727], pp 15–16. Only fourteen emigrants passed through Kingstown in 1912.
63 Crowe (ed.), *Dublin 1911*, p. 22.
64 *Census of Ireland, 1911. General report*, Table 75.
65 Crowe (ed.), *Dublin 1911*, p. 23.
66 *Census of Ireland, 1911*, City of Dublin, Table XXVI.
67 David Fitzpatrick, *The Americanization of Ireland: migration and settlement, 1841–1925* (Cambridge, 2019), pp 26–37.
68 Ruth McManus, 'Dublin's lodger phenomenon in the early twentieth century', *Irish Economic and Social History*, 45:1 (2018), 23–41.
69 Housing report, p. 3.
70 Dickson, *Dublin*, p. 397.
71 Lynd, *Rambles*, p. 275.
72 Dickson, *Dublin*, pp 397–8.
73 Categorization of housing was based on the quality of building material, number of rooms and number of front windows, but not the state of repair.
74 Housing report, pp 3–5.
75 1911 census, enumerator's abstract, Henrietta Street, Dublin (http://census.nationalarchives.ie/) (accessed 15 June 2020).
76 See, for example, Jacinta Prunty, *Dublin slums, 1800–1925: a study in urban geography* (Dublin, 1988).
77 Housing report, pp 4–5.
78 Quoted in Moody, *Church Street*, p. 41.
79 Kearns, *Dublin tenement life*, pp 14–17.
80 Clear, 'Social conditions', p. 159; Moody, *Church Street*, pp 47–9.
81 Housing report, pp 5–6.
82 Ciara Breathnach and Brian Gurrin, 'A tale of two cities – infant mortality and cause of infant death, Dublin, 1864–1910', *Urban History*, 44:4 (2017), 649.
83 *Census of Ireland, 1911*, County of Dublin, Table IX.
84 Ibid., Table VIII.
85 *Census of Ireland, 1911*, County of Dublin, xi–xiii; David Fitzpatrick, 'The geography of Irish nationalism, 1910–1921', *Past & Present*, 78 (1978), 138–9.
86 Buildings were designated as first-class houses based on the number of rooms, windows and the quality of building materials. Quality of accommodation was based on the quality of the house and the number of families sharing that house. To be deemed first-class accommodation, for instance, a house had to be first class with only one family living in it.
87 *EH*, 24 Nov. 1913.
88 Coyle, 'Larkinism', 177; *Untenanted lands (Ireland). A return of untenanted lands in rural districts, distinguishing demesnes on which there is a mansion house showing: (1) rural district and electoral division; (2) townland; (3) area in statute acres; (4) valuation (poor law); (5) names of occupiers as in valuation lists*, HC, 1906 [paper number 250], pp 117–21.
89 Heard repeated variations of this in almost all of his reports between 1912 and 1914 (The National Archives (hereafter TNA), CO 904/89–94).
90 *Royal Irish Constabulary and Dublin Metropolitan Police. Report of the committee of inquiry, 1914*, HC, 1914 [Cd. 7421] (hereafter RIC and DMP committee), p. 35.

91 General monthly return of the regimental strength of the British army, Jan. 1912 (TNA, WO 73/90). I am grateful to Dr Seamus Cullen for sharing this file with me.
92 RIC and DMP committee, Appendix VIII, p. 341.
93 *Judicial statistics, Ireland, 1912*, HC, 1913 [Cd. 7064], xv, xxiv, Table 12; RIC and DMP committee, Appendix VIII, p. 341.
94 *Judicial statistics, Ireland, 1912*, Tables 19, 20 and 23; Statistical tables of the Dublin Metropolitan Police for the year 1912, HC, 1913 [Cd. 6860], Table I. Simple and minor larceny accounted for 2,178 of a total of 3,122 indictable offences for the year in the city. There were 81 cases in the county.
95 *FJ*, 11 Jan. 1912.
96 *Judicial statistics, Ireland, 1912*, Tables E, 19 and 20.
97 *Statistical tables of the Dublin Metropolitan Police for the year 1912*, v.
98 *Judicial statistics, Ireland, 1912*, xv, Table E. The latter records the rate per 100,000 people and the city comparison is based on a figure of 3,615 non-indictable offences where drunkenness was included.
99 O'Brien, *Dear, dirty Dublin*, pp 64–6.
100 Dickson, *Dublin*, pp 346–7, 386–7.
101 Stephanie Rains, *Commodity culture and social class in Dublin, 1850–1916* (Dublin, 2010), pp 168–9.
102 MacDowel Cosgrave & Strangways, *The dictionary of Dublin*, pp viii–ix, 178–9; Dickson, *Dublin*, pp 326–7, 387. The number of cases of drunk driving are reported in *Statistical tables of the Dublin Metropolitan Police for the year 1912*, v.
103 Patrick Maume, 'Murphy, William Martin', *DIB*, DOI: https://doi.org/10.3318/dib. 06106.v1.
104 Readership figures and other information on the press is drawn from the following: O'Brien, *Dear, dirty Dublin*, p. 60; Brian Ó Conchubhair, 'The Gaelic League and Irish Ireland' in Bartlett (ed.), *Cambridge history of Ireland*, iv, pp 206–7; Patrick Maume, 'Moran, David Patrick ('D.P.')', *DIB*, DOI: https://doi.org/10.3318/dib.005957.v1; Crowe (ed.), *Dublin 1911*, p. 122; Louise Ryan, 'The *Irish Citizen*, 1912–1920', *Saothar*, 17 (1992), 105–11.
105 Andrews, *Dublin made me*, p. 15.
106 *The seventy-ninth report of the commissioners of national education in Ireland, school year 1912–13*, HC, 1913 [Cd. 7141].
107 Maguire, 'Socio-economic analysis of the Dublin Protestant working-class', 44, 49–50.
108 Dickson, *Dublin*, pp 340, 391–2, 400–1.
109 Brendan Power, 'The functions of association football in the Boys' Brigade in Ireland, 1888–1914' in Leeann Lane and William Murphy (eds), *Leisure and the Irish in the nineteenth century* (Liverpool, 2016), pp 41–2.
110 For an engaging account of the sort of fare offered in all of these venues in the early twentieth century, see O'Brien, *Dear, dirty Dublin*, pp 44–50.
111 One of the executed leaders of the 1916 Rising, Michael Mallin, was said to have run a short-lived cinematograph around this time, possibly an unlicensed one: Brian Hughes, *16 lives: Michael Mallin* (Dublin, 2012), pp 76–8.
112 O'Brien, *Dear, dirty Dublin*, pp 50–3, 56; Roy Foster, 'The Irish literary revival' in Bartlett (ed.), *Cambridge history of Ireland*, iv, pp 185–6; Shane Kenna, *16 lives: Thomas MacDonagh* (Dublin, 2014), pp 126–34.
113 MacDowel Cosgrave & Strangways, *The dictionary of Dublin*, pp 134–5, 143. O'Brien, *Dear, dirty Dublin*, pp 57–9; Dickson, *Dublin*, p. 416.
114 Crowe (ed.), *Dublin 1911*, pp 191–7.
115 Power, 'Boys' Brigade', pp 42, 46.
116 Conor Curran, *Soccer and society in Dublin: a history of association football in Ireland's capital* (Dublin, 2023), pp 65–71.

117 Dickson, *Dublin*, pp 409–10.
118 O'Brien, *Dear, dirty Dublin*, pp 62–3.
119 Power, 'Boys' Brigade', p. 48.
120 Paul Rouse, *Sport in Ireland: a history* (Oxford, 2015), pp 151–2.
121 Aaron Ó Maonaigh, '"Who were the shoneens?": Irish militant nationalists and association football, 1913–1923', *Soccer and Society*, 18:5–6 (2017), 632–8. See also, for example, Andrews, *Dublin made me*, pp 117–18.
122 Andrews, *Dublin made me*, p. 113.
123 For the image, see https://digital.ucd.ie/view/ucdlib:30860 (accessed 28 June 2019). For hurling: Kathleen Barry (BMH WS 731, p. 7).
124 Marie Coleman, 'McKee, Dick (Richard)', *DIB*, DOI: https://doi.org/10.3318/dib.005715.v3.
125 Marie Coleman, 'Traynor, Oscar', *DIB*, DOI: https://doi.org/10.3318/dib.008626.v1; Ó Maonaigh, 'Shoneens', 631, 638–9. Much later Traynor was president of the Football Association of Ireland.

CHAPTER TWO *Politics and activism in Dublin, 1912–14*

1 Alvin Jackson, 'The failure of unionism in Dublin, 1900', *Irish Historical Studies*, 26:104 (1989), 377.
2 Brian M. Walker, *Parliamentary election results in Ireland, 1801–1922* (Dublin, 1978), pp 344–9, 355–6, 367–8, 381–2; Marie Coleman, 'Nannetti, Joseph Patrick ('J.P.')', *DIB*, DOI: https://doi.org/10.3318/dib.006135.v1.
3 *II*, 26 Nov. 1913; Frank Whearity, 'The founding of the Irish Volunteers at Dublin's Rotunda Hall, 25 November 1913', *Dublin Historical Record*, 67:1 (2014), 73.
4 Brian Hanley, '"The layers of an onion": reflections on 1913, class and the memory of the Irish Revolution' in Conor McNamara and Padraig Yeates (eds), *The Dublin lockout 1913: new perspectives on class and war & its legacy* (Kildare, 2017), p. 149; *II*, 26 Nov. 1913; Marie Coleman, 'Macken, Peter Paul (Peadar)', *DIB*, DOI: https://doi.org/10.3318/dib.005227.v2.
5 Conor McNamara, 'Glorious forever? The political evolution of the Irish Citizen Army, 1913–1921' in McNamara & Yeates (eds), *Lockout*, pp 124–44.
6 Hanley, '"Layers of an onion"', p. 149. Michael Mallin, second-in-command from 1914, however, was a skilled silk weaver.
7 Thomas J. Morrissey, 'Walsh, William Joseph', *DIB*, DOI: https://doi.org/10.3318/dib.008905.v1.
8 Seamus Cullen, *Kildare: the Irish Revolution, 1912–23* (Dublin, 2020), p. 13; Georgina Clinton and Bridget Hourican, 'Peacocke, Joseph Ferguson', *DIB*, DOI: https://doi.org/10.3318/dib.007243.v1.
9 Nicola K. Morris, 'Traitors to their faith? Protestant clergy and the Ulster covenant of 1912', *New Hibernia Review*, 15:3 (2011), 22–3.
10 *DE*, 13 Jan. 1912, 16 Jan. 1912, 1 Feb. 1912.
11 Ibid., 30 Apr. 1913.
12 Ibid., 21 June 1912.
13 Martin Maguire, '"Our people": the Church of Ireland laity and the culture of community in Dublin since disestablishment' in Raymond Gillespie and W.G. Neely (eds), *The laity and the Church of Ireland, 1000–2000: all sorts and conditions* (Dublin, 2002), pp 280–4; Dickson, *Dublin*, pp 400–1, 470.
14 David Fitzpatrick, 'Instant history: 1912, 1916, 1918' in Fearghal McGarry and Richard S. Grayson (eds), *Remembering 1916: the Easter Rising, the Somme and the politics of memory in Ireland* (Cambridge, 2016), p. 65.

15 *Daily Express* (hereafter *DE*), 28 Sept. 1912.
16 Ibid., 30 Sept. 1912.
17 *Irish Independent* (hereafter *II*), 30 Sept. 1912.
18 *Saturday Herald*, 28 Sept. 1912.
19 *DE*, 28 Sept. 1912.
20 Ibid.
21 Cullen, *Kildare*, p. 13.
22 Morris, 'Traitors', 24–5; *Church of Ireland Gazette*, 20 Sept. 1912.
23 *Saturday Herald*, 28 Sept. 1912; *DE*, 30 Sept. 1912; *II*, 30 Sept. 1912.
24 Public Record Office of Northern Ireland (hereafter PRONI), Ulster Covenant and Women's Declaration digitized signature sheets (https://apps.proni.gov.uk/ulstercovenant/search.aspx) (accessed 22 July 2020). I am grateful to Desmond McCabe at PRONI for confirming that the Dublin covenant signatories have not survived.
25 *DE*, 30 Sept. 1912; PRONI, Ulster Covenant and Women's Declaration digitized signature sheets (https://apps.proni.gov.uk/ulstercovenant/search.aspx) (accessed 22 July 2020).
26 *Census of Ireland, 1911*, City (or County Borough) of Dublin, Table XXIV; County of Dublin, Table XXIV.
27 *DE*, 30 Sept. 1912.
28 Ibid.; *IT*, 30 Sept. 1912.
29 1901 and 1911 census returns, Hugh Robert Topping, Dublin (http://census.nationalarchives.ie/) (accessed 20 Sept. 2020).
30 *DE*, 29 Nov. 1912; 1911 census returns, Arthur E. Pomeroy, Dublin (http://census.nationalarchives.ie/) (accessed 20 Sept. 2020).
31 *1919 Annual report of the City of Dublin & Pembroke Unionist Association* (Dublin, 1919).
32 See, for example, attendees at the CDUA annual meeting in 1913 and members elected to the board of management: *DE*, 31 Mar. 1913.
33 Frank Barry, 'The southern unionist business community and the economics of home rule and secession' in Brian Hughes and Conor Morrissey (eds), *Southern Irish loyalism, 1912–1949* (Liverpool, 2020), pp 95–113.
34 *IT*, 30 Dec. 1912.
35 Ibid., 8 Jan. 1913.
36 Ibid., 10 May 1913.
37 *DE*, 28 Mar. 1914.
38 Dickson, *Dublin*, p. 434.
39 *DE*, 5 Jan. 1912.
40 Martin Maguire, 'The organization and activism of Dublin's Protestant working class, 1883–1935', *Irish Historical Studies*, 29:113 (1994), 70.
41 *IT*, 29 Nov. 1913; IUA, *Unionist demonstration: Dublin, 28 Nov. 1913* (Dublin, 1913), p. 45.
42 Wallace, 'Fighting for unionist home rule', 934; Maguire, 'Our people', pp 280–1.
43 *IT*, 27 Sept. 1912; *II*, 27 Sept. 1912.
44 Maguire, 'Our people', p 283.
45 *DE*, 19 Feb. 1912; 16 Nov. 1912.
46 Maguire, 'Protestant working class', 77.
47 *IT*, 10 Nov. 1913.
48 Ibid., 14 June 1935; *IT*, 25 Aug. 1964. The *Evening Herald* report on the find noted 120 to 140 rifles.
49 *DE*, 30 Sept. 1912.
50 Patrick Buckland, *Irish Unionism I: the Anglo-Irish and the new Ireland* (Dublin, 1972), pp 58–9.
51 David Fitzpatrick, *Descendancy: Irish Protestant histories since 1795* (Cambridge, 2014), pp 40–1.
52 Maguire, 'Our people', p. 281.

53 Buckland, *Irish Unionism I*, p. 28; R.B. McDowell, *Crisis and decline: the fate of the southern unionists* (Dublin, 1997), 52–3.
54 Conor Morrissey, *Protestant nationalists in Ireland, 1900–1923* (Cambridge, 2019), p. 16.
55 Ibid., pp 93, 110.
56 Senia Pašeta, *Irish nationalist women, 1900–1918* (Cambridge, 2013), pp 99–100.
57 Martin Maguire, 'Protestant republicans in the revolution and afterwards' in Ian d'Alton and Ida Milne (eds), *Protestant* and *Irish: the minority's search for place in independent Ireland* (Cork, 2019), pp 191–212; Foster, *Vivid faces*, pp 8–9.
58 Whearity, 'Irish Volunteers', 68.
59 Ibid., 66–81; CI Dublin, May 1913 (TNA, CO 904/93).
60 CI Dublin, May 1914, June 1914 (TNA, CO 904/93).
61 Ibid., June 1914.
62 Whearity, 'Irish Volunteers', 73.
63 Pašeta, *Nationalist women*, pp 128–47.
64 Jackson, 'Failure of unionism', 378–9.
65 Cullen, *Kildare*, p. 11; Declan Brady, *Culture, politics and local government in Fingal, 1891–1914* (Dublin, 2017), p. 33.
66 Brady, *Fingal*, p. 36.
67 *II*, 8 May 1914, 13 May 1914, 15 May 1914; *FJ*, 18 May 1914, 6 June 1914; *Dublin Evening Telegraph*, 9 June 1914; *DE*, 10 June 1914; *Drogheda Independent*, 14 June 1914.
68 Marie O'Neill, 'Dublin Corporation and the troubled times, 1914–1924', *Dublin Historical Record*, 47:1 (1994), 56.
69 Pašeta, *Nationalist women*, p. 18.
70 O'Neill, 'Corporation', 56; Diarmaid Ferriter, 'Harrison, Sarah Cecilia', *DIB*, DOI: https://doi.org/10.3318/dib.003826.v2.
71 Pašeta, *Nationalist women*, p. 80.
72 Frank Whearity, 'Mary Ellen "Molly" Adrien (1873–1949): Cumann na mBan volunteer', *Dublin Historical Record*, 69:2 (2016), 226–7.
73 Mary Sheahan, 'Dockrell, Margaret Sarah', *DIB*, DOI: https://doi.org/10.3318/dib.002647.v1. She was elected to Dublin County Council fourteen years later.
74 *IT*, 10 May 1913, 28 Apr. 1914.
75 Ibid., 17 Nov. 1913, 28 Apr. 1914.
76 Ibid., 30 Dec. 1912.
77 See IWSLGA minute books, 1912–1914 (https://www.nationalarchives.ie/article/minute-book-dublin-womens-suffrage-association-irish-womens-suffrage-local-government-association-1876-1913/) (accessed 27 Jan. 2022).
78 McDowell, *Crisis*, p. 33.
79 Pašeta, *Nationalist women*, pp 63–80. For pro-suffrage Dublin MPs, see pp 71, 225, 262.
80 Ibid., p. 76.
81 Crowe (ed.), *Dublin 1911*, pp 71–6.
82 Pašeta, *Nationalist women*, pp 72–3, 79–80.
83 Daly, *Deposed capital*, pp 72–3.
84 Hanley, 'Farm labourers', 143–9.
85 Padraig Yeates, *Lockout: Dublin 1913* (Dublin, 2000), pp xiii–xxiv.
86 Hughes, *16 lives: Michael Mallin*.
87 The seminal account of the lockout remains Yeates, *Lockout*. See also, McNamara & Yeates (eds), *The Dublin lockout*, which includes a very useful descriptive chronology and Dickson's concise and insightful discussion in *Dublin*, pp 428–42.
88 Hanley, 'Layers', pp 144–5.
89 Yeates, *Lockout*, p. 27.
90 Cullen, *Kildare*, pp 19–22.

91 Hanley, 'Farm labourers', 150–2.
92 Brady, *Fingal*, pp 37–9.
93 CI Dublin, Apr. 1912 (TNA, CO 904/89); CI Dublin, Oct. 1913 (TNA, CO 904/91).
94 CI Dublin, Sept. 1913 (TNA, CO 904/91).
95 Hanley, 'Farm labourers', 152–3.
96 CI Dublin, Nov. 1913 and Dec. 1913 (TNA, CO 904/91).
97 Coyle, 'Larkinism', 176–90; Yeates, *Lockout*, pp 241, 258.
98 Yeates, *Lockout*, p. 154.
99 CI Dublin, June 1914 (TNA, CO 904/93).
100 Dickson, *Dublin*, p. 433.
101 Anastasia Dukova, *The history of the Dublin Metropolitan Police and its legacy* (London, 2016), p. 114.
102 Daly, *Deposed capital*, p. 319.
103 Eunan O'Halpin and Daithí Ó Corráin, *The dead of the Irish Revolution* (New Haven and London, 2020), p. 26.
104 Coyle, 'Larkinism', 185.
105 Holmpatrick to George Fowler, 7 July 1914 (FCCLA, Holmpatrick Estate papers (hereafter HEP) HEP/NA/11–13).
106 Holmpatrick to George Fowler, 5 July 1914 (ibid.).
107 CI Dublin, June 1914 (TNA, CO 904/93).
108 Ibid., July 1914, Aug. 1914 (TNA, CO 904/94).
109 Ibid., July 1914 (TNA, CO 904/94).
110 Dickon, *Dublin*, p. 433; Richard S. Grayson, *Dublin's great wars: the First World War, the Easter Rising and the Irish Revolution* (Cambridge, 2018), pp 21–2.
111 Quoted in Donal Fallon, 'Remembering – and forgetting – Bachelor's Walk' (https://comeheretome.com/2019/10/28/remembering-and-forgetting-bachelors-walk/) (accessed 10 July 2023).
112 Minutes of quarterly meeting of Dublin County Council, 31 July 1914 (Fingal County Council Archives (hereafter FCCA), CC/01/14).
113 Fallon, 'Bachelor's Walk'.
114 Hanley, 'Farm labourers', 161–2.

CHAPTER THREE *Dublin's response to war, 1914–16*

1 Thomas King Moylan, 'A Dubliner's diary 1914–1918' (National Library of Ireland (hereafter NLI), MS 9,620).
2 Catriona Pennell, 'Going to war' in John Horne (ed.), *Our war: Ireland and the Great War* (Dublin, 2008), pp 38–9.
3 'Dubliner's diary' (NLI, MS 9,620).
4 *DE*, 5 Aug. 1914.
5 *II*, 5 Aug. 1914.
6 *IT*, 5 Aug. 1914.
7 *Evening Herald* (hereafter *EH*), 5 Aug. 1914.
8 *II*, 5 Aug. 1914.
9 *DE*, 5 Aug. 1914.
10 'Dubliner's diary' (NLI, MS 9,620).
11 Grayson, *Great wars*, p. 32.
12 *IT*, 6 Aug. 1914.
13 'Dubliner's diary' (NLI, MS 9,620).
14 *IT*, 6 Aug. 1914.
15 Catriona Pennell, *A kingdom united: popular responses to the outbreak of the First World War in Britain and Ireland* (Oxford, 2012), pp 165–7.

16 'Dubliner's diary' (NLI, MS 9,620).
17 *EH,* 10 Aug. 1914.
18 CI Dublin, Aug. 1914 (TNA, CO 904/94).
19 Séamus Ó Maitiú, 'The home front: the Dublin townships and the First World War', *Dublin Historical Record*, 69:1 (2016), 71–3.
20 Minutes of adjourned quarterly meeting of Dublin County Council, 27 Aug. 1914 (FCCA, CC/01/14).
21 Ibid., 24 Sept. 1914.
22 Terence Dooley, *Burning the Big House: the story of the Irish country house in a time of war and revolution* (New Haven and London, 2022), p. 39.
23 Buckland, *Unionism I*, p. 35.
24 Ian d'Alton, 'Loyal to what? Identity and motivation in southern Irish Protestant involvement in two world wars' in Hughes and Morrissey (eds), *Southern Irish loyalism*, p. 120.
25 Buckland, *Unionism I*, pp 32–5.
26 *II*, 14 Aug. 1914.
27 Holmpatrick to George Fowler, 24 Apr. 1914, May 1914 (FCCA, HEP/NA/11–13).
28 *II*, 28 May 1915; *IT*, 27 May 1915.
29 Holmpatrick to George Fowler, 7 Aug. 1914 (FCCA, HEP/NA/11–13).
30 *IT*, 6 Mar. 1915.
31 *II*, 28 May 1915; *IT*, 27 May 1915.
32 *FJ*, 17 July 1915.
33 Fionnuala Walsh, *Irish women and the Great War* (Cambridge, 2020), pp 25–9.
34 Niamh Gallagher, *Ireland and the Great War: a social and political history* (London, 2020), p. 37.
35 Eileen Reilly, 'Women and voluntary war work' in Adrian Gregory and Senia Paŝeta (eds), *Ireland and the Great War: 'a war to unite us all'* (Manchester, 2002), pp 53–4.
36 Monica Roberts collection (https://repository.dri.ie/catalog/v9807j056) (accessed 29 June 2023).
37 Gallagher, *Great War*, p. 32.
38 Ibid., pp 35–7.
39 Padraig Yeates, *A city in wartime: Dublin, 1914–1918* (Dublin, 2011), p. 29.
40 Joseph V. Lawless (BMH WS 1,043, pp 11–13).
41 Michael Laffan, *The resurrection of Ireland: the Sinn Féin party, 1916–1923* (Cambridge, 1999), pp 128–9; Daithí Ó Corráin and Gerard Hanley, *Cathal Brugha: 'an indomitable spirit'* (Dublin, 2022), pp 46–7.
42 Voting by battalions and companies for and against Redmond, Dublin City Volunteers, *c.*Sept. 1914 (NLI, Maurice Moore papers, MS 10,548/4/101). Oscar Traynor remembered that in his company the split was 'something like 80 to 50 in favour of the National Volunteers', and in Moore's figures 'F' Company, 2nd battalion split 100 to 15: Oscar Traynor (BMH WS 340, p. 1).
43 Analysis of voting for and against Mr Redmond among County Dublin Volunteer Corps, *c.*Sept. 1914 (NLI, Moore papers, MS 10,548/4/101).
44 CI Dublin, Nov. 1914 (TNA, CO 904/95).
45 Ó Corráin & Hanley, *Brugha*, p. 47.
46 CI Dublin, Sept. 1914 (TNA, CO 904/95).
47 Joseph V. Lawless (BMH WS 1,043, p. 14).
48 Thomas Peppard (BMH WS 1,399, p. 2).
49 Joseph O'Connor (BMH WS 157, p. 12).
50 Gerald Byrne (BMH WS 143, p. 4).
51 CI Dublin, Sept. 1914 (CO 904/95).

52 See correspondence in Maurice Moore papers, MS 10,544/1, MS 10,548/4 and MS 10,548/5, including, for example, Laurence Nugent to Maurice Moore, 18 Dec. 1914 regarding a miniature rifle for Dundrum company (MS 10,548/4/19).
53 Laurence Kettle to Maurice Moore, 2 Jan. 1915; M. Donnell to Fitzroy Hemphill, 3 Feb. 1915 (NLI, Moore papers, MS 10,548/4/26).
54 P. McEntee to Moore, 6 Aug. 1915 (NLI, Moore papers, MS 10,548/4/48).
55 Frank O'Curran to Moore, 10 Dec. 1915 (NLI, Moore papers, MS 10,548/4/69).
56 J. O'Donovan to Moore, 13 Feb. 1916 (NLI, Moore papers, MS 10,548/4/71).
57 Colonel C. Phillips to Moore, 17 Feb. 1916; Moore to Phillips, 18 Feb. 1916 (NLI, Moore papers, MS 10,548/4/81).
58 CI Dublin, Aug. 1914 to Dec. 1915 (TNA, CO 904/94–8).
59 Grayson, *Great wars*, p. 38; Keith Jeffery, *Ireland and the Great War* (Cambridge, 2000), p. 39.
60 Grayson, *Great wars*, pp 47–8.
61 CI Dublin, Oct. 1914, Nov. 1914, Dec. 1914 (TNA, CO 904/95).
62 Grayson, *Great wars*, p. 33.
63 Mark Tierney, Paul Bowen and David Fitzpatrick, 'Recruiting posters' in David Fitzpatrick (ed.), *Ireland and the First World War* (Dublin, 1986), pp 47–58.
64 Quoted in Grayson, *Great wars*, p. 33.
65 *IT*, 24 Sept. 1914.
66 Ibid., 25 Sept. 1914.
67 Thomas J. Morrissey, *William J. Walsh, archbishop of Dublin, 1841–1921* (Dublin, 2000), p. 271.
68 Jérôme aan de Wiel, 'Archbishop Walsh and Mgr. Curran's opposition to the British war effort in Dublin, 1914–1918', *Irish Sword*, 22:88 (2000), 195; *IT*, 10 May 1915.
69 Gallagher, *Great War*, p. 34; Walsh, *Irish women*, p. 34.
70 Grayson, *Great wars*, pp 38–42.
71 Yeates, *Wartime*, p. 61.
72 Reilly, 'Women', p. 54; Certificate from the Red Cross Society to Edward Lee, 1919 (DCLA, AR/ADD/014/02/02/08). See also certificates presented to Annie Lee (Dublin City Library and Archive (hereafter DCLA) DCLA/AR/ADD/ 104/02/02/05–07).
73 Grayson, *Great wars*, pp 33–8.
74 Timothy Bowman, William Butler and Michael Wheatley, *The disparity of sacrifice: Irish recruitment to the British armed forces, 1914–1918* (Liverpool, 2020), p. 57.
75 Grayson, *Great wars*, pp 40, 368.
76 See Chapter 5.
77 Grayson, *Great wars*, p. 40.
78 Fingal Roll of Honour (FCCA).
79 Tom Burke, 'Whence came the Royal Dublin Fusiliers?', *Irish Sword*, 24 (2005), 451–8.
80 Bowman et al., *Disparity*, p. 56.
81 See Corporal Henry Kavanagh Collection, 1894–1916 (DCA, RDFA/003).
82 Grayson, *Great wars*, pp 45–6.
83 Lar Joye, 'The fighting Irish, 1914–1916', *Defence Forces Review* (2016), 56–7.
84 Yeates, *Wartime*, pp 56–63.
85 Ibid., pp 44–8.
86 David Fitzpatrick, 'The logic of collective sacrifice: Ireland and the British army, 1914–1918', *Historical Journal*, 38:4 (1995), 1029–30.
87 Death scroll honouring Corporal Henry Kavanagh, 1916 (DCA, RDFA/003/16).
88 Grayson, *Great wars*, pp 40, 98.

CHAPTER FOUR *Dublin city's 1916 Rising*

1 'The personal experience of Miss L. Stokes during the Sinn Féin Rebellion of 1916' (Trinity College Dublin (hereafter TCD), MS 11,507). The account was later published in *Nonplus*, Winter 1960.

2 F.X. Martin, 'The 1916 Rising: a "coup d'état or a bloody protest"?', *Studia Hibernica*, 8 (1968), 132.
3 The most authoritative accounts of the origins, organization and outbreak of the Rising are Brian Barton and Michael Foy, *The Easter Rising* (2nd ed., Dublin, 2011); Charles Townshend, *Easter 1916: the Irish rebellion* (London, 2005); Fearghal McGarry, *The Rising: Ireland: 1916* (2nd ed., Oxford, 2016).
4 Brian Hughes, Billy Campbell and Susan Schreibman, 'Contested memories: revisiting the Battle of Mount Street Bridge, 1916', *British Journal for Military History*, 4:1 (2017), 2–22.
5 Stokes diary (TCD, MS 11,507).
6 McGarry, *Rising*, pp 79–119.
7 Wesley Hanna to his family, 27 Apr.–2 July 1916 (Private, http://letters1916.maynooth university.ie/).
8 Elsie Mahaffy's 'book' of the Easter Rising, *c.*June 1917 (TCD, MS 2,074).
9 Alfred Fannin to Edward Fannin, 10 May 1916 (TCD, MS 10,841).
10 Alfred Fannin to Edward Fannin, 25 Apr.–6 May 1916 (ibid.).
11 James Stephens, *The insurrection in Dublin* (Dublin, 1916), pp 13, 19.
12 Elsie Mahaffy book (TCD, MS 2,074).
13 *Irish Life*, 12 May 1916, p. 118. See also *'Irish Life': A record of the Irish rebellion of 1916* (Dublin, 1916), p. 33.
14 *IT*, 2 May 1916.
15 John Dillon to Elizabeth Mathew, Apr. 1916 (unsent) (TCD, MS 9820).
16 *IT*, 25 Apr. 1916.
17 Ibid., 27 Apr. 1916.
18 See also Alvin Jackson, 'Mrs Foster and the rebels: Irish unionist approaches to the Easter Rising, 1916–2016', *Irish Historical Studies*, 42:161 (May 2018), 146–7.
19 O'Halpin & Ó Corráin, *Dead*, pp 65–6.
20 Dot to Cecil Harmsworth, 11 May 1916 (NLI, MS 46,627).
21 'Returns of persons killed and wounded by the rebels' (TNA, WO 35/69/1); Padraig Yeates, *A city in wartime: Dublin, 1914–1918* (Dublin, 2011), pp 108–9.
22 Glasnevin Trust, *1916 Necrology 485*. See, for example, Elsie Mahaffy's reference to a young woman who 'had only left her poor house to try and buy food for her 6 hungry children' and was 'mortally wounded': Elsie Mahaffy book (TCD, MS 2074); Sir John Robert O'Connell in Mick O'Farrell (ed.), *1916: what the people saw* (Cork, 2013), p. 176.
23 O'Halpin & Ó Corráin, *Dead*, p. 87.
24 Yeates, *Wartime*, p. 110; Las Fallon, *Dublin Fire Brigade and the Irish Revolution* (Dublin, 2012), pp 40–52.
25 'Unarmed persons killed or wounded in the D[ublin].M[etropolitan]. Police District', 26 May 1916 (TNA, WO 35/69/1).
26 *DE*, 10 May 1916.
27 See, for example, James McGuire (ed.), '"To tell you all about it": a letter from Mrs Marion Kelleher to her family written in the immediate aftermath of the Easter Rising in Dublin', *Analecta Hibernica*, 47 (2016), 108; Stephens, *Insurrection*, p. 7.
28 O'Farrell (ed.), *What the people saw*, pp 271–3.
29 Lucy McDiarmid, *At home in the revolution: what women said and did in 1916* (Dublin, 2015), Chapter 2.
30 Monica Roberts' diary of Easter Rising 1916 (DCLA, Royal Dublin Fusiliers Association papers, 01/08/048); Denis Johnston, 'A schoolboy in the Rebellion' (TCD, MS 10,066/179).
31 Isabelle Fleming, 'Dublin during the reign of terror: at the cross roads', typescript, n.d. (NLI, MS 46,267).
32 *DE*, 8 May 1916.

33 *IT*, 2 May 1916.
34 Alf Fannin to Edward Fannin, 25 Apr.–6 May 1916 (TCD, MS 10,841); W.G. Smith's account of the Easter Rising, n.d. (NLI, MS 24,952).
35 Jackson, 'Mrs Foster and the rebels', 148.
36 Monica Roberts' diary of Easter Rising 1916 (DCLA, Royal Dublin Fusiliers Association papers, 01/08/048).
37 Townshend, *Easter*, pp 183–213.
38 Stephens, *Insurrection*, p. 40.
39 *DE*, 8 May 1916.
40 Alf Fannin to Ed Fannin, 10 May 1916 (TCD, MS 10,841).
41 McGuire (ed.), 'Kelleher', 113.
42 See, for example, Mary Martin diary, 26 Apr. 1916 (NLI, MS 34,356A); Eileen Chance diary, 24 Apr. 1916–2 May 1916, typescript (TCD, Misc photocopy 181) and *Sunday Independent*, 23 Apr. 1989; Clara Cullen (ed.), *The world upturning: Elsie Henry's Irish wartime diaries, 1913–1919* (Dublin, 2012), pp 146, 149.
43 Frances Taylor diary, 24 Apr.–4 May, typescript (TCD, MS 9,932/60). See also, Frederick William Kidd to George Kidd, 29 Apr.–4 May 1916 (TCD, MS 9,932/135/2).
44 John Dillon to Elizabeth Mathew (TCD, MS 9,820).
45 Henry Robinson, *Memories: wise and otherwise* (London, 1923), pp 238–9; Horace Curzon Plunkett diary, 28 & 29 Apr., 1 May 1916 (NLI, Horace Plunkett papers, MS 42,222/36); Yeates, *Wartime*, p. 119.
46 John Dillon to Elizabeth Mathew (TCD, MS 9,820).
47 Margaret Mitchell to Flora, 24–7 Apr. 1916 (NLI, MS 24,553/1); Cullen (ed.), *World upturning*, p. 149.
48 Douglas Hyde diary, Easter 1916 (NLI, Douglas Hyde papers, MS 17,770).
49 Typescript letter from member of the Shackleton family, Lucan to 'C', 25 Apr.–4 May 1916 (Private, http://letters1916.maynoothuniversity.ie/).
50 *DE*, 15 May 1916.
51 Margaret Mitchell to Flora (NLI, MS 24,553/1); Dorothy Stopford diary (NLI, MS 16,063).
52 Eileen Chance diary (TCD, Misc photocopy 181).
53 Frances Taylor diary (TCD, MS 9,932/60); Alf Fannin to Ed Fannin, 25 Apr.–6 May 1916 (TCD, MS 10,841).
54 Sarah Harden to Donald Harden, 27 Apr.–4 May 1916 (Private, http://letters1916.maynoothuniversity.ie/).
55 Nellie May Preston to Albert Woodman, 4 May 1916 (ibid.).
56 Eileen Chance diary (TCD, Misc photocopy 181).
57 Dorothy Stopford diary (NLI, MS 16,063).
58 Thomas Johnson diary, Easter 1916, manuscript (NLI, Thomas Johnson papers, MS 17,116(1)).
59 John Dillon to Elizabeth Mathew (TCD, MS 9,820).
60 Keith Jeffery (ed.), *The GPO and the Easter Rising* (Dublin, 2006), p. 73.
61 Fred Kidd to George Kidd (TCD, MS 9,932/135/2).
62 John White, 'Insult and the locked-out workers of 1913' in McNamara & Yeates (eds), *Lockout*, p. 85.
63 Thomas Johnson diary (NLI, Johnson papers, MS 17,116(1)).
64 Mary Martin diary, 26 Apr. 1916 (http://dh.tcd.ie/martindiary/); 'The personal experience of Miss L. Stokes' (TCD, MS 11,507); Margaret Mitchell to Flora [May 1916] (NLI, MS 24,553/1); John Dillon to Elizabeth Mathew (TCD, MS 9,820); Fred Kidd to George Kidd (TCD, MS 9,932/135/2).
65 *Evening Mail*, 4 May 1916.
66 Jeffery (ed.), *GPO*, pp 78–9.

67 Douglas Hyde diary (NLI, Hyde papers, MS 17,770); 'The personal experience of Miss L. Stokes' (TCD, MS 11,507); Frances Taylor diary (TCD, MS 9,932/60); O'Farrell (ed.), *What the people saw*, p. 210; *DE*, 6 May 1916.
68 Stephens, *Insurrection*, p. 26.
69 McGarry, *Rising*, pp 144–8.
70 *Irish Life*, 12 May 1916, p. 142; John Joly, *Reminiscences and anticipations* (Dublin, 1920), p. 260. See also Eileen Costello (BMH WS 1,184, p. 6); John Dillon to Elizabeth Mathew (TCD, MS 9,820); Elsie Mahaffy book (TCD, MS 2,074); *DE*, 6 May 1916.
71 *DE*, 11 May 1916.
72 See *DE*, 11 May, 12 May 1916.
73 Ibid., 11 May 1916.
74 Yeates, *Wartime*, p. 98.
75 Blair Carphin to Jo Carphin, 28 Apr. 1916 (Private, http://letters1916.maynoothuniversity.ie/).
76 Monica Roberts' diary of Easter Rising 1916 (DCLA, Royal Dublin Fusiliers Association papers, 01/08/048).
77 *IT*, 2 May 1916.
78 Justin Dolan Stover, *Enduring ruin: environmental destruction during the Irish Revolution* (Dublin, 2022), pp 8–18.
79 Elsie Mahaffy book (TCD, MS 2,074).
80 Jeffrey, *The GPO*, p. 79; Wesley Hanna letter (Private, http://letters1916.maynoothuniversity.ie/).
81 Gladys Johnson to Ellen Vickery, 15 May 1916 (Private, http://letters1916.maynoothuniversity.ie/).
82 Nellie May Preston to Albert Woodman (Private, http://letters1916.maynoothuniversity.ie/).
83 John Ross, *The years of my pilgrimage: random reminiscences* (London, 1924), p. 264.
84 *IT*, 25 Apr. 1916, 26 Apr. 1916; O'Farrell (ed.), *What the people saw*, p. 108.
85 Tomás Irish, *Trinity in war and revolution, 1912–1923* (Dublin, 2015), pp 141–2, 150.
86 Mary Martin diary, 28 Apr. 1916 (http://dh.tcd.ie/martindiary/).
87 *Sinn Féin Rebellion Handbook: Easter 1916*, published by the *Weekly Irish Times* (Dublin, 1917), p. 253.
88 Horace Plunkett diaries, 28 Apr. 1916 (NLI, Plunkett papers, MS 42,222/36). Alfred Charles William Harmsworth, Viscount Northcliffe, owner of the *Daily Mail*, was born in Dublin.
89 Monica Roberts' diary of Easter Rising 1916 (DCLA, Royal Dublin Fusiliers Association papers, 01/08/048).
90 'The personal experience of Miss L. Stokes' (TCD, MS 11,507); Eileen Chance diary (TCD, Misc photocopy 181); Frances Taylor diary (TCD, MS 9,932/60).
91 Douglas Hyde diary (NLI, Hyde papers, MS 17,770). The three-line notice is found as a cutting in Elsie Mahaffy book (TCD, MS 2,074). See, also, Stephens, *Insurrection*, p. 21; Alfred Fannin to Edward Fannin, 25 Apr.–6 May 1916 (TCD, MS 10,841); Frederick William Kidd to Eric Kidd, 25 Apr.–2 May 1916 (TCD, MS 9,932/135/1) and Sarah Harden to Donald Harden (Private, http://letters1916.maynoothuniversity.ie/). Frances Taylor recorded in her diary that she was unable to obtain a copy: Frances Taylor diary (TCD, MS 9,932/60).
92 *Sinn Féin Rebellion Handbook*, p. 253.
93 *IT*, 19 Apr. 1976. It is the uncensored copy that is currently available on the Pro Quest Irish Times Digital Archive for that date.
94 Mark O'Brien, *Th*e Irish Times: *a history* (Dublin, 2008), pp 48–9. James Stephens and Horace Plunkett seem to have read Wednesday's edition, but are unusual in remarking on this: Stephens, *Insurrection*, p. 34; Horace Plunkett diaries, 26 Apr. 1916 (NLI, Plunkett papers, MS 42,222/36).
95 See Stephens, *Insurrection*, pp 23–4, 28–30, 33–4, 49–52, 56.
96 Douglas Hyde diary (NLI, Hyde papers, MS 17,770).

97 Horace Curzon Plunkett diaries, 28 Apr. 1916 (NLI, Plunkett papers, MS 42,222/36).
98 Townshend, *Easter*, pp 204–5, 243–68.
99 Cullen (ed.), *The world upturning*, p. 161; Dorothy Stopford diary (http://dh.tcd.ie/pricediary/).
100 *EM*, 4 May 1916.
101 *DE*, 6 May 1916; Yeates, *A city in wartime*, p. 120.
102 Stephens, *Insurrection*, p. 73; Jeffery, *The GPO*, p. 89.
103 Ronald Nesbitt, *At Arnott's of Dublin, 1843–1993* (Dublin, 1993), pp 65–9.
104 *DE*, 4 May, 8 May, 9 May, 10 May 1916. Several other traders in the city placed similar advertisements in the papers.
105 Charles E. Jacob to James Brennan, 6 May 1916 (NAI, Chief Secretary's Office Registered Papers (hereafter CSORP) CSORP/1916/7645/1); *DE*, 6 May 1916.
106 Alfred Millar to Major General L.B. Friend, 10 May 1916 (TNA, WO 35/69/1); *Evening Mail*, 8 May 1916.
107 Padraig Yeates, 'The politics of Dublin City Council and the 1916 Rising' in John Gibney (ed.), *Dublin City Council and the 1916 Rising* (Dublin, 2016), pp 23–5.
108 Daithí Ó Corráin, '"They blew up the best portion of our city and … it is their duty to replace it": compensation and reconstruction in the aftermath of the Easter Rising', *Irish Historical Studies*, 39:154 (Nov. 2014), 272–95.
109 'Prevention of Epidemic', May 1916 (NLI, POL/1910-20/2).
110 Elsie Mahaffy book (TCD, MS 2074); see also *DE*, 14 May.
111 Yeates, *Wartime*, p. 118.
112 McGuire (ed.), 'Kelleher', 118.
113 Thomas Johnson diary (NLI, Johnson papers, MS 17,116(1)).
114 See, for example, Tom to Kitty, 2 May 1916 (TCD, Misc photocopy 184); Blair Carphin to Jo Carphin (Private, http://letters1916.maynoothuniversity.ie/); Dot to Cecil Harmsworth (NLI, MS 46,627); Wesley Hanna letter (Private, http://letters1916.maynoothuniversity.ie/); Wesley Hanna letter (Private, http://letters1916.maynoothuniversity.ie/); Cullen (ed.), *World upturning*, p. 161.
115 Elsie Mahaffy book (TCD, MS 2,074); Jackson, 'Mrs Foster and the rebels', 147–8; Denis Johnston, 'A schoolboy in the Rebellion' (TCD, MS 10,066/179); Fitzpatrick, 'Instant histories', p. 70.
116 Elsie Mahaffy book (TCD, MS 2,074); Jeffery (ed.), *GPO*, pp 25, 36, 41, 69.
117 Thomas King Moylan, 'A Dubliner's diary, 1914–1918' (NLI, MS 9,620).
118 Richard Hoskin diary (TCD, MS 10,073); Notice and agenda for a meeting of the Irish Builders Co-operative Society, n.d. (NLI, MS 16,650/1/22); O'Farrell, *People*, p. 22.
119 Shackleton letter (Private, http://letters1916.maynoothuniversity.ie/).
120 Jackson, 'Mrs Foster and the rebels', 149.
121 *EM*, 4 May 1916.
122 Wesley Hanna letter (Private, http://letters1916.maynoothuniversity.ie/).
123 McGuire (ed.), 'Kelleher', 120.
124 Yeates, *Wartime*, p. 106.
125 Edward H. Andrews to Arthur Bigge, 5 May 1916 (NAI, CSORP/1916/5611).
126 Ó Corráin, 'Compensation', 272.
127 *IT*, 28 Apr.–1 May 1916, 6 May, 10 May 1916; *FJ*, 26 Apr.–5 May 1916, 8 May 1916; *II*, 10 May, 12 May 1916.
128 *DE*, 11 May 1916.
129 Ibid., 16 May 1916.
130 *The Times*, 6 May 1916; *DE*, 6 May 1916; Thomas J. Morrissey, 'Walsh, William Joseph', *DIB*, DOI: https://doi.org/10.3318/dib.008905.v1.

131 Yeates, *Wartime*, pp 127–8.
132 Minutes of special meeting of Dublin County Council, 9 May 1916 (FCCA, CC/01/16).
133 Yeates, *Wartime*, p. 125.
134 *Sinn Féin Rebellion Handbook*, p. 253.
135 Darragh Gannon, *Proclaiming a republic: Ireland, 1916 and the national collection* (Dublin, 2016).
136 *EM*, 13 May 1916.
137 Charles Dalton, *With the Dublin Brigade: espionage and assassination with Michael Collins' intelligence unit* (Cork, 2014 [1929]), p. 51.
138 Elsie Mahaffy book (TCD, MS 2074).
139 Tom Dolan to Dolly Dolan, 11 May 1916 (Private, http://letters1916.maynoothuniversity.ie/).
140 McGarry, *Rising*, p. 282.
141 Brian Hughes, '"Well may we be proud of him": living with the deaths of the Easter Rising leaders, 1916–17' in Lisa Marie Griffith and Ciarán Wallace (eds), *Grave matters: death and dying in Dublin, 1500 to the present* (Dublin, 2016), pp 187–97.
142 Caoimhe Nic Dháibhéid, 'The Irish National Aid Association and the radicalization of public opinion in Ireland, 1916–1918', *Historical Journal*, 55:3 (2012), 705–29.
143 Elsie Mahaffy book (TCD, MS 2074).
144 *IT*, 23 Apr. 2005.
145 Andrew McDonnell (BMH WS 1,768, p. 23).
146 Joseph V. Lawless (BMH WS 1,043, pp 68–77); James O'Connor (BMH WS 142, pp 2–3); Michael McAllister (BMH WS 1,494, pp 7–9); Charles Weston (BMH WS 149, pp 7–9).
147 Peter F. Whearity, *The Easter Rising of 1916 in north Co. Dublin: a Skerries perspective* (Dublin, 2013).
148 *Drogheda Independent*, 13 May 1916.
149 CI Dublin, May–Dec. 1916 (TNA, CO 904/100–101).
150 CI Dublin, Feb. 1917 (TNA, CO 904/102).
151 T.W. Lyster to Edward O'Farrell, 8 May 1916 (NAI, CSORP/1916/5611).

CHAPTER FIVE *Sinn Féin and its enemies: from the GPO to the Dáil, 1916–18*

1 Buckland, *Unionism I*, pp 39–40.
2 D.G. Boyce, 'British opinion, Ireland and the war, 1916–1918', *Historical Journal*, 17:3 (1974), 579–84; Alvin Jackson, *Judging Redmond & Carson* (Dublin, 2018), pp 188–90.
3 *II*, 25 July 1916; *EH*, 25 July 1916.
4 Charles Townshend, *The partition: Ireland divided, 1885–1925* (London, 2022), pp 102–3.
5 Jackson, *Judging*, p. 190.
6 Jérôme aan de Wiel, 'Archbishop Walsh and Mgr Curran's opposition to the British war effort in Dublin, 1914–1918', *Irish Sword*, 22:88 (2000), 193.
7 *IT*, 25 July 1916.
8 Yeates, *Wartime*, p. 165.
9 *DE*, 7 July 1917.
10 Yeates, *Wartime*, p. 177.
11 Laffan, *Resurrection*, pp 49–56.
12 *Hansard (Commons)*, 23 May 1916, vol. 82, cols. 1955–9.
13 Ibid., vol. 82, cols. 1955–9, 1961–3, 1964; 24 May 1916, vol. 82, cols. 2077-81; 25 May 1916, vol. 82, col. 2265; 31 May 1916, vol. 82, cols. 2681-6.
14 Ibid., 12 July 1916, vol. 84, cols. 320–1.
15 Ibid., 10 May 1916, vol. 82, cols. 629–30.

16 *II*, 23 Dec. 1916.
17 Yeates, *Wartime*, p. 157.
18 Ibid., pp 188–9.
19 Irish, *Trinity*, p. 185; Charles Townshend, *The republic: the fight for Irish independence* (London, 2013), p. 4.
20 Townshend, *Partition*, p. 117.
21 *II*, 25 July 1917.
22 *EH*, 25 July 1917.
23 Jackson, *Judging*, p. 193.
24 Buckland, *Irish Unionism I*, pp 83–145.
25 *IT*, 10 Apr. 1917.
26 Ibid., 9 Apr. 1917.
27 *IT*, 10 Apr. 1917.
28 Ibid.
29 Thomas J. Morrissey, *Archbishop William J. Walsh: archbishop of Dublin, 1841–1921* (Dublin, 2000), pp 300–1; 'Archbishop Walsh writes that Ireland has been sold. A call for votes for Joe McGuinness', May 1917 (NLI, EPH C88).
30 CI Dublin, Apr. 1916–July 1917 (TNA, CO 904/99–103).
31 CI Dublin, Sept. 1917 (TNA, CO 904/104).
32 Townshend, *Republic*, p. 5.
33 Grayson, *Great wars*, pp 232–3; O'Halpin and Ó Corráin, *Dead*, p. 102.
34 *Hansard (Commons)*, 11 June 1917, vol. 94, cols. 595–7.
35 *EH*, 15 June 1916.
36 Yeates, *Wartime*, p. 196.
37 See, for example, 'Crowds on Westland Row in Dublin waiting to meet prisoners released under general amnesty, taken from the railway bridge at Westland Row Station' (NLI Keogh Photographic Collection, KE 125); 'Arrival of train with released prisoners at Pearse Station, crowds on platform' (NLI, Keogh Photographic Collection, KE 126); 'Released prisoners outside Pearse Station [*sic*], crowds, taken from elevated vantage point' (NLI, Keogh Photographic Collection, KE 128).
38 Yeates, *Wartime*, pp 196–7.
39 *EH*, 18 June 1916.
40 Ibid., 19 June 1916.
41 *II*, 22 June 1916.
42 Yeates, *Wartime*, pp 144–6.
43 CI Dublin, Oct. 1917, Mar. 1918, Oct. 1918 (TNA, CO 904/104, 105, 107).
44 Bowman et al., *Disparity*, pp 76–7.
45 CI Dublin, July 1918 (TNA, CO 904/106).
46 Ibid., June 1917 (TNA, CO 904/103).
47 Ibid., May–June 1916 (TNA, CO 904/100).
48 Ibid., Sept. 1916 (TNA, CO 904/101).
49 Ibid., Feb. 1918, June 1918 (TNA, CO 904/105, 106).
50 Yeates, *Wartime*, pp 67, 137, 186–7.
51 *Hansard (Commons)*, 7 June 1917, vol. 94, cols. 309–10.
52 Ibid., 12 June 1917, vol. 94, cols. 759–60.
53 *EH*, 1 Dec. 1917.
54 *Hansard (Commons)*, 21 Nov. 1917, vol. 94, cols. 654–5.
55 Ibid., 29 Nov. 1917, vol. 99, cols. 2325–6w.
56 *EH*, 1 Dec. 1917.
57 *II*, 1 Dec. 1917.

58 *IT*, 1 Dec. 1917.
59 *EH*, 1 Dec. 1917.
60 Dickson, *Dublin*, pp 457–8.
61 Yeates, *Wartime*, pp 134–5, 258–63.
62 *Constabulary Gazette*, 24 Feb. 1917.
63 Diary of Mary Martin, 1 Jan.–25 May 1916 (NLI, MS 34,256A).
64 Grayson, *Great wars*, pp 228–9, 256.
65 *IT*, 3 Apr. 1918.
66 CI Dublin, Oct. 1917 (TNA, CO 904/104).
67 Ibid., Nov. 1917 (Ibid.).
68 Townshend, *Republic*, p. 5.
69 CI Dublin, Dec. 1918 (TNA, CO 904/107).
70 Frank Henderson (BMH WS 821, p. 6).
71 Thomas Tormey, 'Scotland's Easter Rising veterans and the Irish Revolution', *Studi Irlandesi*, 9 (2019), 285.
72 Andrews, *Dublin made me*, pp 99–101.
73 Based on a sample of 150 Dublin men who applied for military service pensions for Easter Rising service only.
74 See Eunan O'Halpin, 'Cosgrave, William Thomas', *DIB*, DOI: https://doi.org/10.3318/dib.002077.v1; Patrick Maume, 'O'Kelly, Seán Thomas (Ó Ceallaigh, Seán Tomás)', *DIB*, DOI: https://doi.org/10.3318/dib.006840.v1.
75 Frank Henderson (BMH WS 821, pp 6–7).
76 Sworn statement by Frank Shouldice to the advisory committee, 8 Mar. 1937 (IMA, MSPC, 21841); MSP application, Peadar Dunne (IMA, MSPC, 342414).
77 Brian Hanley, 'The Irish Citizen Army after 1916', *Saothar*, 28 (2003), 37–47; McNamara, 'Glorious forever?', pp 133–9.
78 Sworn statement made by Mrs Kathleen Barrett before advisory committee, 5 Oct. 1936 (IMA, MSPC, 342198).
79 'The Fifth Battalion (Engineers)' in National Association of the Old IRA, *Iris Drong Átha Cliath: Dublin Brigade Review* (Dublin, 1939), p. 53.
80 Voice recording, Oscar Traynor (IMA, BMH S 1412); Liam Archer pension application (IMA, MSPC, 24SP1019).
81 Frank Henderson (BMH WS 821, pp 37–8).
82 C.J. Woods and William Murphy, 'Ashe, Thomas (Tomás Ághas)', *DIB*, DOI: https://doi.org/10.3318/dib.000247.v1; Ronan Fanning, 'Richard Mulcahy', *DIB*, DOI: https://doi.org/10.3318/dib.006029.v2; Ida Milne, *Stacking the coffins: influenza, war and revolution in Ireland, 1918–19* (Manchester, 2018), pp 209–14.
83 Pašeta, *Nationalist women*, p. 219; Townshend, *Republic*, pp 47–8.
84 Annie and Lily Cooney (BMH WS 805, p. 17). Only one branch used military ranks in 1916: Rose McNamara (BMH WS 483, p. 2).
85 'Scheme of organization', n.d., *c.*1919/20 (IMA, BMH CD/167/3).
86 Cumann na mBan Nominal Rolls, Dublin City Council (IMA, CMB/126).
87 Mary Adrien to Department of Defence, 12 Dec. 1934; Sworn statement before the advisory committee by Mary Adrien, 4 Dec. 1936 (IMA, MSPC, 34152). Adrien was later presented with a bicycle in recognition of this work.
88 Summary of sworn evidence before the interviewing officers by Ann McGuinness, 29 Apr. 1941 (IMA, MSPC, 59512).
89 Gallagher, *Great War*, pp 150–3.
90 Laffan, *Resurrection*, p. 129.
91 Grayson, *Great wars*, p. 231.

92 Yeates, *Wartime*, p. 70.
93 Laffan, *Resurrection*, p. 134.
94 Dickson, *Dublin*, p. 457.
95 CI Dublin, Apr. 1918 (TNA, CO 904/105).
96 Ibid., Sept. 1918 (TNA, CO 904/107).
97 Ibid., Sept.–Oct. 1918 (ibid.).
98 Morrissey, *Walsh*, p. 302; *EH*, 22 June 1917.
99 Gallagher, *Great War*, pp 86–90.
100 CI Dublin, Oct. 1918 (TNA, CO 904/107).
101 Yeates, *Wartime*, pp 231–2.
102 *II*, 12 Oct. 1918; *IT*, 19 Oct. 1918; Yeates, *Wartime*, pp 253–4.
103 *II*, 5 Oct. 1918.
104 Dickson, *Dublin*, p. 459.
105 John Dorney, 'The rabble and the republic', *Saothar*, 41 (2016), 104–6; Yeates, *Wartime*, p. 115.
106 Dickson, *Dublin*, p. 459.
107 CI Dublin, Nov. 1918 (ibid.).
108 Ibid., Oct. 1918 (ibid.).
109 Milne, *Coffins*, pp 60–80.
110 Elaine Callinan, *Electioneering and propaganda in Ireland, 1917–21: votes, violence and victory* (Dublin, 2020), pp 32–42.
111 DMP 'Report on activities of extremists during month of October, 1918', 4 Nov. 1918 (TNA, CAB 24/70/94).
112 Townshend, *Republic*, pp 58–60.
113 Yeates, *Wartime*, p. 289.
114 Dickson, *Dublin*, p. 459.
115 Anne Dolan, 'Byrne, Alfred ('Alfie')', *DIB*, DOI: https://doi.org/10.3318/dib.001318.v1; 'Harbour division: vote for Philip Shanahan [Sinn Fein candidate] and strike a blow for complete independence', Dec. 1918 (NLI, EPH F426).
116 Walker, *Parliamentary election results*, pp 188, 388–9.
117 Joseph V. Lawless (BMH WS 1,043, pp 9–10).
118 Gerard Hogan, 'Duffy, George Gavan', *DIB*, DOI: https://doi.org/10.3318/dib.002810.v1.
119 'To the electors of South County Dublin', 1918 (NLI, EPH C67).
120 Brian M. Walker, *Parliamentary election results in Ireland, 1918–92* (Dublin and Belfast, 1992), p. 6.
121 Callinan, *Electioneering*, p. 91.
122 'Fellow electors of Rathmines! Carson has thrown you over for the "six counties"! …' (NLI, D145).
123 Yeates, *Wartime*, p. 290; *II*, 30 Dec. 1918.
124 *Belfast News-Letter*, 30 Dec. 1918.
125 *II*, 30 Dec. 1918.
126 Walker, *Election results, 1918–92*, pp 6–7.
127 Elaine Callinan, 'Voting to maintain the Union in 1918: "One of the strongest pillars upon which they stood"' in Hughes & Morrissey (eds), *Southern Irish loyalism*, pp 56–7.

CHAPTER SIX *The IRA at war in Dublin, 1919–21*

1 Staff memorandum, 'The war as a whole', 24 Apr. 1921 (UCDA, Richard Mulcahy papers, P7/A/17).
2 CI Dublin, Sept. 1919 (TNA, CO 904/110). See also CI Dublin, Jan., Oct. 1919, Jan., Feb., June, Aug., Nov. 1920 (TNA, CO 904/108–112).

3 Peter Hart, 'The geography of revolution in Ireland, 1917–1923', *Past & Present*, 155:1 (1997), 147–55. Hart does not explicitly describe Kildare as passive, though its rate of violence is identical to Meath by his calculations. It is also not clear how exactly Hart defines the county as opposed to the city, but it is likely based on the DMP and RIC areas of jurisdiction.
4 Joost Augusteijn, *From public defiance to guerrilla warfare: the experience of ordinary volunteers in the Irish War of Independence, 1916–1921* (Dublin, 1996), p. 94; Patrick McCrea (BMH WS 413, pp 6–7).
5 Joseph V. Lawless (BMH WS 1,043, pp 283, 346–8).
6 Frank Henderson (BMH WS 821, p. 117).
7 Joseph V. Lawless (BMH WS 1,043, p. 346); 'With the Sixth Battalion (South County Dublin)' in *Dublin's fighting story, 1913–1921: told by the men who made it* (1st ed., Tralee, n.d., *c.*1948), p. 185.
8 Oscar Traynor (UCDA, Ernie O'Malley notebooks, P17b/96 and P17b/98). See also Patrick McCrea (BMH WS 413, pp 42–3); Tom MacMahon (UCDA, O'Malley notebooks, P17b/86).
9 Todd Andrews to secretary, Office of Referee, 2 Feb. 1935 (IMA, Military Service Pensions Collection (hereafter MSPC), 34815).
10 Andrews, *Dublin made me*, pp 174–5.
11 Oscar Traynor (BMH WS 340, p. 40).
12 'Report by the General Officer Commanding-in-Chief on the Situation in Ireland for the Week Ending February 5th, 1921' (TNA, CAB/24/119/69).
13 Voice recording, Oscar Traynor (IMA, BMH S 1412).
14 *Census of Ireland, 1911. Areas, houses and population*, City of Dublin, Table XIX; Peter Hart, *The IRA at war, 1916–1923* (Oxford, 2003), p. 119.
15 Discussion of occupations among IRA fatalities is based on a survey of forty-eight men from the Dublin and Fingal brigades and drawn from a wide range of sources, including the MSPC, newspapers, census returns, birth, marriage and death records. For occupations in Dublin in this period see Chapter 1.
16 Unsigned note dated 4 Nov. 1920 (IMA, CP-05-01-13).
17 David Flood, 'Dublin Corporation employees involved in 1916 Rising: with biographical notes' in Gibney (ed.), *Dublin City Council in 1916*, pp 219–94.
18 Frank Henderson (UCDA, O'Malley notebooks, P17b/99). For clustering of workers in the city, see Chapter 1.
19 James Foley (BMH WS 744, p. 1); Seán O'Neill (BMH 1,154, p. 2); Gerald Davis (BMH WS 1,361, pp 1–2); Michael Cremin (BMH WS 563, p. 13); 'The Third Battalion' in *Dublin Brigade Review*, p. 31.
20 Voice recording, Oscar Traynor (IMA, BMH S 1412).
21 1901 and 1911 Census of England and Wales (https://www.findmypast.ie/) (accessed 4 July 2019); *IT*, 11 May 1920; *II*, 11 May 1920.
22 Pauric J. Dempsey, 'Clancy, Peadar', *DIB*, DOI: https://doi.org/10.3318/dib.001679.v1.
23 1911 census return, Savage household (http://census.nationalarchives.ie/) (accessed 4 July 2019); Dependents' pension claim, Martin Savage (IMA, MSPC, W1D107).
24 Pat McHale, Sligo, 12 Feb. 1924 (IMA, MSPC, W1D107).
25 Bridget Whelan, n.d., c. 1923 (IMA, MSPC, 1D125).
26 *Saorstát Éireann. Census of population, 1926, Vol. 2. Occupations of males and females in each province, county, county borough, urban and rural district* (1928), Table 10A, pp 162–3. Based on a list of brigade and battalion officers and company captains named on nominal rolls for 11 July 1921 who could be satisfactorily traced using 1911 census returns.
27 Hart, *IRA at war*, p. 115.
28 Drawn from a range of sources available online, including 1901 and 1911 census returns, military service pensions records, birth, marriage and death certificates, and newspaper reports.
29 Daniel Killian 1911 census return (http://census.nationalarchives.ie/) (accessed 13 Jan. 2020); Thomas Peppard (BMH WS 1,399, p. 1).

30 Michael Lynch (BMH WS 511, pp 1, 122); Joseph V. Lawless (BMH WS 1,043, p. 316).
31 Andy McDonnell interview (UCDA, O'Malley notebooks, P17b/100); Andrew McDonnell (BMH WS 1,768, p. 26).
32 Michael Chadwick pension application form (IMA, MSPC, 3418109); Niall MacNeill pension application form (IMA, MSPC, 24SP10285).
33 Patrick Kavanagh pension application form (IMA, MSPC, 3438420).
34 Andrew McDonnell (BMH WS 1,768, p. 36).
35 The outlier was 'G' company, 4th Battalion with 203 listed members.
36 Nominal Rolls, Dublin Brigade, 11 July 1921 (IMA, MSPC, RO1–RO9); Oscar Traynor (BMH WS 340, p. 40).
37 Nominal Rolls, Fingal Brigade, 11 July 1921 (IMA, MSPC, RO519).
38 Nominal Rolls, 1st and 3rd Meath Brigades, 11 July 1921 (IMA, MSPC, RO479–83, RO489).
39 Thomas Peppard (BMH WS 1,399, p. 14).
40 References supplied for Andy McDonnell by Michael Tannam, Simon Donnelly, Ernie O'Malley (IMA, MSPC, 34REF16644). For an outline of the officers and company areas of the 6th Battalion, see Patrick Brennan (BMH WS 1,773, pp 3–5).
41 Lawrence William White, 'Boland, Gerald', *DIB*, DOI: https://doi.org/10.3318/dib.000762.v1.
42 7th Battalion Nominal Rolls, 11 July 1921 (IMA, MSPC, RO8). These are the figures verified by a brigade committee and differ slightly from those provided elsewhere in the file. For Kildare/Wicklow men, see Patrick O'Carroll (BMW WS 1161, pp 4–5).
43 Cuman na mBan Nominal Rolls, Dublin City Council (IMA, CMB/126).
44 Eve Morrison, 'The Bureau of Military History and female republican activism, 1913–1923' in Maryann Gialanella Valiulis (ed.), *Gender and power in Irish history* (Dublin, 2009), p. 62.
45 CI Dublin, Jan. 1919–Sep. 1921 (TNA, CO 904/108–115). It was not unusual for the RIC to have inaccurate figures and to fail to update branch and membership numbers for nationalist and unionist organizations.
46 North County Dublin (Fingal) Cumann na mBan Nominal Rolls (IMA, MSPC, CMB124); Lists of members of branches of Cumann na mBan in Fingal (FCCA, CMN/038/1–12).
47 Summary of Cumann na mBan activities in North County Dublin by Kathleen McAllister and Mary J. Weston, n.d. *c.*1934 (IMA, MSPC, CMB124).
48 Quartermaster Fingal Brigade to Brigid Connolly, 29 June 1921 (FCC, CMN/006).
49 South County Dublin Cumann na mBan Nominal Rolls (IMA, MSPC, CMB125).
50 Micheál Hodgins, 'Remembering the forgotten Cumann na mBan in South County Dublin', *Dun Laoghaire Journal*, 27 (2018), 76–84.
51 Sworn statement by Lily [O']Brennan before the advisory committee, 29 Mar. 1935 (IMA, MSPC, CMB/126).
52 Mary Flannery Woods (BMH WS 624, p. 25).
53 Lily Mernin (BMH WS 441, pp 1–7); Signed statement by Lily Mernin, n.d.; Statement by Frank Saurin, 6 Apr. 1933 (IMA, MSPC, 34REF4945).
54 Statement of activities of Annie May Smith (née Brennan), n.d. (IMA, MSPC, 3423407).
55 Sworn statement to the advisory committee by Eilis McNamara, 29 May 1946; Sworn statement to the advisory committee by Mrs P. O'Flanagan, Mrs O'Doherty, Seán Budds, George White, 12 June 1946 (IMA, MSPC, 3460726).
56 Supplementary statement by Teresa Redmond, 9 May 1942; Summary of sworn evidence given before the secretary by Teresa Redmond, 11 May 1942 (IMA, MSPC, 3459927).
57 Morrison, 'The Bureau of Military History and female republican activism', pp 61–2.
58 Catherine Rooney, née Byrne (BMH WS 648, p. 19).
59 Rose McNamara (BMH WS 482, p. 13).
60 Maureen McGavock (BMH WS 385, p. 7).

61 Summary of Cumann na mBan activities in North County Dublin by Kathleen McAllister and Mary J. Weston, n.d. *c.*1934 (IMA, MSPC, CMB124).
62 Ann McGuinness (IMA, MSPC, 3459512) carried despatches between Dublin and Barnacullia for Andy McDonnell and Maureen Twomey (IMA, MSPC, 3420401) did the same between Donnybrook and Dundrum.
63 Sworn statement before the advisory committee by Mairéad Duke, 10 May 1940 (IMA, MSPC, 3414710).
64 Cumann na mBan Nominal Rolls, Fingal (IMA, MSPC, 124); Aidan Collins, 'Fleury, Eleonora Lilian', *DIB*, DOI: https://doi.org/10.3318/dib.008796.v2.
65 Sworn statement before the advisory committee by Thomasina Lynders (née Weston), 14 May 1938 (IMA, MSPC, 3421421).
66 Hodgins, 'Remembering', p. 77.
67 In only one monthly report was Cumann na mBan included among a list of 'active' organizations in the county: CI Dublin, July 1920 (TNA, CO 904/112).
68 Reference for Daniel Brophy by James Lawless, 15 Jan. 1925 (IMA, MSPC, 241950).
69 Joseph V. Lawless (BMH WS 1,043, p. 316).
70 Summary of sworn evidence by Michael Lynch, 24 Mar. 1941 (IMA, MSPC, 349462); Michael Lynch (BMH WS 511, p. 145); Joseph V. Lawless (BMH WS 1,043, pp 316–17).
71 Reference for Daniel Brophy by James Lawless, 15 Jan. 1925 (IMA, MSPC, 241950).
72 Joseph V. Lawless (BMH WS 1,043, p. 349).
73 O/C Fingal to chief of staff, 23 Mar. 1921 (UCDA, Mulcahy papers, P7/A/17).
74 Quartermaster to chief of staff, 4 Apr. 1921 (ibid.).
75 Chief of staff to O/C Fingal, 6 Apr. 1921 (ibid.).
76 O/C Fingal to chief of staff, 9 Apr. 1921 (ibid.).
77 List of operations carried out by Fingal Brigade, IRA (IMA, MCPS, A64); Thomas Peppard (BMH WS 1,399, pp 16–17).
78 *Evening Mail*, 18 June 1921.
79 Sworn statement made before the advisory committee by Andrew McDonnell on behalf of Thomas Watkins, 19 Oct. 1936 (IMA, MSPC, 344154).
80 Andrew McDonnell (BMH WS 1,768, p. 63); Sworn statement made before the advisory committee by Thomas Watkins, 17 Jan. 1936 (IMA, MSPC, 344154).
81 See 'Events of importance in connection with the Dublin Brigade activities from 1914 to 1922' (IMA, MSPC, A85); Andy McDonnell interview (UCDA, O'Malley notebooks, P17a/100).
82 D.M. Leeson, *The Black & Tans: British police and Auxiliaries in the Irish War of Independence* (Oxford, 2011), p. 234, n. 81.
83 Michael Rock (BMH WS 1,398, pp 10–14).
84 Walter Brown (BMH WS 1,436, pp 9–10).
85 Patrick J. Brennan (BMH WS 1,773, pp 6–9).
86 Chadwick, 'Sixth Battalion', p. 185. Casualties described in Andy McDonnell's BMH statement tend not to align with reported casualties in the press. Patrol Reports submitted to GHQ often record 'Not Known' for enemy casualties (UCDA, Mulcahy papers, P7/A/17). Also compare Patrick J. Brennan (BMH WS 1,773, p. 27) with *Evening Mail*, 4 July 1921.
87 See, for example, James Foley (BMH WS 774, p. 7).
88 *EH*, 9 July 1920.
89 War Diaries, General Staff, HQ Dublin District, December 1920–May 1921 (TNA, WO 30/90/2).
90 Nevil Macready, *Annals of an active life, vol. II* (London, 1924), pp 453–4.
91 *General monthly return of the regimental strength of the British army*, May, June 1921 (TNA, WO 73/114).

92 *The Irish Republican Army – from captured documents only*, June 1921 (TNA, WO 141/40). It was ultimately decided that this, and an earlier companion piece, would not be circulated to the troops.
93 Padraig Yeates, *A city in turmoil: Dublin, 1919–21* (Dublin, 2012), pp 168–9.
94 Jim Herlihy, *The Dublin Metropolitan Police: a short history and genealogical guide* (Dublin, 2001), pp 178–181.
95 Macready, *Annals*, p. 439.
96 Yeates, *Turmoil*, pp 91, 161; Leeson, *Black and Tans*, pp 103–18; https://theauxiliaries.com/ (accessed 8 July 2020).
97 'Report by the General Officer Commanding-in-Chief on the Situation in Ireland for the Week Ending February 19th, 1921' (TNA, CAB/24/120/25); Dependents' pension application, Peter Freyne (IMA, MSPC, W1D472).
98 Raid and search reports, Dublin District, Oct.–Dec. 1920 (TNA, WO 35/75); Search reports, Jan.–Jun. 1921 (TNA, WO 35/86B/1); F Co. ADRIC, raids completed, Apr.–Jul. 1921 (TNA, WO 35/86B/5); Leeson, *Black and Tans*, pp 34–7.
99 Susan Byrne, '"Keeping company with the enemy": gender and sexual violence against women during the Irish War of Independence and Civil War, 1919–1923', *Women's History Review*, 30:1 (2021), 111.
100 Affidavit by William Gorman, 1921 (UCDA, Mulcahy papers, P7/A/18).
101 Byrne, 'Keeping company', 111.
102 Yeates, *Turmoil*, pp 161, 251–2.
103 Thomas Peppard (BMH WS 1,399, p. 15).
104 Patrick J. Brennan (BMH WS 1,773, p. 29).
105 Sworn statement before the advisory committee by Michael Chadwick, 1 May 1936 (IMA, MSPC, 3418109).
106 Unsigned, typescript note, n.d. in Brigade activity report, 6th Battalion, Dublin Brigade (IMA, MSPC, A72).
107 McSweeney, 'The fight in the Bray area' in *Dublin's fighting story*, p. 185.
108 1911 census returns for Bray No. 1 and No. 2 DEDs (http://census.nationalarchives.ie/) (10 July 2020); McSweeney, 'The fight in the Bray area', p. 186. McSweeney's statement is confirmed, to some extent at least, by the listed occupations of men over the age of fifty as returned on 1911 census forms.
109 Hart, 'Geography of revolution', 160.
110 1911 census returns for Clonmethan DED (http://census.nationalarchives.ie/) (10 July 2020); Thomas Peppard (BMH WS 1,399, pp 14–15).
111 Thomas Peppard (BMH WS 1,399, p. 13).
112 Hart, *IRA at war*, p. 230.
113 Joseph Leonard (BMH WS 547, p. 1).
114 Yeates, *Turmoil*, pp 103–6.
115 Dominic Price, *We bled together: Michael Collins, the Squad and the Dublin Brigade* (Cork, 2017), p. 115.
116 Augusteijn, *Public defiance*, pp 140–2.
117 Anne Dolan, 'Killing and Bloody Sunday, November 1920', *Historical Journal*, 49:3 (2006), 792.
118 Jane Leonard, '"English dogs" or "poor devils"? The dead of Bloody Sunday morning' in David Fitzpatrick (ed.), *Terror in Ireland, 1916–1923* (Dublin, 2012), pp 102–40.
119 Christie Byrne (UCDA, O'Malley notebooks, P17b/96).
120 Charlie Dalton (BMH WS 434, p. 21).
121 Dolan, 'Killing', 792; Fergus O'Farrell, *Cathal Brugha* (Dublin, 2018), p. 60.
122 David Leeson, 'Death in the afternoon: the Croke Park massacre, 21 November 1920', *Canadian Journal of History*, 38 (2003), 49–50.

123 See Michael Foley, *The bloodied field: Croke Park, Sunday 21 November 1920* (Dublin, 2014).
124 Eunan O'Halpin, 'Counting terror: Bloody Sunday and the *Dead of the Irish Revolution*' in Fitzpatrick (ed.), *Terror*, pp 143–4; Foley, *Bloodied field*, p. 82.
125 *FJ*, 22 Nov. 1920. See also Leeson, 'Death', pp 52–4.
126 Leeson, 'Death', p. 45.
127 Foley, *Bloodied field*, pp 183–4. A different account of Ryan's death is given in the file for his wife's application for a dependent's pension (IMA, MSPC, DP7168). Thomas Hogan was a member of the Limerick IRA (IMA, MSPC, DP25659).
128 References by Peadar McNulty and H. Murphy (IMA, MSPC, 2RB4005); 'The First Battalion' in *Dublin Brigade Review*, p. 19.
129 Joseph Traynor (IMA, MSPC, DP9656). Traynor's father Michael's application for a dependent's pension was rejected in 1937 as his father stated on the form that he was not a member of an eligible organization, but an earlier letter had stated 'he was a member of the IRA and did much for the freedom of his country'. Following an application from Traynor's brother in the 1940s, a posthumous Service (1917–21) Medal was awarded (IMA, MSPC, MD1794). Traynor does not appear on the surviving nominal rolls for his company, but this may have been an oversight (IMA, MSPC, RO5).
130 O'Halpin, 'Counting terror', pp 142–3. See also Moira McKee (UCDA, O'Malley notebooks, P17b/103).
131 Townshend, *Republic*, pp 201–10; Patrick McCrea (BMH WS 413, pp 20–1). Conor Clune, a Volunteer and member of the Gaelic League from County Clare, was probably just in the wrong place at the wrong time and was also killed.
132 Augusteijn, *Public defiance*, pp 115–16.
133 Frank Henderson (UCDA, O'Malley notebooks, P17b/99).
134 Andrews, *Dublin made me*, p. 185.
135 'Deputation consisting of Messrs Holohan, Seán O'Moore, P. O'Connor and Michael Byrne, 1st Battalion, Dublin Brigade, 9th Sept. 1940' in Brigade activity report, 1st Battalion, Dublin Brigade (IMA, MSPC, A73).
136 'Operation summary from 1 December 1920', Headquarters, Dublin District (TNA, WO 30/90/1).
137 William Sheehan, *Fighting for Dublin: the British battle for Dublin, 1919–1921* (Cork, 2007), pp 143–4.
138 'The First Battalion' in *Dublin Brigade Review*, p. 20; IRA Nominal Rolls, 11 July 1921, Dublin Brigade (IMA, MSPC, RO2–6).
139 Andrews, *Dublin made me*, pp 143–4.
140 J.J. Devoy pension application (IMA, MSPC, 3481).
141 Thomas Peppard (BMH WS 1,399, p. 23); Michael Rock (BMH WS 1,398, p. 27); Walter Brown (BMH WS 1,436, p. 13); Thomas Markey (BMH WS 1,446, p. 17); John Gaynor (BMH WS 1,447, p. 37).
142 Thomas Peppard (BMH WS 1,399, p. 13).
143 Sworn statement before the advisory committee by Thomasina Lynders (née Weston), 14 May 1938 (IMA, MSPC, 3421421); Sworn statement before the advisory committee by Mary Julia Lynders, 14 May 1938 (IMA, MSPC, 3422083).
144 Walter Brown (BMH WS 1,436, p. 13).
145 Thomas Peppard (BMH WS 1,399, p. 23).
146 Eunan O'Halpin, 'Problematic killing during the War of Independence and its aftermath: civilian spies and informers' in James Kelly and Mary Ann Lyons (eds), *Death and dying in Ireland, Britain and Europe: historical perspectives* (Dublin, 2013), p. 328. Padraig Óg Ó Ruairc, *Truce: murder, myth and the last days of the Irish War of Independence* (Cork, 2016), pp 101–2

gives a total of fifteen civilian 'spies' executed in Dublin city and county with nine having formerly served in the army (eight) or the navy.

147 List of operations, B Company, 2nd Battalion, Apr. 1921 (NLI, MS 901/112).

148 Paddy Rigney (UCDA, O'Malley notebooks, P17b/105); George White (UCDA, O'Malley notebooks, P17b/99).

149 Paddy Rigney interview (UCDA, O'Malley notebooks, P17b/90, P17b/105).

150 O'Halpin & Ó Corráin, *Dead*, p. 289.

151 Pádraig Ó Conchubhair and Paddy Rigney, 'The Active Service Unit' in *Dublin Brigade Review*, p. 75; Pádraig Ó Conchubhair (BMH WS 813, p. 15); John Anthony Caffrey (BMH WS 569, p. 9).

152 Sworn statement before advisory committee by Leo Duffy, 17 July 1935 (IMA, MSPC, RO9).

153 Price, *Bled together*, pp 199–200; *EH*, 13 Jan. 1921.

154 Dalton, *Dublin Brigade*, p. 45; Yeates, *Turmoil*, p. 239; Leeson, *Black and Tans*, pp 77, 97.

155 Quartermaster Fingal Brigade to Mary Derham, 28 Sept. 1921 (FCCA, CMN/018).

156 Sworn statement by Lily [O']Brennan before the advisory committee, 29 Mar. 1935 (IMA, MSPC, CMB/126).

157 James Harpur (BMH WS 536, p. 3).

158 Seán Ryan, 'Frank Flood and the Drumcondra ambush', *History Ireland*, 26:2 (2018), 8–9.

159 Quoted in Thomas Tormey, 'Guerrilla warfare and the dynamics of violence in the Irish War of Independence' (PhD, TCD, 2020), p. 58.

160 Military inquiry in lieu of inquest, Daniel Carew (TNA, WO 35/147A/35).

161 Quoted in Price, *Bled together*, p. 201.

162 Oscar Traynor (UCDA, O'Malley notebooks (hereafter OMN), P17b/98).

163 *EH*, 7 Apr. 1921; *FJ*, 11 Apr. 1921; Military inquiry in lieu of inquest, Michael Daly (TNA, WO35/148/75).

164 Death certificates for Terence McGlynn, Daniel Carew and Michael Daly (www.irish genealogy.ie) (accessed 15 July 2019).

165 Grayson, *Great wars*, p. 297.

166 *FJ*, 9 Mar. 1921.

167 *EH*, 13 May 1921.

168 O'Halpin & Ó Corráin, *Dead*, p. 324.

169 Yeates, *Turmoil*, p. 171; Michael Rock (BMH WS 1,389, pp 11–12).

170 Ross O'Mahoney, 'Sack of Balbriggan and tit-for-tat terror' in Fitzpatrick (ed.), *Terror*, pp 58–75; David Fitzpatrick, 'The price of Balbriggan', in Fitzpatrick (ed.), *Terror*, pp 75–101.

171 Dependents' pension claim, James Lawless (IMA, MSPC, 1D486); 1911 census returns, James Lawless (http://census.nationalarchives.ie/) (accessed 4 July 2019); marriage certificate, James Lawless (www.irishgeneology.ie) (accessed 4 July 2019), *II*, 22 Sept. 1920. Both men are described as Volunteers in Michael Rock (BMH WS 1,398, p. 12); John Gaynor (BMH WS 1,447, p. 20); Michael Lynch (BMH WS 511, p. 143).

172 Michael Rock (BMH WS 1,398, p. 13); *Evidence on conditions in Ireland comprising the complete testimony, affidavits and exhibits presented before the American Commission on Conditions in Ireland*, annotated and translated by Albert Coyle (Washington, DC, 1921), pp 92–120; RTÉ Archives, Cashman Collection (https://stillslibrary.rte.ie/).

173 Death certificate, William Straw, 1920 (www.irishgeneology.ie) (accessed 4 July 2019); *IT*, 1 Nov. 1920.

174 *EH*, 27 Oct. 1920.

175 Military inquiry in lieu of inquest on Thomas Hand (TNA, WO 35/151A/22).

176 Michael Rock (BMH WS 1,398, p. 13).

177 Weekly Summaries, Apr. 1920 (TNA, CO 904/148). He is misnamed as Thomas Lawless and aged forty-eight, but described as a barber. James Lawless is the only barber or hairdresser with that surname listed on the 1911 census so it is likely the same man.
178 John Gaynor (BMH WS 1,447, pp 15–16).
179 *II*, 23 Nov. 1920.
180 *FJ*, 6 Dec. 1920; Francis Whearity, 'Thomas Hand', *Time & Tide*, 4 (2001), 47–9.
181 O'Mahoney, 'Sack of Balbriggan', p. 68; Richard Abbott, *Police casualties in Ireland, 1919–1922* (Cork, 2019; [2000]), pp 244, 252, 283, 312. See also Brigade activity report, Fingal Brigade (MAI, MSPC, A64), which contains a number of incorrect details and describes incidents for which no other information has been found.
182 Robinson quoted in Yeates, *Turmoil*, p. 274.
183 James Slattery (BMH WS 445, pp 16–17); James Slattery pension application (IMA, MSPC, WA117).
184 Yeates, *Turmoil*, pp 272–5; Grayson, *Great wars*, pp 294–6.
185 *ET*, 25 May 1921.
186 Yeates, *Turmoil*, p. 275.
187 Grayson, *Great wars*, p. 296.
188 'Custom House seized, 1978' (https://www.rte.ie/archives/2021/0518/1222363-burning-of-the-custom-house/) (accessed 25 May 2021).
189 Diary of operations, 'D' Co. 2nd Battalion, May 1921 (NLI, MS 902/1).
190 Diary of operations of the Dublin Brigade for June 1921 (UCDA, Mulcahy papers, P7/A/21).

CHAPTER SEVEN *Labour, politics and the counter-state in Dublin, 1919–21*

1 Máire Comerford, *On dangerous ground: a memoir of the Irish Revolution*, ed. Hilary Dully (Dublin, 2021), p. 98.
2 CI Dublin, Jan. 1919, May 1919 (TNA, CO 904/108-109).
3 Francis Devine, 'Irish Transport & General Workers' Union: organization in Dublin city and county, 1918–1928', *Saothar*, 34 (2009), 91–4.
4 Ibid., p. 91; Cormac Murphy, 'Revolution and radicalism in county Dublin, 1913–21' in Myrtle Hill and Sarah Barber (eds), *Aspects of Irish studies* (Belfast, 1990), p. 17.
5 CI Dublin, Feb. 1919 (TNA, CO 904/108).
6 Ibid., Jan. 1919 (ibid.); *Irish Opinion: The Voice of Labour* (hereafter *Irish Opinion*), 1 Feb. 1920.
7 Carters were also demanding 18*s.* a day and a minimum of stonebreakers 2*s.* 6*d.* per yard: *Irish Opinion*, 8 Feb. 1920.
8 CI Dublin, Jan., Feb. 1919 (TNA, CO 904/108).
9 Ibid., Mar., Apr. 1919 (ibid.), May, June 1919 (TNA, CO 904/109); *FJ*, 8 Aug. 1919.
10 Ibid., Jan. 1919 (TNA, CO 904/108); *Irish Opinion*, 14 Feb. 1919.
11 *Irish Opinion*, 14 Feb. 1919. The payment was made in February: *Irish Opinion*, 22 Feb. 1919.
12 Ibid., 8 Feb. 1919. C. Desmond Greaves, *The Irish Transport and General Workers' Union: the formative years, 1909–1923* (Dublin, 1982), pp 233–4; Yeates, *Turmoil*, pp 10–12.
13 CI Dublin, Mar. 1919 (TNA CO 904/108).
14 Ibid., Apr., June 1919 (TNA, CO 904/109).
15 *FJ*, 14 July 1919.
16 CI Dublin, July 1919 (TNA, CO 904/109).
17 Ibid., Aug. 1919 (ibid.).
18 *Irish Opinion*, 30 Aug. 1919.
19 Callinan, *Electioneering*, p. 46.
20 Laffan, *Resurrection*, p. 325.
21 Yeates, *Turmoil*, p. 63; *II*, 16 June 1920.
22 Yeates, *Turmoil*, pp 76–7.

23 Laffan, *Resurrection*, p. 325.
24 *EH*, 19 Jan. 1920.
25 Callinan, *Electioneering*, p. 49.
26 Yeates, *Turmoil*, pp 64, 76–80.
27 Ibid., pp 70–1, 76; *EH*, 19 Jan. 1920.
28 *EH*, 19 Jan. 1920.
29 *II*, 19 Jan. 1920.
30 File copy of *Irish Bulletin*, 17 May 1920 (NAI, DÉ/2/81).
31 Yeates, *City in turmoil*, p. 81.
32 Callinan, *Electioneering*, p. 48.
33 *EH*, 19 Jan. 1920; Yeats, *Turmoil*, p. 80.
34 *EH*, 17 Jan. 1920, 19 Jan. 1920; *II*, 20 Jan. 1920; Yeates, *Turmoil*, p. 80.
35 *FJ*, *ET*, *II*, 8, 9 June 1920.
36 *II*, 9 June 1920; *EH*, 10 June 1920.
37 R.J.C. Adams, *Shadow of a taxman: who funded the Irish Revolution?* (Cambridge, 2022), p. 80.
38 Ormonde Winter, *Winter's tale: an autobiography* (London, 1955), p. 299.
39 Mitchell, *Revolutionary government*, p. 63.
40 Adams, *Taxman*, p. 301.
41 Winter, *Winter's tale*, p. 300.
42 Griffith and Collins to (?) Count Plunkett, 9 Apr. 1920 (NLI Count Plunkett papers, MS 11,404).
43 Yeates, *Turmoil*, p. 104.
44 Adams, *Taxman*, pp 28–37, 301.
45 Michael Rock (BMH WS 1,398 p. 5); Thomas Markey (BMH WS 1,446, p. 5); Adams, *Taxman*, p. 301.
46 Adams, *Taxman*, p. 79.
47 Yeates, *Turmoil*, pp 104–5.
48 Townshend, *Republic*, pp 94–5.
49 'Dáil Éireann Report on the Propaganda Department', n.d. [*c*. June 1920] (NAI, DÉ/2/10).
50 William Murphy, 'FitzGerald, (Thomas Joseph) Desmond', *DIB*, DOI: https://doi.org/10.3318/dib.003136.v1.
51 Comerford, *Dangerous ground*, p. 108.
52 Francis J. Costello, 'The role of propaganda in the Anglo-Irish War 1919–1921', *Canadian Journal of Irish Studies*, 14:2 (1989), 7.
53 'Dáil Éireann Report on the Propaganda Department'.
54 D.S. Johnson, 'The Belfast Boycott, 1920–1922' in L.A. Clarkson and J.M. Goldstrom (eds), *Irish population, economy and society: essays in honour of the late K.H. Connell* (Oxford, 1981), pp 287–307; Arthur Mitchell, *Revolutionary government in Ireland: Dáil Éireann, 1919–22* (Dublin, 1995), pp 168–72.
55 Johnson, 'Belfast boycott', p. 307; Robert Lynch, *The northern IRA and the early years of partition, 1920–1922* (Dublin, 2006), p. 44.
56 'Labour Department Report' n.d. [*c*.July 1921] (IMA, Collins papers, A/602).
57 Joseph Kinsella (BMH WS 476, p. 13).
58 Dublin Brigade monthly report, Apr. 1921 (UCDA, Donal O'Donoghue papers, P106/1921(44–45)).
59 Dublin Brigade diary of operations, Mar. 1921 (UCDA, Mulcahy papers, P7/A/39).
60 William James Stapleton (BMH WS 822, p. 27).
61 'Belfast Boycott, Resume', 20 Jan. 1921 (NAI, DÉ/2/110).
62 Yeates, *Turmoil*, pp 143–4.

63 *EH*, 8 Apr. 1920, 10 Apr. 1920. Prisoners had already gone on hunger strike in Wormwood Scrubs in March: *EH*, 20 Mar. 1920.
64 *EH*, 15 Apr., 20 Apr. 1920; W.H. Kautt (ed.), *Ground truths: British army operations in the Irish War of Independence* (Kildare, 2014), pp 43–4. See also William Murphy, *Political imprisonment and the Irish, 1912–23* (Oxford, 2014), pp 164–7.
65 Andrews, *Dublin made me*, pp 148–55, quote at p. 155; Andrew McDonnell (BMH WS 1,768, p. 45).
66 *EH*, 15 Apr. 1920.
67 *II*, 12 May 1920; *Chicago Tribune*, 20 June 1920.
68 Murphy, *Political imprisonment*, p. 191.
69 Yeates, *Turmoil*, pp 234–5.
70 Ibid., p. 267.
71 *EH*, 7 July 1920.
72 *FJ*, 21 July, 26 July 1920.
73 Brian Hughes, *Defying the IRA? Intimidation, coercion and communities during the Irish Revolution* (Liverpool, 2016), pp 55–82.
74 Robin J.C. Adams, 'Tides of change and changing sides: the collection of rates in the Irish War of Independence, 1919–21' in Douglas Kanter and Patrick Walsh (eds), *Taxation, politics and protest in Ireland, 1662–2016* (Cham, 2019), pp 253–69; *II*, 6 Jan. 1921; Patrick J. Brennan (BMH WS 1,773, p. 15); Andrew McDonnell (BMH WS 1,767, pp 69–70).
75 Minutes of adjourned quarterly meeting of Dublin County Council, 20 Jan. 1921 (NAI, DÉLG/9/18).
76 Peter Ennis pension application (IMA, MSPC, 24/SP5580); Joseph Kinsella pension application (IMA, MSPC, 24/SP4685); James Sweeney pension application (IMA, MSPC, 34/10168).
77 Yeates, *Turmoil*, pp 224–5.
78 Quote in Thomas Peppard (BMH WS 1,399, p. 12). See also Walter Browne (BMH WS 1,436, p. 5); John Gaynor (BMH WS 1,447, p. 14).
79 Brigade activity report F company, 6th Battalion, Dublin Brigade (IMA, MSPC, A72); *EH*, 13 June 1921.
80 Joseph Kinsella (BMH, WS 476, pp 4–5). In Kinsella's statement this took place around 1918, though was much more likely to have been later.
81 Liam O'Carroll (BMH, WS 594, pp 10–11); *EH*, 25 Sept. 1920. See also 'The Sons of Dawn – Dublin's "midnight crawlers"' (https://comeheretome.com/2017/09/12/the-sons-of-dawn-dublins-midnight-crawlers/) (accessed 28 Sept. 2022).
82 Joseph Kinsella to secretary, Military Service Pensions Board, 7 Apr. 1936 (IMA, MSPC, 3410168). In a reference for Joseph Sweeney, Kinsella gives a detailed description of flogging carried out by Sweeney (though does not mention this in his own statement to the BMH).
83 *EH*, 27 Sept. 1920.
84 Townshend, *Republic*, pp 266–7.
85 *Chicago Tribune*, 27 July 1920.
86 Stack to Mulcahy, 6 Apr. 1921 (UCDA, Mulcahy papers, P7/A/17).
87 Mitchell, *Revolutionary government*, p. 210.
88 O'Hegarty to each department, 31 May 1921; Collins to O'Hegarty, 2 June 1921 (NAI, DÉ/2/36).
89 'Standing orders', n.d. [Apr. 1921] (NAI, DÉ/2/36).
90 O'Hegarty to each minister, 24 Apr. 1921 (NAI, DÉ/3/36).
91 McSweeney, 'Bray area', p. 192.
92 Weekly summaries, July 1920; Mar. 1921 (TNA, CO 904/148–9).
93 Weekly summaries, May, July 1920 (TNA, CO 904/148).

94 Weekly summaries, Aug. 1920 (TNA, CO 904/149).
95 Lawrence McBride, *The greening of Dublin Castle: the transformation of bureaucratic and judicial personnel in Ireland, 1892–1922* (Washington, 1991), pp 287–8.
96 Campbell, 'Irish administration', 623, 641–42.
97 Sir H. A. Robinson claim (TNA, CO 762/32/24).
98 Robinson, *Memories*, pp 303–6.
99 Cabinet conclusions, 13 Aug. 1920 (TNA, CAB/23/22).
100 Michael Hopkinson (ed.), *The last days of Dublin Castle: the Mark Sturgis diaries* (Dublin, 1999), p. 9.
101 'Periscope' [G.C. Duggan], 'The last days of Dublin Castle', *Blackwood's Magazine*, 212 (1922), 173.
102 Donal O'Kelly, 'The Dublin scene: war amid the trappings of peace' in *With the IRA in the fight for freedom: 1919 to the truce, the red path of glory* (Dublin, 2010 ed.), p. 55.
103 Kautt, *Ground truths*, p. 39.
104 Dickson, *Dublin*, pp 462–3.
105 *EH*, 22 Nov. 1921.
106 *Evening Mail*, 24 June 1921.

CHAPTER EIGHT *From truce to Civil War, 1922–3*

1 *EH*, 9 July 1921.
2 Padraig Yeates, *A city in civil war: Dublin, 1921–24* (Dublin, 2015), pp 1–2.
3 *Forty years of* Dublin Opinion: *a selection from all the drawings and writings which have appeared in Ireland's magazine of humour from the time of its foundation* (Dublin, *c.*1962), p. 14.
4 Townshend, *Republic*, p. 331.
5 John Dorney, *The Civil War in Dublin: the fight for the Irish capital, 1922–1924* (Dublin, 2017), p. 2.
6 *II*, 11 July 1921.
7 *EH*, 11 July 1921.
8 *II*, 12 July 1921.
9 CI Dublin, July 1921 (TNA, CO 904/116).
10 Breaches of the Truce, Dublin (TNA, CO 904/152).
11 O'Halpin & Ó Corráin, *Dead*, pp 521–42.
12 *II*, 12 Nov. 1922; Dependents' pension application, James Henry Doyle (IMA, MSPC, 1D206).
13 Joseph O'Connor (BMH WS 544, p. 1).
14 Dorney, *Civil War*, p. 19; Patrick Mooney to Pensions Board, 17 Dec. 1939 (IMA, MSPC, 3421452).
15 Price, *Bled together*, pp 223–4.
16 *II*, 27 July 1921.
17 Mark Sturgis diary, 19 Jan. 1922 (TNA, PRO 30/59/5).
18 Andrews, *Dublin made me*, pp 236, 241–2.
19 Laffan, *Resurrection*, p. 384.
20 Minutes of special meeting, 2 Jan. 1922; Minutes of quarterly meeting, 4 Feb. 1922 (FCC, CC/01/20).
21 Four independent unionists were also elected to Dublin University and separately attended the only meeting of the parliament for southern Ireland constituted under the Act.
22 *II*, 9 Jan. 1922.
23 Dickson, *Dublin*, pp 467–8.
24 *IT*, 10 Dec. 1921.

25 *Church of Ireland Gazette*, 13 Jan. 1922.
26 Irish, *Trinity*, p. 222.
27 Martin Maguire, '16 January 1922, the "surrender" of Dublin Castle: administering Ireland' in Darragh Gannon and Fearghal McGarry (eds), *Ireland 1922: independence, partition, civil war* (Dublin, 2022), pp 15–17.
28 *II*, 17 Jan. 1922.
29 *IT*, 17 Jan. 1922.
30 John Gibney and Kate O'Malley, *The handover: Dublin Castle and the British withdrawal from Ireland, 1922* (Dublin, 2022).
31 Dorney, *Civil War*, p. 24; *II*, 1 Feb. 1922; *FJ*, 2 Feb. 1922.
32 Liz Gillis, *The fall of Dublin* (Cork, 2011), p. 23.
33 I am grateful to John Dorney for clarification on the handover of Dublin barracks.
34 Dorney, *Civil war*, p. 21.
35 Jack Kavanagh, 'Re-mapping the Irish Civil War: the role of the National army' (PhD, Maynooth University, 2021), pp 59–60.
36 Gillis, *Fall*, pp 28–9; Dorney, *Civil war*, pp 40–2.
37 Michael Fewer, *The battle of the Four Courts: the first days of the Irish Civil War* (London, 2018), p. 42.
38 Ó Corráin & Hanley, *Brugha*, pp 145–9.
39 Dorney, *Civil War*, pp 43–4.
40 *II*, 18 Jan. 1922; *FJ*, 19 Jan. 1922.
41 *FJ*, 20 Jan. 1922.
42 *II*, 21 Jan. 1922.
43 *FJ*, 23 Jan. 1922.
44 Yeates, *Civil War*, p. 43.
45 Dorney, *Civil War*, pp 41–2.
46 Robert Lynch, *The partition of Ireland, 1918–1925* (Cambridge, 2019), pp 175–96; Dorney, *Civil War*, pp 52–4; Yeates, *Civil War*, p. 66.
47 Laffan, *Resurrection*, pp 396–7.
48 Michael Gallagher, 'The pact general election of 1922', *Irish Historical Studies*, 21:84 (1979), 404–14.
49 Laffan, *Resurrection*, p. 406.
50 Gallagher, 'Pact', 415–17; Dorney, *Civil War*, pp 59–62; Yeates, *Civil War*, pp 72–4.
51 Tom Tormey, '"The parting of the way": the 1922 split in the Dublin IRA and the foundation of the modern army', *Defence Forces Review* (2016), 46.
52 Charles Joseph McHenry pension application (IMA, MSPC, 3421187).
53 Joe McHenry interview (UCDA, O'Malley notebooks, P17b/95).
54 Tormey, 'Split', 48.
55 *An tÓglach*, 25 Apr. 1922.
56 Tormey, 'Split', 48.
57 Oscar Traynor interview (UCDA, O'Malley notebooks, P17b/98).
58 Tormey, 'Split', 46–7.
59 Larry Nugent interview (UCDA, O'Malley notebooks, P17b/88).
60 Archie Doyle interview (ibid., P17b/105).
61 Nominal Rolls, Dublin No. 2 Brigade (IMA, MSPC, RO20).
62 Andie McDonnell interview (UCDA, O'Malley notebooks, P17b/100).
63 Dorney, *Civil War*, pp 163–5.
64 Nominal Rolls, Fingal Brigade (IMA, MSPC, RO519).
65 Michael Lynch military service pension application form (IMA, MSPC, 3422070); Michael Rock military service pension application form (IMA, MSPC, 349462).

66 Joseph Vincent Lawless military service pension application form (IMA, MSPC, 242912); James Crenigan military service pension application form (IMA, MSPC, 246186); Thomas Peppard military service pension application form (IMA, MSPC, 24323); Daniel Brophy military service pension application form (IMA, MSPC, 241950).
67 Dorney, *Civil War*, pp 166–7.
68 These figures are drawn from research by Dr Jack Kavanagh in the 1922 National Army Census. I am grateful to Dr Kavanagh for sharing them with me.
69 Michael Kenny military service application form (IMA, MSPC, 2411980). Kenny applied for the periods 1916–21 but was unsuccessful.
70 Mary McAuliffe, '"An idea has gone abroad that all the women were against the Treaty": Cumann na Saoirse and pro-Treaty women' in Liam Weeks and Micheál Ó Fathartaigh (eds), *The Treaty: debating and establishing the Irish state* (Dublin, 2018), p. 161; Townshend, *Republic*, p. 364.
71 McAuliffe, 'Cumann na Saoirse', pp 169–79. The organization ceased in October 1923, after the end of the Civil War.
72 Dorney, *Civil War*, pp 66–7.
73 'Easter Week Repeats Itself', 1922 (NLI, EPH F292).
74 Dorney, *Civil War*, pp 101–2; Fewer, *Four Courts*, pp 235, 255.
75 Price, *Bled together*, pp 321–2.
76 Unpublished figures courtesy of John Dorney. I am grateful to John for sharing this information with me.
77 *IT*, 5 July 1922.
78 Fewer, *Four Courts*, pp 224–45.
79 Comerford, *Dangerous ground*, p. 266.
80 Ó Corráin & Hanley, *Brugha*, pp 155–62.
81 Dorney, *Civil War*, p. 97.
82 Dickson, *Dublin*, p. 470.
83 Fionnuala Walsh, '9 August 1922, the reopening of Clery's department store: the mundane and the traumatic: ordinary life in extraordinary times' in Gannon & McGarry (eds), *1922*, pp 215–20.
84 Diarmaid Ferriter, *Between two hells: the Irish Civil War* (London, 2022), p. 49.
85 David Fitzpatrick, 'Boland, Henry James ('Harry')', *DIB*, DOI: https://doi.org/10.3318/dib.000763.v1.
86 Dorney, *Civil War*, pp 116–20.
87 Brian Hanley, '26 August 1922: the killing of Seán Cole and Alf Colley: state terror' in Gannon & McGarry (eds), *1922*, pp 239–40.
88 Dorney, *Civil War*, pp 169–75.
89 Hanley, 'State terror', pp 240–3; Dorney, *Civil War*, pp 177–90, 259.
90 Townshend, *Republic*, pp 437–42.
91 *II*, 9 Dec. 1922; *IT*, 9 Dec. 1922.
92 *EH*, 11 Dec. 1922.
93 Dorney, *Civil War*, pp 174–6.
94 *FJ*, 9 Dec. 1922.
95 Daithí Ó Corráin, '10 October 1922: the bishops condemn the republican campaign. Weaponing the sacraments: the Roman Catholic Church and Civil War' in Gannon & McGarry (eds), *1922*, pp 273–7.
96 Brian Hughes, 'Mallin, (Ó Mealláin), Séamus', *DIB*, DOI: https://doi.org/10.3318/dib.009773.v1.
97 Yeates, *Civil War*, pp 202–3.

98 Gemma Clark, *Everyday violence in the Irish Civil War* (Cambridge, 2014), p. 70; *II*, 2 Oct. 1922.
99 *IT*, 14 Jan., 25 Jan. 1922.
100 Ibid., 16 Mar. 1922.
101 Ibid., 5 Apr. 1922.
102 Ibid., 8 Apr. 1922; *Cork Examiner*, 8 Apr. 1922.
103 *IT*, 18 July 1922.
104 Ibid., 18 Aug. 1922; *The Times*, 18 Aug. 1922.
105 *IT*, 18 Aug. 1922.
106 *Weekly Irish Times*, 2 Sept. 1922.
107 *The Times*, 18 Aug. 1922.
108 Anthony Kinsella, '"Goodbye Dublin": the British military evacuation, 1922', *Old Dublin Journal*, 51:1 (1998), 21–4.
109 'Brief summary of the work of the Royal Irish Constabulary Tribunal', Apr. 1928 (TNA, HO 45/13029).
110 Alfred Cope to Michael Collins, 28 Mar. 1922 (NAI, FIN 1/506); Henry Tudor to Hamar Greenwood, 5 Apr. 1922 (TNA, HO 351/95); Walsh to assistant under-secretary and secretary, RIC Tribunal, 22 Apr. 1922 (TNA, HO 351/98); *Church of Ireland Gazette*, 24 Feb. 1922; *Constabulary Gazette*, 28 Jan. 1922.
111 O'Sullivan, *Constabularies*, p. 368.
112 Abbott, *Police casualties*, pp 275–91.
113 Dorney, *Civil War*, p. 45.
114 Unpublished figures courtesy of John Dorney.
115 Ruth McManus, *Dublin, 1910–1940: shaping the city and suburbs* (revised ed. Dublin 2021, [2001]), p. 78.

CHAPTER NINE *Legacies of Dublin's revolution*

1 Patrick O'Daly military service pension application form (IMA, MSPC, 24242).
2 Joseph Leonard military service pension application form (IMA, MSPC, 242671).
3 Typescript of speech by Joe Leonard, 16 Apr. 1955 (IMA, Joe Leonard papers, PRCN/0022/07/01/01).
4 Ferriter, *Two hells*, p. 107; Dublin Guard Nominal Roll, Feb.–Apr. 1922 (IMA, uncatalogued). I am grateful to Dr Jack Kavanagh for sharing this source.
5 Ferriter, *Two hells*, pp 107–9.
6 Linda Connolly, 'Sexual violence in the Irish Civil War: a forgotten war crime?', *Women's History Review*, 30:1 (2021), 136–9.
7 Katriona Goldstone, 'The Kahn/Goldberg murders 1923 in cultural memory: comparisons with Limerick 1904' in Seán William Gannon and Natalie Wynn (eds), *The Limerick Boycott in context* (forthcoming, 2025). I am grateful to Katrina Goldstone and Seán Gannon for permission to reference this forthcoming chapter. See also, James Conroy application (IMA, MSPC, W24SP80).
8 Mel Farrell, *Party politics in a new democracy: the Irish Free State, 1922–37* (Cham, 2017), pp 88–9.
9 Dorney, *Civil War*, pp 266–7.
10 Farrell, *Party politics*, pp 119–27.
11 Ferriter, *Two hells*, pp 161–5.
12 By-elections to the 4th Dáil (https://electionsireland.org/results/general/04dail.cfm) (accessed 5 Apr. 2023).
13 *Forty years of* Dublin Opinion, p. 14.

14 Ferriter, *Two hells*, p. 136.
15 Ibid., p. 128.
16 Andrews, *Dublin made me*, pp 132–3.
17 Tom Garvin, 'Andrews, Christopher Stephen ('Todd')', *DIB*, DOI: https://doi.org/10.3318/dib.000155.v1.
18 Dependents' pension application for Dermot O'Dwyer (IMA, MSPC, 1D364).
19 Col. B. Byrne to AG, 8 Feb. 1924, Superintendent J.J. Meehan, 7 Mar. 1924, Dependents' application form, Patrick and Margaret O'Connell (IMA, MSPC, 1D90).
20 Claim for dependents' allowance or gratuity, Peadar S. Doyle, 1924 (IMA, MSPC, 1D28); Death certificate, John (Séan) Doyle (https://www.irishgenealogy.ie/en/) (28 Oct. 2019); James O'Connor & Co. Solicitors to Ministry of Finance, 3 Jan. 1923 (IMA, MSPC, 597/15).
21 Letter from Sergeant Pat McHale, Sligo, 12 Feb. 1924 (IMA, MSPC, W1D107).
22 Report from inspector, Bridewell, 24 Feb. 1924 (IMA, MSPC, W1D142).
23 Dependents' pension application for Bernard O'Hanlon (IMA, MSPC, 1D95).
24 Patrick Magee to Cosgrave, 13 Feb. 1925 (IMA, MSPC, 1D73).
25 Brigid Breen to Joe Leonard, 3 June 1961 (IMA, Joe Leonard papers, PRCN-0082-02-01-14(1)).
26 Military service pension application, Brigid Breen (née Malone) (IMA, MSPC, 34281 1). Leonard was called to give evidence on Breen's application on 28 May 1941.
27 File on James Joseph Grace (IMA, MSPC, W1P421).
28 Anne Dolan, '"I have lost a lot by fighting for my country": reckoning with the Irish Revolution', *Contemporary European History*, 32:4 (2023), 587–603.
29 Paul Taylor, *Heroes or traitors? Experiences of southern Irish soldiers returning from the Great War, 1919–1939* (Liverpool, 2015), pp 137–68.
30 *IT*, 27 Jan. 1925.
31 Minutes of Southern Irish Loyalists Relief Association Irish advisory committee, 1922–1928 (PRONI, IUA papers, D989/B/1/2); John E. Walsh to Major I.G.H. White, 19 Nov. 1925 (ibid., D989/B/3/5).
32 McManus, *Dublin*, pp 75–83.
33 James Edward Terrett claim (TNA, IGC, CO 762/11/6).
34 Dorney, *Civil War*, p. 56.
35 J.C. Murray claim (TNA, IGC, CO 762/9/11).
36 R.H. Murray claim (TNA, IGC, CO 762/8/11); Irish, *Trinity*, p. 222.
37 John Murphy claim (TNA, CO 762/49/13).
38 John Egan claim (TNA, CO 762/160/9).
39 Timothy Doona claim (TNA, CO 762/60/20).
40 Maguire, 'Dublin Protestant working class', 50–3.
41 Lynch, *Partition*, p. 172.
42 See, for example, Seamus McKenna (BMH WS 1,016) and Roger McCorley (BMH WS 389).
43 Pauric J. Dempsey and Shaun Boylan, 'Dockrell, Sir Maurice Edward', *DIB*, DOI: https://doi.org/10.3318/dib.002648.v1.
44 Maguire, 'Our people', 281.
45 *Irish Press*, 5 Dec., 12 Dec., 25 Dec. 1931; 2 Jan., 7 Jan., 14 Jan., 27 Jan., 6 Feb., 15 Feb. 1932.
46 d'Alton, 'Protestant "belongings"', p. 28.
47 Maguire, 'Our people', 284.
48 Brian Inglis, *West Briton* (London, 1962), p. 15.
49 McDowell, *Crisis and decline*, p. 167.
50 d'Alton, 'Protestant "belongings"', p. 29.
51 Ian d'Alton, '"A vestigial population?" Perspectives on southern Irish Protestants," *Éire-Ireland*, 44:3&4 (2009), 39.

52 Jane Leonard, 'The twinge of memory: Armistice Day and Remembrance Sunday in Dublin since 1919' in Richard English and Graham Walker (eds), *Unionism in modern Ireland: new perspectives on politics and culture* (Basingstoke, 1996), p. 102; Mandy Link, *Remembrance of the Great War in the Irish Free State, 1914–1937* (Cham, 2019), pp 135–46.

53 *IT*, 5 May 1924.

54 Taylor, *Heroes or traitors?*, p. 213.

55 *Cork Examiner*, 12 Nov. 1928.

Select bibliography

PRIMARY SOURCES

A. MANUSCRIPTS

Belfast

Public Record Office of Northern Ireland

Irish Unionist Alliance papers.

Ulster Covenant and Women's Declaration signature sheets (online).

Dublin

Dublin City Library and Archive

Royal Dublin Fusiliers Association papers.

Fingal Local Studies and Archives

Cumann na mBan papers.

Dublin County Council minute books.

Hamilton Estate, Abbotstown papers.

Fingal Roll of Honour.

Irish Military Archives

Bureau of Military History.

Collins papers.

Dublin Guard Nominal Roll.

Joe Leonard papers.

Military Service Pensions Collection.

National Archives of Ireland

Chief Secretary's Office Registered Papers.

Dáil Éireann papers.

Dáil Éireann Local Government papers.

Department of Finance papers.

Irish Women's Suffrage and Local Government Association minute books (online).

National Library of Ireland

Dublin Brigade, IRA, 2nd Battalion papers.

Douglas Hyde papers.

Keogh Photographic Collection.

Maurice Moore papers.

Count George Noble Plunkett papers.

Horace Plunkett papers.

Pamphlets and ephemera.

Miscellaneous collections of papers and accounts relating to the Irish Revolution.

RTÉ Archives
Cashman Photographic Collection.
Interview with Emmet Dalton, 1978.

Trinity College Dublin Manuscripts and Archives
Eileen Chance diary, 1916.
Letter from John Dillon to Lady Elizabeth Mathew, 1916.
Fannin letters.
Richard Hoskin diary, 1916.
Denis Johnston papers.
Two letters written by Frederick William Kidd during the Easter Rising 1916.
Elsie Mahaffy's 'book' of the Easter Rising, *c.* June 1917.
'The personal experience of Miss L. Stokes during the Sinn Féin Rebellion of 1916'.
Francis Taylor diary, 1916.
Letter from 'Tom' to 'Kitty', 1916.

University College Dublin Archives
Desmond FitzGerald photographs.
Richard Mulcahy papers.
Donal O'Donoghue papers.
Ernie O'Malley notebooks.

London
National Archives of the United Kingdom
Cabinet papers.
Colonial Office papers.
Home Office papers.
Irish Grants Committee.
Mark Sturgis diary.
War Office papers.

B. OFFICIAL RECORDS

1901 and 1911 Census of Ireland returns (online)
1911 Census of England and Wales returns (online)
Census of Ireland, 1911. General report with tables and appendix, HC, 1912 [Cd. 6663].
Census of Ireland, 1911, Areas, houses, and population; also the ages, civil condition, occupations, birthplaces, religion, and educations of the people. Province of Leinster, HC, 1912 [Cd. 6049].
Emigration statistics of Ireland for the year 1912. Report and tables showing the number, ages, conjugal condition, and destinations of the emigrants from each county and province in Ireland during the year 1912; Also the occupations of the emigrants, and the number of emigrants who left each port in each month of the year, HC, 1913 [Cd. 6727].
Hansard (Commons)
Judicial statistics, Ireland, 1912, HC, 1913 [Cd. 7064].

Report of the departmental committee appointed by the Local Government Board for Ireland to enquire into the housing conditions of the working classes in the city of Dublin, HC, 1914 [Cd. 7273].

Royal Irish Constabulary and Dublin Metropolitan Police. Report of the committee of inquiry, 1914, HC, 1914 [Cd. 7421].

Saorstát Éireann. Census of population, 1926, Vol. 2. Occupations of males and females in each province, county, county borough, urban and rural district (1928).

Statistical tables of the Dublin Metropolitan Police for the year 1912, HC, 1913 [Cd. 6860].

The seventy-ninth report of the commissioners of national education in Ireland, school year 1912–13, HC, 1913 [Cd. 7141].

Untenanted lands (Ireland). A return of untenanted lands in rural districts, distinguishing demesnes on which there is a mansion house showing: (1) rural district and electoral division; (2) townland; (3) area in statute acres; (4) valuation (poor law); (5) names of occupiers as in valuation lists, HC, 1906 [250].

C. NEWSPAPERS AND PERIODICALS

Belfast News-Letter
Chicago Tribune
Church of Ireland Gazette
Constabulary Gazette
Cork Examiner
Daily Express (Dublin)
Dublin Evening Telegraph
Drogheda Independent
Evening Herald
Evening Mail
Freeman's Journal
Irish Independent
Irish Life
Irish Opinion: The Voice of Labour
Irish Press
Irish Times
Saturday Herald
The Times (London)
Weekly Irish Times

D. PRINTED PRIMARY & CONTEMPORANEOUS MATERIAL

1919 Annual report of the City of Dublin & Pembroke Unionist Association (Dublin, 1919).

Chart, D.A., 'Unskilled labour in Dublin', *Journal of the Statistical and Social Inquiry Society of Ireland*, 23 (1913–14), 160–75.

Comerford, Máire, *On dangerous ground: a memoir of the Irish Revolution*, ed. Hilary Dully (Dublin, 2021).

Cullen, Clara (ed.), *The world upturning: Elsie Henry's Irish wartime diaries, 1913–1919* (Dublin, 2012).

Dalton, Charles, *With the Dublin Brigade: espionage and assassination with Michael Collins' intelligence unit* (Cork, 2014 [1929]).

Dublin's fighting story, 1913–1921: told by the men who made it (1st ed., Tralee, n.d., *c.*1948).

Evidence on conditions in Ireland comprising the complete testimony, affidavits and exhibits presented before the American Commission on Conditions in Ireland, annotated and translated by Albert Coyle (Washington, DC, 1921).

Forty years of Dublin Opinion*: a selection from all the drawings and writings which have appeared in Ireland's magazine of humour from the time of its foundation* (Dublin, *c.*1962).
Gwynn, Stephen, *The famous cities of Ireland* (Dublin, 1915).
'Irish Life': A record of the Irish rebellion of 1916 (Dublin, 1916).
Joly, John, *Reminiscences and anticipations* (Dublin, 1920).
Lynd, Robert, *Rambles in Ireland* (London, 1912).
MacDowel Cosgrave, E. and Leonard R.F. Strangways, *The dictionary of Dublin: being a comprehensive guide to the city and its neighbourhood* (Dublin, 1908).
Macready, Nevil, *Annals of an active life, vol. II* (London, 1924).
McGuire, James (ed.), '"To tell you all about it": a letter from Mrs Marion Kelleher to her family written in the immediate aftermath of the Easter Rising in Dublin', *Analecta Hibernica*, 47 (2016), 105–23.
National Association of the Old IRA, *Iris Drong Átha Cliath: Dublin Brigade Review* (Dublin, 1939).
'Periscope' [G.C. Duggan], 'The last days of Dublin Castle', *Blackwood's Magazine*, 212 (1922), 137–90.
Robinson, Sir Henry, *Memories: wise and otherwise* (London, 1923).
Ross, John, *The years of my pilgrimage: random reminiscences* (London, 1924).
Sinn Féin Rebellion Handbook: Easter 1916, published by the *Weekly Irish Times* (Dublin, 1917).
Stephens, James, *The insurrection in Dublin* (Dublin, 1916).
With the IRA in the fight for freedom: 1919 to the truce, the red path of glory (Dublin, 2010 ed.).

SELECT SECONDARY SOURCES

D. PUBLISHED WORKS

aan de Wiel, Jérôme, 'Archbishop Walsh and Mgr. Curran's opposition to the British war effort in Dublin, 1914–1918', *Irish Sword*, 22:88 (2000), 193–204.
Andrews, C.S., *Dublin made me* (Dublin, 2001 [1979]).
Abbott, Richard, *Police casualties in Ireland, 1919–1922* (Cork, 2019 ed.).
Adams, R.J.C., *Shadow of a taxman: who funded the Irish Revolution?* (Cambridge, 2022).
Augusteijn, Joost, *From public defiance to guerrilla warfare: the experience of ordinary volunteers in the Irish War of Independence, 1916–1921* (Dublin, 1996).
Bartlett, Thomas (ed.), *The Cambridge history of Ireland, vol. IV: 1880 to the present* (Cambridge, 2018).
Barton, Brian and Michael Foy, *The Easter Rising* (2nd ed., Dublin, 2011).
Bowman, Timothy, William Butler and Michael Wheatley, *The disparity of sacrifice: Irish recruitment to the British armed forces, 1914–1918* (Liverpool, 2020).
Boyce, D.G., 'British opinion, Ireland and the war, 1916–1918', *Historical Journal*, 17:3 (1974), 575–93.
Brady, Declan, *Culture, politics and local government in Fingal, 1891–1914* (Dublin, 2017).
Brady, Joseph and Anngret Simms (eds), *Dublin through space and time* (Dublin, 2001).
Breathnach, Ciara and Brian Gurrin, 'A tale of two cities – infant mortality and cause of infant death, Dublin, 1864–1910', *Urban History*, 44:4 (2017), 647–77.

Buckland, Patrick, *Irish Unionism I: the Anglo-Irish and the new Ireland* (Dublin, 1972).

Burke, Tom, 'Whence came the Royal Dublin Fusiliers?', *Irish Sword*, 24 (2005), 451–8.

Byrne, Susan, '"Keeping company with the enemy": gender and sexual violence against women during the Irish War of Independence and Civil War, 1919–1923', *Women's History Review*, 30:1 (2021), 108–25.

Callinan, Elaine, *Electioneering and propaganda in Ireland, 1917–21: votes, violence and victory* (Dublin, 2020).

Campbell, Fergus, 'Who ruled Ireland? The Irish administration, 1879–1914', *Historical Journal*, 50:3 (2007), 633–44.

Clark, Gemma, *Everyday violence in the Irish Civil War* (Cambridge, 2014).

Clarkson, L.A. and J.M. Goldstrom (eds), *Irish population, economy and society: essays in honour of the late K.H. Connell* (Oxford, 1981).

Clear, Caitríona, *Social change and everyday life in Ireland, 1850–1922* (Manchester, 2007).

Connolly, Linda, 'Sexual violence in the Irish Civil War: a forgotten war crime?', *Women's History Review*, 30:1 (2021), 126–43.

Costello, Francis J., 'The role of propaganda in the Anglo-Irish War 1919–1921', *The Canadian Journal of Irish Studies*, 14:2 (1989), 5–24.

Coyle, Eugene A., 'Larkinism and the 1913 County Dublin farm labourers' dispute', *Dublin Historical Record*, 58:2 (2005), 176–90.

Crowe, Catriona (ed.), *Dublin 1911* (Dublin, 2011).

Cullen, Seamus, *Kildare: the Irish Revolution, 1912–23* (Dublin, 2020).

Curran, Conor, *Soccer and society in Dublin: a history of association football in Ireland's capital* (Dublin, 2023).

d'Alton, Ian and Ida Milne (eds), *Protestant* and *Irish: the minority's search for place in independent Ireland* (Cork, 2019).

Daly, Mary E., 'Social structure of the Dublin working class, 1871–1911', *Irish Historical Studies*, 23:90 (1982), 121–33.

——, *Dublin, the deposed capital: a social and economic history* (Cork, 1984).

Devine, Francis, 'Irish Transport & General Workers' Union: organization in Dublin city and county, 1918–1928', *Saothar*, 34 (2009), 85–98.

Dukova, Anastasia, *The history of the Dublin Metropolitan Police and its legacy* (London, 2016).

Dickson, David, *Dublin: the making of a capital city* (London, 2014).

Dolan, Anne, 'Killing and Bloody Sunday, November 1920', *Historical Journal*, 49:3 (2006), 789–810.

——, '"I have lost a lot by fighting for my country": reckoning with the Irish Revolution', *Contemporary European History*, 32:4 (2023), 587–603.

Dolan Stover, Justin, *Enduring ruin: environmental destruction during the Irish Revolution* (Dublin, 2022).

Dooley, Terence, *Burning the Big House: the story of the Irish country house in a time of war and revolution* (New Haven and London, 2022).

Dorney, John, 'The rabble and the republic', *Saothar*, 41 (2016), 101–9.

——, *The Civil War in Dublin: the fight for the Irish capital, 1922–1924* (Dublin, 2017).

English, Richard and Graham Walker (eds), *Unionism in modern Ireland: new perspectives on politics and culture* (Basingstoke, 1996).

Farrell, Mel, *Party politics in a new democracy: the Irish Free State, 1922–37* (Cham, 2017).
Fewer, Michael, *The battle of the Four Courts: the first days of the Irish Civil War* (London, 2018).
Fitzpatrick, David, 'The geography of Irish nationalism, 1910–1921', *Past & Present*, 78 (1978), 113–44.
—— (ed.), *Ireland and the First World War* (Dublin, 1986).
——, 'The logic of collective sacrifice: Ireland and the British army, 1914–1918', *Historical Journal*, 38:4 (1995), 1017–30.
—— (ed.), *Terror in Ireland, 1916–1923* (Dublin, 2012).
——, *Descendancy: Irish Protestant histories since 1795* (Cambridge, 2014).
——, *The Americanization of Ireland: migration and settlement, 1841–1925* (Cambridge, 2019).
Fallon, Las, *Dublin Fire Brigade and the Irish Revolution* (Dublin, 2012).
Ferriter, Diarmaid, *Between two hells: the Irish Civil War* (London, 2022).
Foley, Michael, *The bloodied field: Croke Park, Sunday 21 November 1920* (Dublin, 2014).
Foster, R.F., *Vivid faces: the revolutionary generation in Ireland, 1890–1923* (London, 2015).
Gallagher, Michael, 'The pact general election of 1922', *Irish Historical Studies*, 21:84 (1979), 404–21.
Gallagher, Niamh, *Ireland and the Great War: a social and political history* (London, 2020).
Gannon, Darragh and Fearghal McGarry (eds), *Ireland 1922: independence, partition, civil war* (Dublin, 2022).
Gannon, Darragh, *Proclaiming a republic: Ireland, 1916 and the national collection* (Dublin, 2016).
Gibney, John and Kate O'Malley, *The handover: Dublin Castle and the British withdrawal from Ireland, 1922* (Dublin, 2022).
Gibney, John (ed.), *Dublin City Council and the 1916 Rising* (Dublin, 2016).
Gillespie, Raymond and W.G. Neely (eds), *The laity and the Church of Ireland, 1000–2000: all sorts and conditions* (Dublin, 2002).
Gillis, Liz, *The fall of Dublin* (Cork, 2011).
Grayson, Richard S., *Dublin's great wars: the First World War, the Easter Rising and the Irish Revolution* (Cambridge, 2018).
Greaves, C. Desmond, *The Irish Transport and General Workers' Union: the formative years, 1909–1923* (Dublin, 1982).
Gregory, Adrian and Senia Pašeta (eds), *Ireland and the Great War: 'a war to unite us all'* (Manchester, 2002).
Griffith, Lisa Marie and Ciarán Wallace (eds), *Grave matters: death and dying in Dublin, 1500 to the present* (Dublin, 2016).
Hanley, Gerard, '"Let the harvest go to blazes": farm labourers in north County Dublin and the 1913 lockout', *Studia Hibernica*, 40 (2014), 135–64.
Hart, Peter, 'The geography of revolution in Ireland, 1917–1923', *Past & Present*, 155:1 (1997), 142–76.
——, *The IRA at war, 1916–1923* (Oxford, 2003).
Herlihy, Jim, *The Dublin Metropolitan Police: a short history and genealogical guide* (Dublin, 2001).

Hill, Myrtle and Sarah Barber (eds), *Aspects of Irish studies* (Belfast, 1990).

Hodgins, Micheál, 'Remembering the forgotten Cumann na mBan in south County Dublin', *Dun Laoghaire Journal*, 27 (2018), 142–76.

Horne, John (ed.), *Our war: Ireland and the Great War* (Dublin, 2008).

Hughes, Brian and Conor Morrissey (eds), *Southern Irish loyalism, 1912–1949* (Liverpool, 2020).

Hughes, Brian, *16 lives: Michael Mallin* (Dublin, 2012).

——, *Defying the IRA? Intimidation, coercion and communities during the Irish Revolution* (Liverpool, 2016).

——, '"Well may we be proud of him": living with the deaths of the Easter Rising leaders, 1916–17' in Lisa Marie Griffith and Ciarán Wallace (eds), *Grave matters: death and dying in Dublin, 1500 to the present* (Dublin, 2016), pp 187–97.

——, Campbell, Billy and Susan Schreibman, 'Contested memories: revisiting the Battle of Mount Street Bridge, 1916', *British Journal for Military History*, 4:1 (2017), 2–22.

Inglis, Brian, *West Briton* (London, 1962).

Irish, Tomás, *Trinity in war and revolution, 1912–1923* (Dublin, 2015).

Jackson, Alvin, 'The failure of unionism in Dublin, 1900', *Irish Historical Studies*, 26:104 (1989), 377–95.

——, *Judging Redmond & Carson* (Dublin, 2018).

——, 'Mrs Foster and the rebels: Irish unionist approaches to the Easter Rising, 1916–2016', *Irish Historical Studies*, 42:161 (May 2018), 143–60.

Jeffery, Keith, *Ireland and the Great War* (Cambridge, 2000).

—— (ed.), *The GPO and the Easter Rising* (Dublin, 2006).

Joye, Lar, 'The fighting Irish, 1914–1916', *Defence Forces Review* (2016), 53–61.

Kanter, Douglas and Patrick Walsh (eds), *Taxation, politics and protest in Ireland, 1662–2016* (Cham, 2019).

Kautt, W.H. (ed.), *Ground truths: British army operations in the Irish War of Independence* (Kildare, 2014).

Kelly, James and Mary Ann Lyons (eds), *Death and dying in Ireland, Britain and Europe: historical perspectives* (Dublin, 2013).

Kenna, Shane, *16 lives: Thomas MacDonagh* (Dublin, 2014).

Kinsella, Anthony, '"Goodbye Dublin": the British military evacuation, 1922', *Old Dublin Journal*, 51:1 (1998), 4–24.

Laffan, Michael, *The resurrection of Ireland: the Sinn Féin party, 1916–1923* (Cambridge, 1999).

Lane, Leeann and William Murphy (eds), *Leisure and the Irish in the nineteenth century* (Liverpool, 2016).

Leeson, D.M., 'Death in the afternoon: the Croke Park massacre, 21 November 1920', *Canadian Journal of History*, 38 (2003), 43–67.

——, *The Black & Tans: British police and Auxiliaries in the Irish War of Independence* (Oxford, 2011).

Link, Mandy, *Remembrance of the Great War in the Irish Free State, 1914–1937* (Cham, 2019).

Lynch, Robert, *The northern IRA and the early years of partition, 1920–1922* (Dublin, 2006).

——, *The partition of Ireland, 1918–1925* (Cambridge, 2019).

Maguire, Martin, 'A socio-economic analysis of the Dublin Protestant working class, 1870–1926', *Irish Social and Economic History*, 20 (1993), 65–87.

Martin, F.X., 'The 1916 Rising: a "Coup d'État or a Bloody Protest"?', *Studia Hibernica*, 8 (1968), 106–37.

——, 'The organization and activism of Dublin's Protestant working class, 1883–1935', *Irish Historical Studies*, 29:113 (1994), 65–87.

——, '"Our people": the Church of Ireland laity and the culture of community in Dublin since disestablishment' in Raymond Gillespie and W.G. Neely (eds), *The laity and the Church of Ireland, 1000–2000: all sorts and conditions* (Dublin, 2002), pp 277–303.

McBride, Laurence, *The greening of Dublin Castle: the transformation of bureaucratic and judicial personnel in Ireland, 1892–1922* (Washington, 1991).

McDiarmid, Lucy, *At home in the revolution: what women said and did in 1916* (Dublin, 2015).

McDowell, R.B., *Crisis and decline: the fate of the southern unionists* (Dublin, 1997).

McGarry, Fearghal and Richard S. Grayson (eds), *Remembering 1916: the Easter Rising, the Somme and the politics of memory in Ireland* (Cambridge, 2016).

McGarry, Fearghal, *The Rising: Ireland: 1916* (2nd ed., Oxford, 2016).

McNamara, Conor and Padraig Yeates (eds), *The Dublin lockout 1913: new perspectives on class and war & its legacy* (Kildare, 2017).

McManus, Ruth, *Dublin 1910–1940: shaping the city and suburbs* (revised ed. Dublin, 2021 [2001]).

——, 'Dublin's lodger phenomenon in the early twentieth century', *Irish Economic and Social History*, 45:1 (2018), 23–46.

Milne, Ida, *Stacking the coffins: influenza, war and revolution in Ireland, 1918–19* (Manchester, 2018).

Mitchell, Arthur, *Revolutionary government in Ireland: Dáil Éireann, 1919–22* (Dublin, 1995).

Moody, Janet, *The tenement dwellers of Church Street, Dublin, 1911* (Dublin, 2017).

Morris, Nicola K., 'Traitors to their faith? Protestant clergy and the Ulster covenant of 1912', *New Hibernia Review*, 15:3 (2011), 16–35.

Morrissey, Conor, *Protestant nationalists in Ireland, 1900–1923* (Cambridge, 2019).

Morrissey, Thomas J., *Archbishop William J. Walsh: archbishop of Dublin, 1841–1921* (Dublin, 2000).

Murphy, William, *Political imprisonment and the Irish, 1912–23* (Oxford, 2014).

Nesbitt, Ronald, *At Arnott's of Dublin, 1843–1993* (Dublin, 1993).

Nic Dháibhéid, Caoimhe, 'The Irish National Aid Association and the radicalization of public opinion in Ireland, 1916–1918', *Historical Journal*, 55:3 (2012), 705–29.

O'Brien, James V., *Dear, dirty Dublin: a city in distress, 1899–1916* (Berkeley, 1982).

O'Brien, Mark, *The* Irish Times*: a history* (Dublin, 2008).

Ó Corráin, Daithí, '"They blew up the best portion of our city and … it is their duty to replace it": compensation and reconstruction in the aftermath of the Easter Rising', *Irish Historical Studies*, 39:154 (Nov. 2014), 272–95.

—— and Gerald Hanley, *Cathal Brugha: 'an indomitable spirit'* (Dublin, 2022).

O'Farrell, Fergus, *Cathal Brugha* (Dublin, 2018).

O'Farrell, Mick, *1916: what the people saw* (Cork, 2013).

O'Halpin, Eunan and Daithí Ó Corráin, *The dead of the Irish Revolution* (New Haven and London, 2020).
Ó Maitiú, Séamas, *Dublin's suburban towns* (Dublin, 2003).
Ó Maonaigh, Aaron, '"Who were the shoneens?': Irish militant nationalists and association football, 1913–1923', *Soccer and Society*, 18:5–6 (2017), 631–47.
——, 'The home front: the Dublin townships and the first world war', *Dublin Historical Record*, 69:1 (2016), 71–83.
O'Neill, Marie, 'Dublin Corporation and the troubled times, 1914–1924', *Dublin Historical Record*, 47:1 (1994), 56–70.
Ó Ruairc, Pádraig Óg, *Truce: murder, myth and the last days of the Irish War of Independence* (Cork, 2016).
O'Sullivan, Donal J., *The Irish constabularies, 1822–1922: a century of policing in Ireland* (Kerry, 1990).
Pašeta, Senia, *Irish nationalist women, 1900–1918* (Cambridge, 2013).
Pennell, Catriona, *A kingdom united: popular responses to the outbreak of the First World War in Britain and Ireland* (Oxford, 2012).
Price, Dominic, *We bled together: Michael Collins, the Squad and the Dublin Brigade* (Cork, 2017).
Prunty, Jacinta, *Dublin slums, 1800–1925: a study in urban geography* (Dublin, 1988).
Rains, Stephanie, *Commodity culture and social class in Dublin, 1850–1916* (Dublin, 2010).
Reynolds, John, *46 dead men: the Royal Irish Constabulary in County Tipperary, 1919–1922* (Cork, 2016).
Rouse, Paul, *Sport in Ireland: a history* (Oxford, 2015).
Ryan, Louise, 'The *Irish Citizen*, 1912–1920', *Saothar*, 17 (1992), 105–11.
Sheehan, William, *Fighting for Dublin: the British battle for Dublin, 1919–1921* (Cork, 2007).
Taylor, Paul, *Heroes or traitors? Experiences of southern Irish soldiers returning from the Great War, 1919–1939* (Liverpool, 2015).
Tormey, Thomas, 'Scotland's Easter Rising veteran's and the Irish Revolution', *Studi Irlandesi*, 9 (2019), 271–302.
——, '"The parting of the way": the 1922 split in the Dublin IRA and the foundation of the modern army', *Defence Forces Review* (2016), 45–53.
Townshend, Charles, *Easter 1916: the Irish rebellion* (London, 2005).
——, *The republic: the fight for Irish independence* (London, 2013).
——, *The partition: Ireland divided, 1885–1925* (London, 2022).
Valiulis, Maryann Gialanella (ed.), *Gender and power in Irish history* (Dublin, 2009).
Wallace, Ciarán, 'Civil society in search of state: Dublin 1898–1922', *Urban History*, 45:3 (2018), 426–52.
Walsh, Fionnuala, 'Fighting for unionist home rule: competing identities in Dublin 1800–1929', *Journal of Urban History*, 38:5 (2012), 932–49.
——, *Irish women and the Great War* (Cambridge, 2020).
Walker, Brian M., *Parliamentary election results in Ireland, 1801–1922* (Dublin, 1978).
——, *Parliamentary election results in Ireland, 1918–92* (Dublin and Belfast, 1992).
Weeks, Liam and Mícheál Ó Fathartaigh (eds), *The Treaty: debating and establishing the Irish state* (Dublin, 2018).

Whearity, Frank, 'Thomas Hand', *Time & Tide*, 4 (2001), 47–9.
——, *The Easter Rising of 1916 in north Co. Dublin: a Skerries perspective* (Dublin, 2013).
——, The founding of the Irish Volunteers at Dublin's Rotunda Hall, 25 November 1913, *Dublin Historical Record*, 67:1 (2014), 66–81.
——, 'Mary Ellen "Molly" Adrien (1873–1949): Cumann na mBan volunteer', *Dublin Historical Record*, 69:2 (2016), 223–35.
Whelan, Yvonne, 'The construction and destruction of a colonial landscape: monuments to British monarchs in Dublin before and after independence', *Journal of Historical Geography*, 28:4 (2002), 508–33.
Winter, Ormonde, *Winter's tale: an autobiography* (London, 1955).
Yeates, Padraig, *Lockout: Dublin 1913* (Dublin, 2000).
——, *A city in wartime: Dublin 1914–1918* (Dublin, 2011).
——, *A city in turmoil: Dublin, 1919–21* (Dublin, 2012).
——, *A city in civil war: Dublin, 1921–24* (Dublin, 2015).

E. THESES AND UNPUBLISHED WORK

Kavanagh, Jack, 'Re-mapping the Irish Civil War: the role of the National army' (PhD, Maynooth University, 2021).
Tormey, Thomas, 'Guerrilla warfare and the dynamics of violence in the Irish War of Independence' (PhD, TCD, 2020).

F. ONLINE SOURCES

Birth, Marriage, Death records, irishgenealogy.ie.

Come Here to Me blog, comeheretome.com.

Dictionary of Irish Biography, dib.ie.

Electionsireland.org.

UCD Digital Library, digital.ucd.ie.

Ulster Covenant and Women's Declaration online, PRONI, nidirect.gov.uk/services/search-ulster-covenant.

Index